A Woman of Firsts

Margaret Heckler, Political Trailblazer

Kimberly Heckler

LYONS
PRESS

Essex, Connecticut

An imprint of The Globe Pequot Publishing Group, Inc.
64 South Main Street
Essex, CT 06426
www.globepequot.com

Distributed by NATIONAL BOOK NETWORK

British Library Cataloguing in Publication Information Available

Library of Congress Cataloging-in-Publication Data

Names: Heckler, Kimberly, author.
Title: A woman of firsts : Margaret Heckler, political trailblazer / Kimberly Heckler.
Description: Essex, Connecticut : Lyons Press, [2025] | Includes bibliographical
    references and index.
Identifiers: LCCN 2024031563 (print) | LCCN 2024031564 (ebook) | ISBN
    9781493086085 (cloth) | ISBN 9781493086092 (ebook)
Subjects: LCSH: Heckler, Margaret. | Women legislators—United States—Biography.
    | Women ambassadors—United States—Biography. | Health ministers—United
    States—Biography. | Republican Party (U.S. : 1854–) | United States—Politics and
    government—20th century.
Classification: LCC E840.8.H433 H43 2025 (print) | LCC E840.8.H433 (ebook) |
    DDC 328.73/092 [B]—dc23/eng/20241029
LC record available at https://lccn.loc.gov/2024031563
LC ebook record available at https://lccn.loc.gov/2024031564

♾™ The paper used in this publication meets the minimum requirements of American
National Standard for Information Sciences—Permanence of Paper for Printed Library
Materials, ANSI/NISO Z39.48-1992.

I would like to dedicate this book to the Heckler family:
my husband, John M. Heckler Jr.;
my children, John III, Amanda, and Elizabeth Heckler;
my nephew, John Mulliken IV;
my brother-in-law, John Mulliken III;
my sister-in-law, Alison Heckler-Haensler;
my brother-in-law, Mick Haensler;
but most importantly, Belinda Heckler Mulliken,
Margaret's eldest daughter, who has come alongside me
over the last seven-year journey.
Belinda has been my partner and confidant.
Without her love and support, personal insights,
and practical attention to detail, this book would not have been possible.

Contents

PART III: Appointments 1982–1989

Foreword

In recent years, significant strides have been made in women's representation in the highest public offices across the United States. Record numbers of women have run for and won elected office, moving the needle ever closer to equal representation. As I write this in the summer of 2024, a woman serves as vice president, women make up just over a quarter of members of the US Congress (150 out of 535), and two state legislatures have achieved gender parity. A third of all state legislative seats nationwide are held by women.

A broader historical context, however, reflects lingering disparity and highlights the magnitude of the impact of early women officeholders like Margaret Heckler. To date, almost thirteen thousand people have served in Congress, yet only 419 of them have been women. When Heckler first took the oath of office as a member of Congress in 1967, she became just the seventy-fifth woman to do so in our nation's then 150-year history. At the time, she served alongside eleven other women, making them just one in every fifty members: a stark contrast to today's ratio of one in four.

History books have traditionally lionized male leaders, while the stories of pioneering women like Heckler are often overlooked. *A Woman of Firsts* offers a compelling exploration of Heckler's life, providing both an intimate look at her personal journey and an inspiring narrative for those dedicated to advancing women's representation in politics and elsewhere. For students, scholars, candidates, officeholders, and advocates, Heckler's story is enlightening and motivational.

Throughout her political career, Heckler endured relentless media scrutiny about her gender and perpetual questions from reporters about her family responsibilities. The challenges she encountered as a new member of Congress—including the absence of a women's bathroom near the House floor, intraparty conflicts, unwelcome advances from male colleagues, and pervasive institutional sexism—underscore the fortitude of the women of her era who forged a new path in the halls of government.

Preserving and sharing these stories is crucial, both for inspiration and for the practical lessons they offer. As she rose up the ladder in government, Heckler wielded her influence to make change wherever possible for the most vulnerable members of society. During her time in Congress, Heckler was an unwavering advocate for issues such as financial and legal equality for women, affordable childcare for working families, the Equal Rights Amendment, Title IX, and veterans' rights, despite numerous political and legislative obstacles in her way.

Research by political scientists has shown that women legislators bring unique and impactful contributions to governance. They are more likely than their male counterparts to champion bills focused on issues important to women, draw from distinct life experiences at policymaking tables, and work across party lines to build consensus. Heckler was an early leader in working across party lines—she cofounded the Congresswomen's Caucus (currently known as the Bipartisan Women's Caucus), considered by scholars and observers to be one of the most effective bipartisan organizations in Congress. Heckler understood early on that as a Republican in a predominantly Democratic Massachusetts delegation, her success would depend on her ability to build bridges. Her foresight and dedication to collaboration across party lines made her a true stateswoman and a model for future leaders. Moreover, in a current era of hyperpartisanship and polarization, Heckler's approach serves as a reminder of what can be achieved when public leaders put their country's and constituents' needs first over party politics.

The influence of the relatively small number of women serving in Congress during the 1960s and 1970s on shaping the legislative agenda—particularly in advancing women's rights—was profound. Heckler's leadership in crafting and advocating for the Equal Credit Opportunity Act (ECOA) is a standout example. Passed in 1974, the ECOA prohibited banks and lending institutions from discriminating based on sex or marital status when offering loans, credit, and other financial services. Heckler's determination was fueled by personal experience—despite being an attorney, she was denied a mortgage—as well as memories of being raised by single women. After joining the House Banking Committee, Heckler used her legislative power and diplomatic skills to push the ECOA through countless political and cultural obstacles and to see it signed into law.

The ECOA empowered women to open bank accounts, apply for mortgages, and secure credit in their own names without needing the approval of a husband or father—rights that were previously out of reach. Whenever I cite the ECOA as an example of the transformative power of women in office, younger audiences are often shocked to learn that such basic financial freedoms were once denied to women. Heckler's legacy is a powerful reminder of how one woman's courage and persistence can reshape the lives of millions. Her work on the Equal Credit Opportunity Act not only expanded financial freedoms for women but also set a lasting precedent for the role of women in driving forward social and economic progress.

After being appointed secretary of the US Department of Health and Human Services (HHS)—at the time, only the ninth woman in the country's history to be appointed to a presidential cabinet position—Heckler continued her tenacious approach to policymaking, tackling issues and problems that others resisted. Defying naysayers, she spearheaded the Task Force on Black and Minority Health, a revolutionary effort that led to a report—commonly known as the *Heckler Report*—with shocking data on the persistent health disparities faced by different racial and ethnic groups in the United States. The impact of the *Heckler Report* reverberates to this day through funding, legislation, research, and offices devoted to minority health. During the AIDS crisis, she bucked the White House's approach of largely ignoring the issue, working instead to make AIDS the number one health priority in the country. She also channeled her legislative experience to change the landscape of end-of-life care, making hospice care widely available to the American public via Medicare.

When she was appointed as the US ambassador to Ireland at the tail end of her public career, Heckler did not slow down. Using her considerable work ethic along with her diplomacy and entertaining skills, she advanced peacekeeping efforts, economic opportunities, and American business investments in the country.

As I read this book, I often wondered what Heckler would make of today's political landscape. Perhaps she would reflect on how, despite progress, many challenges are stubbornly persistent. But I imagine that instead of getting discouraged, she would march ahead undeterred. The resilience of and strategies employed by Heckler to advance the causes she cared about continue to serve as a valuable guide for our times.

While there is still quite some distance to go before women are equally represented in the halls of government, the progress made owes much to trailblazers like Margaret Heckler. Their presence in elected and appointed offices throughout the last century fostered shifts in cultural expectations about women's public leadership, and they served as role models for many women who followed in their footsteps. The policies they championed have had a lasting impact on millions of Americans and continue to shape the nation's legislative landscape. Undoubtedly, the world would look different if women like Margaret had not pursued their political aspirations.

Finally, research shows that women win elected office as often as men do in comparable races. The challenge is that women don't *run* for office at the same rates as men do, partially because they are not recruited by party officials or other influential leaders. Margaret Heckler's story of determination is remarkable because she was an early self-starter—she did not wait to be asked, nor did she ask permission. She simply went for it. She also relied on her network of fellow women leaders—another factor we know is critical to success.

Heckler's life story offers both a roadmap and a dose of inspiration for women thinking of throwing their hats into the political ring or striving to make a difference in other fields. Her response to those who repeatedly told her it wasn't her turn—*"I'm not waiting."*—remains a powerful message for all who need encouragement to follow their own ambitions.

Jean Sinzdak
Associate Director, Center for American Women and Politics
Rutgers University–New Brunswick

Introduction

*M*argaret O'Shaughnessy Heckler was one of the most powerful and influential women in the United States throughout much of the 1970s and 1980s.[1] A trailblazing political leader, she was one of only eleven congresswomen when first elected in 1966, then later was appointed by President Ronald Reagan as secretary of health and human services and finally, served as the first woman US ambassador to Ireland, as such, becoming the first woman to earn a "triple crown" in politics.

Driven by compassion and justice rather than vitriolic party politics, Heckler cannot fit into any box, then or now. Under her banner, there is room for all Americans: Republicans, Democrats, Independents, immigrants, veterans, minorities, people of faith, women, the terminally ill, and more. Margaret Heckler was a paragon of a bygone era worthy of emulation.

Her legacy is of successes, both pragmatic and visionary, that continue to have an impact on American lives today. A fierce warrior for women's rights, in 1974 she authored and sponsored the Equal Credit Opportunity Act in the House of Representatives, which for the first time in American history gave women the right to credit in their own name, giving women their own financial power. As one of the primary sponsors of the Equal Rights Amendment, she advocated for women to be enshrined in the Constitution, paving a path for tomorrow's daughters. As secretary of health and human services, Heckler commissioned the *Heckler Report* to address health disparities among American minorities, championed early AIDS research and treatment, and crafted the first federalized hospice program from scratch.

Heckler was acutely aware of the price her Irish immigrant parents paid to become Americans, which instilled in her a deep responsibility to ensure all present and future Americans had access to enjoy a flourishing life in the United States.

Margaret Heckler was one part career trailblazer, one part celebrity, and one part mother of three. A five-foot-two-inch strawberry blonde, she could carry an entire room with her Irish wit, enticing anyone from an immigrant worker in a textile factory to a presidential hopeful in a post-campaign speech backroom.

Not one to bend to any status quo, Heckler broke most social conventions to accomplish the near impossible in the 1950s and 1960s, courageously making her way into rooms where few women had been invited before. Heckler's allure was sincere, and her effect on the best aspects of modern America was monumental. Most of these career-shaping successes found their start in rooms of men who issued firm vetoes to her ideas and legislative goals. When she encountered these barriers, she used her femininity to set others at ease. She knew when to use the velvet glove and when to turn on the fire.[2]

To understand what drove Margaret Heckler's passionate desire for justice, as well as her ascension in national politics at the age of thirty-five, we must first understand the intimate details of her rejection at birth by her father, a poor and troubled young man by the name of John O'Shaughnessy, known to all as Jack. This permanent wound of her father's abandonment—and the inability of her mother, Bridget, to stand up to him—carved Margaret's deep internal wells of compassion, courage, and conviction, which would come to define her bold, bipartisan legacy.

I

EARLY LIFE 1914–1961

Unwanted

Margaret's first birthday with Belinda West,
1932. *Family collection*.

𝓜argaret's father, Jack O'Shaughnessy, grew up in the small town of Askeaton, County Limerick, Ireland. His family's two-room cottage, separated by a large hearth, was a space that could not hide the effects of decades of misery sunk deeply into the soil of the home.

The eldest of Daniel and Maggie O'Shaughnessy's seven children, Jack had long ago assumed the burden of his family's poverty and his father's alcoholism. Ireland was still struggling in the wake of the 1845

Potato Famine, which caused the starvation and death of nearly one million people.[1] Daniel was not unlike other surrounding subsistence farmers: poor, and downcast. And Maggie, like many mothers of her time, did not hold back her desperate reliance on her eldest son.

At twenty-four, Jack tired of the brutal daily grind of tilling fields with horse-drawn plows and cutting peat in bogs by hand. Although many of his descendants were buried under broken graves and Celtic crosses in the Franciscan friary, set on a knoll above the River Deel, the roots of his family weren't enough to keep Jack firmly planted in the old country.

Jack's thoughts drifted increasingly to the idea of going to America. At the same time, Maggie complained that she needed his help, that he didn't spend enough time with the family, and only cared for himself. Jack's relationship with his mother continued to deteriorate.

In August 1914, World War I began. Because the Irish were under British rule, there were real concerns about a German invasion. Jack had no desire to enlist, but he knew the neighbors would soon begin to question why he hadn't yet done so.

The decision was made. He purchased a third-class ticket to America and left in the middle of the night without saying good-bye. Jack never saw or corresponded with his parents again.

In the early 1900s, New York City was a cacophony of urban sounds. Model T Fords honked horns, horses' hooves rattled on cobblestone streets, and the earth trembled when the subway passed underneath. Immigrants spoke in every language imaginable. Twenty-six-year-old Jack had never seen so many people, all with the same vision of the American dream.

As the war raged on, America remained neutral. President Woodrow Wilson was firmly opposed to the war, so with little concern about wartime military service in then-neutral America, Jack joined the navy as a way of increasing his stability and social status. It was common at the time for men to serve for only a brief time, and when his service ended, Jack carried himself with newfound confidence. He was no longer just another Irish immigrant, but a US veteran.

He landed a job as a doorman at The Pierre, a lavish and iconic hotel with unsurpassed hospitality that catered to the rich and famous. Built by E. F. Hutton, The Pierre was located across from The Plaza Hotel. Jack's relationships with some of the hotel residents, particularly the less stodgy anti-Prohibition entrepreneurs, formed into friendships. They told Jack that the future of wealth accumulation was not in a nine-to-five job, but investment in the stock market. They told him, "Buy Coca-Cola, Jack,"

"Go all in on Standard Oil—it's lookin' like a bull market," and "Get in on General Electric now, before it's too late."

The market became Jack's obsession. In the early 1920s, only 10 percent of Americans invested in stocks, few of them immigrants like Jack.[2] He developed a pattern: putting on a performance for the guests at the hotel in the daytime, neurotically watching stocks in the afternoon, and drinking heavily at night. Now in his thirties, Jack O'Shaughnessy was a self-made man.

For many Irish immigrants, the Catholic Church was the epicenter of their lives. It provided access to jobs, community, and other basic resources. But it also fulfilled their spiritual needs and kept their nostalgia for Ireland at bay.

Church dances were a popular social outlet. One night in 1927, a tall, blue-eyed woman glanced sheepishly at thirty-nine-year-old Jack. Jack walked over and asked her to dance.

The soft-spoken, introverted woman, who introduced herself as Bridget McKeon, was more poised than others Jack had known. Bridget hailed from Mohill, County Leitrim in central Ireland. Her father had died of tuberculosis when she was three, leaving her mother with six children and only a small pension from his position as a policeman in the Royal Irish Constabulary.

In May 1912, Bridget, then eighteen, had immigrated with her older brother and sister. In New York, Bridget and her siblings experienced the pervasive prejudice against Irish immigrants. Help-wanted ads read, "Clean Active Girl Wanted to do the housework of a private family, washer and ironer, a plain cook, a Protestant. No Irish Need Apply."[3] Bridget kept looking, eventually securing a job with a wealthy family as an upstairs maid. Now thirty-three, she had spent the last fifteen years sending money back to her mother and younger siblings in Ireland.

Margaret's parents, Bridget and Jack O'Shaughnessy, 1928. *Family collection.*

A deeply committed Catholic who attended Mass daily, Bridget found comfort in having met Jack at a church function. The two began to date and within a few months, Jack and Bridget wed at Saint Vincent's parish in Queens, New York, on September 23, 1928.

Just over a year later, the roaring twenties came to a screeching halt. On October 24, 1929, the stock market crashed. Thousands of brokers and investors crowded outside the doors of the New York Stock Exchange to learn more about the drop in stock prices and whether anything was salvageable.

New York City, once a shining city of promise for immigrants, became a place of hunger and desperation. By 1932, 1.6 million New Yorkers were on government assistance and 33 percent were unemployed.[4] Bread lines grew long, and parents' faces were etched with stress about how to feed their children.

For a decade, Jack had sunk nearly all of his extra earnings into stocks—and in an instant everything was gone. He was able to maintain his job with reduced hours, but the Depression took its toll. He no longer concealed his drinking from Bridget. As his initial softness toward her turned into occasional drunken fits of verbal abuse, Bridget sank deeper into herself and her faith.

Then, amid hardship, another event began quietly, filled with tenderness and vulnerability in Bridget's womb.

Since the start of their relationship, Jack had been clear that he did not want children. Dreading Jack's reaction, Bridget hid her pregnancy. But one night when she was twelve weeks along, Jack came crashing through the apartment earlier than usual and found Bridget in tears. In her emotional state, she admitted to her husband that she was pregnant. Disappointed and enraged, Jack shouted, "There will be no child in our home!"

In the next room, Bridget prayed for the uncertain future of her child. She also prayed that if the baby was a girl, she would be petite, not tall like herself.

Toward the end of Bridget's second trimester, Jack told her to look for someone to take the baby. Through her church, Bridget learned of a potential caregiver: a woman named Belinda West, a recent widow with no children of her own who lived in East Elmhurst, Long Island. She attended Saint Gabriel's, a nearby church in Queens, and was a devout Irish Catholic.

Mrs. West agreed to meet Bridget O'Shaughnessy at Saint Gabriel of the Sorrowful Mother parish. The irony of the church's name was not lost on either the white-haired, elderly woman or the tall mother-to-be. It became obvious to both of them that it was a divinely appointed arrangement and they agreed Mrs. West would raise the baby.

Margaret Mary O'Shaughnessy was born on June 21, 1931, at Flushing Hospital in Queens. Jack named the baby Margaret after his youngest sister, the sibling he had most adored. Jack and Bridget referred to their child as Peggy, a typical Irish nickname.

For Bridget, Jack's insistence that she part with her own child seemed inhumane. In her hospital bed, during the precious few days she'd been granted with her daughter, Bridget silently wept. Meanwhile, in East Elmhurst, Belinda West prepared a room.

When Bridget was discharged from the hospital, Jack hailed a taxi. Carrying their newborn baby, he and Bridget made their way to Mrs. West's house at 2536 Curtis Street. Bridget returned to her job as a private maid and Jack carried on working as a doorman.

Three-day-old Margaret would never again fully belong to her parents. Margaret's journey begins at the crossroads of her father's rejection, her mother's powerlessness, and the extraordinary compassion of an elderly stranger.

East Elmhurst was a few miles from Jack and Bridget's apartment and four miles from Manhattan. The end of Curtis Street sloped down into a vast marshland, which during Margaret's childhood was filled in for the construction of LaGuardia Airport and the Grand Central Parkway.

William West, Mrs. West's husband, had been a Danish immigrant and a building contractor. He'd built their brick house in 1905. It featured a small front yard, a larger backyard, and a garage. A clothesline strung from the rear of the house to the garage was heavily used in every season.

After Mr. West's death, Mrs. West invited her two sisters, also widowed, to live with her. Prior to accepting the job as Margaret's caretaker, Mrs. West had been a laundress—hard labor for a woman in her late sixties; being a full-time caretaker for an infant was much more accommodating for someone her age. Jack O'Shaughnessy would come monthly to pay Mrs. West for the care of his child. The house of widows welcomed the arrival of the swaddled infant. During the worst years of the Great Depression, the West household was given the gift of new life.

Mrs. West washed laundry on washboards, wrung it, and hung it on the line outside. During cold months, she shoveled in coal and took out ashes. She made all of Margaret's clothes by hand. She also extended herself by bringing soup to newly arrived Irish immigrant families and making clothes for neighbors in need.

Margaret age four. *Family collection.*

At the start of the Depression, while Mrs. West was working as a laundress, she became seriously ill. The illness was so severe that she needed someone to take over her job so she could recover. A Black woman named Christina, who worked at the machine next to Belinda, offered to do her work while she recovered.[5] Margaret would fondly remember Christina's generosity and kindness and would often share the story of this act of mercy throughout the rest of her life.

At home, Mrs. West welcomed the opportunity to nurture a child, but it was her niece Catherine who attached herself most strongly to Margaret. Every weekend, after working as an executive secretary in the city, Catherine came out from Manhattan and took Margaret for extended days of play and exploration. In her late twenties, single and childless, Catherine quickly became a substitute mother for Margaret.

Shortly after Margaret turned four, Catherine was diagnosed with tuberculosis. She moved into a spare bedroom at the West house to receive care from her mother and aunts. The older women were meticulous about keeping Margaret at a safe distance. The good care helped Catherine make a seemingly full recovery.

Margaret's early years were filled with the attention and adoration of strong, industrious women. In a time when it was difficult for women to live without the assistance of a man, the West household demonstrated to Margaret that women were capable on their own. But sexual discrimination policies were ingrained into the social, political, and economic fabric of the nation, leaving women with few options to gain stability without a man. Margaret grew up with this awareness, which would shape the woman she would become and the causes she cared passionately about.

Despite the loving household, Margaret's childhood was marked by muddled sadness over her abnormal upbringing. Margaret grew up with a fuzzy understanding of why she did not live with her parents and exactly who Mrs. West was to her. Margaret referred to Mrs. West as "my grandmother," because she looked like a grandmother and Margaret wanted people to believe that she was related to her even though Margaret knew she was only a boarder. The absence of involved, loving parents left a web of complex emotions: fear of abandonment, loneliness, and an unfillable longing to earn the affection of her father. Margaret was emotionally homeless, not fully belonging to anyone.

Jack and Bridget visited once a month, on Sundays after church. Perched awkwardly on the embroidered sofa in Mrs. West's parlor, they were an intimidating presence in Margaret's childhood memories.

Growing up, Margaret could never understand why her mother had not fought harder to keep her. Bridget's only choice was to follow her husband's decision, caught in an era where women were dependent on their husbands financially and because everyone knew that Jack "ruled the roost." At Our Lady of Lourdes, Bridget prayed earnestly for her daughter. When visiting, Bridget observed that Mrs. West, not she, knew Margaret's idiosyncrasies—what she was like when she misbehaved, how she laughed when she was joyful. All Bridget caught were glimpses of a young girl's show-and-tell performances.

During their monthly Sunday visit to then-six-year-old Margaret, Jack pulled Mrs. West aside and said, "Mrs. West, I thank you for your caretaking over the last six years, but the situation will soon change."

He bluntly told Mrs. West that he and Bridget were planning to take Margaret to Ireland, where she would live with their relatives in County Leitrim. This news shattered the West household, leaving Mrs. West feeling powerless. Jack explained that the three of them were scheduled to leave on an ocean liner in the next few weeks. They would stay in Ireland for six months, until the child was acclimated and then he and Bridget would return to New York. Mrs. West was brokenhearted.

The night before Margaret's departure, Mrs. West held the child closely as they said their evening prayers before a few ladies arrived to play cards. Margaret snuck out of bed and crept to the door, where she listened to the ladies' muffled voices. She heard something about President Roosevelt and then the conversation turned serious at the mention of her name. She heard her grandmother say in a hushed voice, "*They are going to take her.*"

Her friends asked, "Is there anything you can do?"

"I have no authority to keep her," Mrs. West replied.

Terrified, Margaret ran back to bed. Her dreams soon turned into nightmares.

The following evening after Mass, Margaret and Mrs. West lit their last candle together and began their long walk home. Suddenly, Margaret felt scared. The narrow alleyways were now filled with tall shadows. She visualized people dressed in black robes, about to grab her. Even her grandmother couldn't protect her.

On the morning of her departure Margaret came downstairs wearing her white taffeta dress, handmade by Mrs. West. It had been decided that Catherine would take Margaret to the ship, and Belinda West would stay behind. "Today we're going on a big trip to New York City," Catherine told Margaret. The child had no idea that the plan was for her to leave the only home she'd ever known—for good.

Mrs. West embraced her, saying tenderly, "I love you very much, my child." She motioned to Catherine that they should leave quickly, before she became inconsolable. She didn't want to frighten Margaret with her tears.

The *Queen Mary* sat majestically in a Manhattan wharf. On the pier, bands were playing and American flags were flying, creating a powerful scene for young Margaret. Women wore wide-brimmed hats and flowing dresses; men wore hats and three-piece suits. People rushed to say good-bye, board the ship, and wave from the deck to their loved ones. Sailors pushed carts of luggage and prepared the ropes for launch.

Catherine scanned the crowd for Jack and Bridget, spotting the distinctly tall couple already aboard the ship. Jack was sporting his best Sunday suit and hat, patting the two round-trip tickets and the one-way ticket for his daughter he kept in his breast pocket. With the assistance of The Pierre Hotel, he'd been able to secure first-class tickets at a substantial discount.

Bridget stood with poise and presence. For the first time, she would share unregulated time with her daughter, spending months in the land of her best memories. She was going home.

Catherine spun Margaret around to face her. "Peggy, you're going on a trip with your parents to Ireland. They'll take good care of you."

Catherine and Mrs. West knew they might have to bribe Margaret onto the ship. Knowing that Margaret's usual weakness was chocolate, Catherine pulled a box of chocolates from her pocketbook as they went up the gangplank.

Margaret took the chocolates and gave Catherine one last hug. As she reached her parents, she turned around and caught a glimpse of Catherine, mustering a smile as she waved. It would be the last image Margaret had of her.

On board the ship, it didn't take long for Jack to charm the captain with his wit and humor, receiving an invitation to sit at the captain's table. Margaret entertained the table guests and the captain by reciting poems and telling jokes. Bridget and Jack watched their child through a different lens. She was gregarious, precocious, and intelligent. A mixture of pride and wonder befell them as they became better acquainted with their own daughter.

For Margaret, spending full days with her parents on an ocean liner was pure delight. Arriving in Ireland via Liverpool, the O'Shaughnessys made their way to County Leitrim to visit Bridget's sister, Jane, with whom they would leave Margaret. It had been almost thirty years since Bridget left home.

Jane and her family lived on the McKeon farm, where Margaret enjoyed playing with her cousins. There were goats, cows, and chickens. On Sundays, everyone attended the local Catholic church. Margaret, her mother, and father rode bikes to church on winding country roads, followed by a visit to the local sweet shop, where Margaret picked out her favorite candy.

After a few weeks in Ireland, Margaret's parents took her to visit the Cloonturk school in Gortnalamph, which Margaret would attend in the fall. As they walked around the school, it did not occur to her that her parents intended to enroll her, and once she was settled, they planned to leave her in Ireland.

The Great Depression had taken a toll on Jack. He began to resent the monthly payments to Mrs. West. But the trip to Ireland was intended to put a stop to all that. Soon, Jack would leave his daughter behind, just as he'd left his mother behind—without any advance notice, vulnerable and alone.

A few months later, the time had come for Jack and Bridget to return to New York—and to tell young Margaret the hard truth. Jack pulled her aside, explaining that she would be staying behind in Ireland. The incredulous news sent Margaret into an uncontrollable fit. She pleaded with her father, "Please don't leave me behind. Take me with you."

"No, Peggy," Jack said. "It has been decided. You will be staying here with your Aunt Jane."

Margaret cried out defiantly, "I won't let you leave me!" But Jack was not budging. Margaret ran into a spare bedroom and began to wail in disbelief. Jack lost his patience with Margaret and stormed out of the house.

Jack needed time to think. He reached the top of a rocky glen, and he was alone. As he was relieving himself, Margaret came upon her father from the rear. In a purely instinctive act to protect his privacy, Jack accidentally threw his hand back, striking Margaret across the head, causing her to fall, hitting her head on a rock. She was knocked unconscious.

At the sight of her motionless body, Jack exclaimed, "What have I done?" Shame overtook him as he feared the worst for his only child. He felt certain he'd killed her.

Margaret remained unresponsive for far too long. Jack cradled his daughter in his arms, sank to his knees, and bargained with God. "*Please God, open her eyes. If you save her, I'll take her back to America, where she will have every opportunity.*"

The Great Peggy

Margaret age seven. *Family collection.*

An ominous black wreath hung on the front door of Mrs. West's home at 2538 Curtis Street, East Elmhurst, when Jack and Bridget dropped Margaret off upon their return from Ireland. She had fully recovered physically from her father's blow yet feeling emotionally wounded by his original plan to leave her in Ireland. Walking into the house, she was met by another shocking turn of events: Catherine had succumbed to tuberculosis at the age of thirty-two.

When Mrs. West told Margaret the news, she was disoriented. After two months in a foreign country, returning to learn that her closest mother figure was gone forever felt incomprehensible to the six-year-old.

The woman who had sung to her and played imagination games would never return. Already suffering from the perplexing rejection of her parents, Margaret's profound sense of abandonment only deepened with Catherine's death. For the second time, she had been robbed of a mother. She knew now that she did not truly belong to anyone.

For weeks, Margaret cried herself to sleep each night. To comfort herself, she kept the pages of The Bobbsey Twins books active in her mind. Catherine's absence created an even tighter bond between Margaret and Mrs. West.

As summer wound to a close, the O'Shaughnessys enrolled Margaret at the local public school. Jack's bargain with God to save Margaret's life generated improvements in her future prospects, among them the ability to live and attend school in the United States rather than in Ireland. It was said of Margaret's mother by the women in her parish back in Ireland that "Bridget was a woman considerably ahead of her time.[1] She would later encourage her daughter to take the steps *to pursue an independent career* at a time when that was not done. "If you work hard during your first years of school," Bridget told Margaret, "you could be eligible for full scholarships."

Margaret took this advice to heart. On an unconscious level, school was a way to potentially earn her parents' affection. It quickly became clear to Margaret's teachers that she was a gifted student who also excelled socially.

At the end of the school year, Mrs. West received a job offer that added an extra dimension to their small, humble world. One of Mrs. West's former laundry clients, Grenville Lindall Winthrop, asked her to become a live-in custodian for his New York City home while he summered at Gorton Place, his estate in Lenox, Massachusetts.

Winthrop was a direct descendant of John Winthrop, the first governor of the Massachusetts Bay Colony. The Winthrops were among the first upper-class settlers in the United States. Painfully shy, Grenville Winthrop had one true passion in life: art. He attended Harvard University, studying geology and art history before going on to receive a law degree. Upon graduation, he cofounded a law firm in New York City but retired in 1896 at the age of thirty-two to commit himself to his love of art. His home at 15 East Eighty-First Street on Manhattan's Upper East Side housed his private collection. Winthrop was the very definition of a wealthy, eccentric art collector. On the rare occasions when a visitor rang his doorbell, the reclusive man pretended to be the butler as he showed them around his private galleries.

Winthrop acquired over four thousand pieces in his lifetime, eventually requiring three stately homes to store the works. Because he refused to loan his treasured possessions to museums, his collection would remain largely unseen by the public until it was donated to Harvard University, his alma mater, after his death in 1943. He possessed more works by Ingres than any other private collector, more than fifty pieces by William Blake, and masterpieces by Pierre-Auguste Renoir, Vincent van Gogh, and Auguste Rodin, among numerous others. Stephan S. Wolohojian, the former curator of Harvard's Fogg Art Museum, remarked that Winthrop's collection was "one of the most important, yet least well-known, collections ever assembled in the United States."[2]

Every summer from 1938 to 1942, Mrs. West and Margaret relocated to the Winthrop mansion. Each day, Mrs. West wore the uniform of a private maid, appearing official when she answered the door for packages or deliveries. She was vigilant about protecting the house and its contents.

While other children spent their summers at family lake houses or playing in the woods, the unwanted daughter of Irish immigrants lived in a private art gallery in the heart of Manhattan. Slowly walking from room to room, Margaret surveyed every inch of the mansion. Each of the five floors of the thirty-six-room home was devoted to a different theme. There was an entire floor of Korean Buddhas and Mesoamerican masks, a room dedicated to French drawings, and Asian art that ran down the center of hallways. Fifty clocks were scattered throughout the house.[3] On the hour, the clocks came alive with chimes ringing on every floor. Alone in the sumptuous space, her only companions were the tomes that lined the library's walls. Margaret paged through Winthrop's collection of early American books, many of which would later be housed in the Library of Congress.

Inside Grenville Winthrop's mansion at 15 East Eighty-First Street. *Private collection.*

The summer days living at the Winthrop mansion did not change Mrs. West's station in life, but they transformed a young girl into an art devotee. During the hot summer days, Margaret remained mostly inside, walking among the masters and soaking in what she saw. Greatness, wealth, and beauty consumed her attention during these early impressionable years.

Often, Mrs. West would catch Margaret lingering, transfixed, around the child's favorite pieces. One of them was *The Family of Lucien Bonaparte*, a drawing by Ingres depicting a mother and her eight children, making Margaret yearn for the affection of a mother and the playful, chaotic joy of siblings.[4]

A John Singer Sargent painting, *The Breakfast Table* (1883–1884), hung in the heart of the mansion.[5] Margaret felt a kinship with the subject of the painting, a young girl reading alone at a table, surrounded by sterling silver teapots and English china. The scene was all too familiar to Margaret during her time at Mr. Winthrop's, where she ate oatmeal alone in the large kitchen, reading in the nook by the window, pausing to watch passersby through the linden trees.

Despite her loneliness, Margaret later described the experience of residing each summer amid luxury and wealth as "a great education" and "a place for me to play in the summer." Years later, in a different but equally opulent setting, Margaret candidly remarked, "I grew up with this," almost as if she could hardly believe it herself.

Those summers, it would turn out, were merely a foretaste of the types of spaces Margaret would someday occupy thanks to her own hard work and determination.

When Mrs. West and Margaret returned to East Elmhurst at the end of the summer, Jack and Bridget resumed their once-a-month visits to Mrs. West's house. With the Great Depression behind him, Jack excelled as a doorman at The Pierre and his interest in the stock market continued. He took the advice of wealthy guests who mentored him. One gentleman even bequeathed to him a seat on the New York Stock Exchange.

During Sunday visits with Margaret, Jack sometimes smelled like liquor, which made Margaret want to hide. For her tenth birthday, a party was organized in Mrs. West's backyard, with friends from school and her parents. When Jack and Bridget arrived, fear ran through Margaret as she heard Jack's slurred words and loud voice ringing out. As he made his way over to greet his daughter, Margaret thought as she smelled the liquor on him, "Do not even come near me."[6] After this occurred, Margaret slipped away and remained in her room until she heard her parents leave.

Jack always wanted to see Margaret's report card and her assignments marked with stars. The stars, a mark of excellence, were an important indicator for him. Margaret felt she did not fully belong to anyone, and understood that her survival depended on the money Jack gave Mrs. West. It was an unspoken exchange: If Margaret worked hard, Jack would pay for her care. Like many aspects of Margaret's life, this arrangement was never verbalized, but she certainly did not want to disappoint him. Reviewing her assignments, Jack always praised her efforts. As a result of this dynamic, Margaret began placing significant pressure on herself. Good grades became essential, as she often heard her father proclaim, "Ireland is the land of saints and scholars."

Mrs. West used the comment as an opportunity to delicately ask whether Jack would consider funding piano lessons for Margaret. For Mrs. West, piano lessons were as important as academics. The ability to read music trained the mind and taught memorization. Seeing merit in the discipline, Jack agreed. "My father would spend money on education and music lessons," Margaret later remembered.

The Italian maestro, Professor Miccu, was hired. Professor Miccu's teaching was advanced, and Mrs. West made sure Margaret practiced daily. This early discipline allowed Margaret to excel rapidly, giving her an advantage and a growing aspiration to become a concert pianist. Performance came easily to her, and she relished entertaining in grand style. Playing in front of an audience energized the budding extrovert and contributed to Margaret's star-like persona.

In light of Margaret's early musical and academic success, it was not long before private school was discussed. Mrs. West, Jack, and Bridget agreed on one thing: they wanted Margaret to advance. But there were the limitations of a doorman's budget to consider. Conveniently, St. Gabriel's Church in Queens opened a new Catholic grammar school that offered subsidized tuition for a few families in need. Margaret acquired a scholarship to enter third grade at St. Gabriel's.

Although strict, the nuns at St. Gabriel's provided a safe, accepting environment, establishing a hunger for learning and a spiritual foundation that became firmly planted in Margaret's constitution. Through example, Mrs. West taught Margaret good manners, kindness, generosity, and service. Every Advent, Mrs. West assembled baskets for the local priests, teaching firsthand lessons of compassion, kindness, and the merits of working hard.

St. Gabriel's school, and the friendships formed there, opened doors for young Margaret into the wealthy and educated social circles of New York City.

By the time Margaret started middle school, her thirst for learning was more than just schoolwork and what she observed at home. She found what she was looking for at the neighboring Farrell house. She used to pass by their house on the way to church. When the maid had a day off, Margaret would babysit the family's three daughters.

Peter T. Farrell was a lawyer and New York State senator. Margaret's favorite room in the home was Mr. Farrell's law library. In the center of the room sat a large wooden desk and leather chair. Bookcases of law books lined the walls, and a wooden ladder rested on rails, allowing access to hard-to-reach books. Margaret even found the smell of the room alluring. "I was very curious about the law books. I was interested in pulling them out, and when I did so, my mind was clicking. It was not hard for me to understand the books' contents. I would get absorbed in them while the children took their naps."[7]

One day, upon discovering Margaret in his library, absorbed in one of his law books, Mr. Farrell said, "Margaret, my little scholar, I had no idea that you could be so enthralled in my law books. The study of law can take you in many different directions and to many places. You are welcome in my law library at any time."[8]

She decided at that moment, in that place, that she would become a lawyer someday. "There was no real reason I wanted to be a lawyer, except that I loved the books, but I didn't really know what a lawyer did."[9] Margaret would later say, "I was always in touch with my destiny."

Mr. Farrell had more influence on the course of Margaret's life than any other man, igniting her passion for the law and confirming her resolve to pursue higher education.

In the 1940s, female lawyers represented only 2.4 percent of all lawyers in America.[10] Having not yet entered her teens, Margaret could not have known that the field of law was not open to women. To Mr. Farrell's credit, he never tried to deter her from her interest in law—in fact, he became Margaret's mentor. When he saw that she could read and understand the content of his law books with ease, he recognized that the child was gifted far beyond her years.

When Mr. Farrell decided to run for a county judgeship in Queens, Margaret did her part to help him get elected. She used her previous volunteer experience at church selling "chances" (a type of raffle ticket) as a model for assisting in Mr. Farrell's campaign. "Every year, the nuns from

St. Gabriel's would hand out boxes of chances to sell for the church fair. People would make contributions. I loved to sell chances. I would take the first book and sell it and the second book, etc. I took my bicycle and went door to door. I found that people were very kind and did not have any hesitation about giving money to me, and I had no hesitation receiving from them. Everyone in my church and neighborhood was under the impression that I didn't have parents, so people were good to me."[11]

Mr. Farrell, a Democrat, provided Margaret with her first opportunity to develop political canvassing skills. She quickly displayed an instinct for grassroot campaign work. For Mr. Farrell's campaign, Margaret went door to door in East Elmhurst, just like she did for the church fairs.

"Hello," she said, as a door was opened. "Did you know that our neighbor, Mr. Peter Farrell, is running for the county judge seat? He is a great man, and he needs your vote."[12] Mr. Farrell handily won, and he served Queens County from 1943 to 1961 before he rose to the New York Supreme Court.

When Margaret graduated from middle school, the Farrells gifted her a beautiful leather journal with her name, Margaret Mary O'Shaughnessy, engraved in gold lettering. It made her feel valued.

Judge Farrell remained a hero to Margaret for the rest of her life. He showed her a more ambitious path to follow than the traditionally female roles offered by Mrs. West and her sisters, who were a laundress, a seamstress, and a baker. But their example of kindness, service, and faith helped build her character.

In September 1945, Margaret started her freshman year at Dominican Academy High School in Manhattan. After abiding her mother's advice to work toward having her own independent career, she earned a full scholarship. Established by Dominican nuns in 1897, Dominican Academy is located in a former mansion at 44 East Sixty-Eighth Street, between Park and Madison Avenues in the heart of New York City.

The mansion was previously owned by Colonel Michael Friedsam, president of B. Altman's, a chain of luxury department stores founded in New York City. Friedsam amassed an art collection that included more than two hundred paintings, including four Rembrandts and multiple Vermeers and Botticellis. To house his collection, Friedsam built the five-story limestone mansion. After his death in 1931, his art collection, valued at $10 million, was dispersed between the Metropolitan Museum of Art and the Brooklyn Museum. Trustees of his estate were tasked with deciding whether to sell or donate his home. Friedsam left only one stipulation: The building had to be used for educational purposes. In 1936, the trustees decided to sell the property (valued at $35 million today) to the Dominican sisters for $1. Dominican Academy still serves as an all-honors Catholic high school for girls in the center of Manhattan.[13]

Walking into the building that first day, Margaret stood in awe. Just like summering in Grenville Winthrop's mansion, going to school in the Friedsam mansion meant being surrounded by opulence beyond her means: dramatic white marble staircases with plush red runners, ornate crown molding, stained glass and plaster ceilings with floral medallions. There were tall arched doorways and fireplaces large enough to stand inside.

In the 1940s and 1950s, few women in the United States received more than a high school education. But the Dominican Sisters' mission, like that of most all-girls Catholic schools at the time, was to prepare students for college. Dressed in habits, the Sisters at Dominican Academy were serious and devout, creating an atmosphere of academic rigor. Chapel prayers and foreign language study, including Latin courses, were expected of every student. However, the nuns did more than just teach academics and religion. Their pupils partook in the full gamut of New York City life experiences, from volunteering at food pantries to sitting in a private box at the Metropolitan Opera House.

This educational experience attracted wealthy, elite Manhattan parents, as well as dignitaries from around the world who searched New York City for the best education for their daughters. In later years, whenever Margaret discussed Dominican Academy, she referred to it as the "tip of the top"—one of the finest high school experiences a girl could receive.

Unlike most Dominican Academy students, Margaret had to earn her way academically via her full, four-year scholarship. Attending Dominican Academy elevated her on a social and intellectual level, in ways she could never have achieved on her own. While she excelled alongside her other classmates, she was thankful for the school uniform, which allowed her to fit in with the other girls. Years of observing both Mrs. West and her own demure, soft-spoken mother had taught Margaret to naturally bear expectations that she not only be intelligent, but also graceful and refined. Her puritan life with Belinda West and her undisclosed scholarship arrangement only made her work harder.

The Sisters at Dominican Academy empowered Margaret, providing her with leadership positions that might not have happened at a co-ed school. The sisters noticed that Margaret embraced public speaking, and she was asked to take on a leadership role during Open House Days at Dominican Academy.

By 1945, the United Nations had been formed, and many of the meetings were taking place in New York City, where UN headquarters were being built. Latin American Catholic diplomats viewed Dominican Academy as a distinguished place of study for their daughters. To attract prospective families, Mother Superior showcased the school. Each Open House program included a brief history of the Academy, choir songs, and an orator.

The first time Margaret was asked to speak about current events, something switched on inside her. The sisters gave her *Newsweek* and *Time* magazines so she could provide a ten-minute report. She later said, "I would speak about what was happening in America. I had half an hour to prepare these speeches, and I was giving them all the time."[14]

Jack O'Shaughnessy had just finished his shift at The Pierre. During their last visit, Margaret had mentioned that she had been asked to give a talk to potential students and their parents. Knowing what a great privilege it was, Jack was anxious to hear her speech.

Stepping into the entrance hall of Dominican Academy, Jack took in the majesty of the space. At the reception desk, he asked proudly, "Where's the great Peggy?"

A girl walking by, books in hand, replied, "I'm Peggy." Another girl lifted her head from the reception desk saying, "I'm also Peggy."

"No, no," he loudly exclaimed, "*The Great Peggy!*"

From the back office, Sister Mary Elizabeth swiftly approached. "May I help you, sir? Many of our young ladies have the name Peggy, Irish as it is. Might you be referring to Peggy O'Shaughnessy?"

"Yes. She's my daughter," Jack responded.

"Why, of course. She's about to begin a presentation for some of our visiting guests. Come with me. I'll take you there."

Motioning to an empty seat in the front row, Sister Mary Elizabeth quietly seated Jack. From the podium, Margaret watched, her cheeks flushed. Jack hadn't told her he would attend. She hoped he was sober.

Margaret launched into her talk, mentioning among other things the upcoming presidential campaign of 1948. "We all know that President Truman is running for reelection. Although all the polls say that Dewey will win, I predict that Truman will," she said. After the intense research she had done on the topic, Margaret was confident in her prediction—and in the end, Truman did win.

After finishing her first-ever extemporaneous speech, she took a seat behind the podium. That day, Margaret became aware of a calling: speaking unrehearsed before an audience. Yet, sitting through the other speeches, Margaret felt unsettled. Her father had shown up unannounced in a place where she was known, and respected, but she had only revealed to a few girls that she did not live with her parents. Although she wasn't close to her father, she did not want her friends to think negatively about him or look down on her.

The estrangement from her father made her work even harder to win scholarships to college. Hard work would help her counteract her fears. She was a survivor. And yet, she would always reflect on the way her father called her "The Great Peggy." She was driven to live up to his high expectations and earn the affection she so desperately craved.

More Than a Debate

Margaret and John (front bottom left) at the Albertus Magnus spring formal, 1953.
Albertus Magnus College.

On Saturday evening, June 19, 1948, two days before her seventeenth birthday, Margaret was slated to perform the piano composition *Kamennoi Ostrow* by Arthur Rubinstein at the town hall in Elmhurst, Long Island. Having just finished her junior year at Dominican Academy and after endless hours of practicing her pieces, Margaret saw this performance as a culmination of all her efforts. She had worked over every note until it was perfect. Tonight, she hoped to fulfill her early childhood dream of becoming a concert pianist.

Under the spotlight, the young woman demonstrated poise and refinement. As her fingers hit the keys, Margaret exuded confidence and elegance. She performed the Rubinstein piece seamlessly.

A week after the recital, at Professor Miccu's studio, Margaret asked her longtime teacher to assess her performance. What she wanted to know was, "Am I good enough to play in an orchestra?"

Miccu's unexpected response crushed her. "Margaret," he said. "Although you are a high-functioning piano professional, you will never be exceptional enough to become a concert pianist. But I could see you becoming a jazz pianist."

Hearing this hard truth and reflecting on all her years of sacrifice, Margaret broke down in tears. She turned away, leaving the studio behind—and with it, her dreams of ever becoming a concert pianist.

Margaret was forced to accept the disappointment of letting go of a dream, but she did not lose hope. If she could not be the best at something, she wanted no part of it. She turned to the public library for solace. There, a great shift occurred. "I happened upon a book, *How to Go into Politics: A Practical and Entertaining Guide* by Senator Hugh Scott, a former veteran," Margaret recalled. "I don't know why I picked out that book, but I read it. None of the advice appealed or applied to me. . . . Each piece of advice was totally male-oriented, such as, 'join your veteran organizations' or 'be active at your post.' Nonetheless, it sparked my interest in government."[1]

It was a serendipitous moment. Remembering all she had learned from Judge Farrell and how she'd felt delivering speeches about current events at Dominican Academy, Margaret realized she was destined for a redirected path: into the exhilarating world of politics. In 1949, during the era of poodle skirts, jukeboxes, and drive-in movie theaters, Margaret enrolled at Albertus Magnus College in New Haven, Connecticut. Located only minutes away from Yale University, Albertus Magnus College was also known for academic excellence. Once again heeding her mother's advice, Margaret earned a full academic scholarship for all four years at the all-girls Catholic school. Established in 1925, Albertus Magnus had high academic standards akin to the Seven Sisters, a group of prestigious, all-women liberal arts colleges in the northeast that sought to give women an education equal to Ivy League schools. For Margaret, Albertus Magnus provided a distinctly faith-based education as well as a rigorous liberal arts curriculum. Every student was required to complete four years of Latin or Greek study.

Albertus Magnus students were academically-minded—a contrast to the typical young female of the time. In the 1950s, only about 1.2 percent of American women attended college.[2] Gender roles were seemingly unmovable: Men were employed outside the home, while most women, if they were economically able, stayed home raising children. Few women challenged these cultural assumptions. With the Depression and World War II only a few years behind them, Americans sought peace, security, and prosperity. This was true even at Albertus Magnus. In pursuing higher education, its students were ahead of their time; nonetheless, many of these young women also viewed their college years as an opportunity to earn their "MRS degree," securing a ring by spring of their senior year from a young man at one of the nearby universities.

Margaret didn't share these goals. She felt called to do more and destined to follow a different path. As she would later say, the idea was not her own. She believed her life trajectory was arranged by God.

According to Sister Dolores Liptak, an Albertus graduate and University of Connecticut professor, Albertus Magnus's academic rigor, coupled with the lack of male competition, left a wide-open field.[3] This environment challenged Margaret with leadership positions not yet open to women in the world beyond her college campus. The Dominican nuns at Albertus Magnus nourished Margaret's critical thinking skills and faith. Much of the parental nurturing that Margaret had been denied throughout her unusual childhood was received via the small, female-focused Catholic schools she attended.

In an article for the Albertus Magnus alumni magazine, *Magnum Opus*, a classmate of Margaret's, Maureen McManus, was interviewed many years later:

> As Maureen was walking into her dorm, McAuliffe Hall, she was awed observing Margaret, who had come in with a fairly large contingent from New York City. It occurred to her that Margaret went to Dominican Academy and they all came in together. Maureen remembers being terribly impressed. It was obvious to her that Margaret was the most serious of the group.
>
> As Maureen recalled, "She wasn't glamorous, none of the girls were, since it was an all-girls' college. Margaret seemed sophisticated, independent, extremely mature and self-possessed." Maureen had come out of Taunton, Massachusetts, a working-class city and Margaret had come out of Long Island, a suburb of New York City. While they worked setting tables in the dining room for dinner, they talked

for hours. When other girls talked about their dates, Margaret talked about public affairs and current issues. She was very driven.

According to Maureen: "Margaret frequently stayed up all night studying. She was tense and anxious about the exams and about whether she'd do well. Living on coffee and little sleep, she was in constant motion. She was a reader, a student, a talker, a debater. She liked discussions and arguments and was the type who took up a cause and once she did, there were no lengths to which she would not go. Margaret had a wonderful ability to laugh at herself . . . a great deal of wit."[4]

Another classmate, Anne Crellin Seggerman, described Margaret's determination: "Margaret was all by herself, building her career, all while the rest of us were doing what college-aged girls do."[5]

Margaret's steps were deliberate, following her natural instinct. It was only a matter of time before she would push her way into rooms few women dared to enter.

By the end of sophomore year, Margaret announced her major in political science and economics. She was featured in Albertus's *Silver Horn* publication, which referred to her as the "female Winston Churchill" and the "Hepburn of legislation."

In the fall of 1951, the Albertus Magnus debate team traveled to a tournament at the University of Connecticut. Margaret arrived with a dozen other Albertus Magnus girls. The high-ceilinged auditorium was arranged with two lecterns at the front, one on each side of the room. Most of the competitors were young men dressed like lawyers. A senior at Fairfield University, a Jesuit all-male institution, John Heckler had gone up against his own classmates and students from other Connecticut schools, winning every debate. Against the other schools, the Fairfield debate team was undefeated.

John's next competitor was not hard to find among the sea of eager young men in gray and black suits. As Margaret stepped to the front of the room, her bright, round face shined and her hazel eyes beamed.

She had written out her arguments and rehearsed them the night before—always doing her homework. For each debate, she was ready to run her opponent into the ground if she could. As she set up papers and materials on her lectern, her Albertus Magnus teammates took seats in the front row, offering support.

Opposite her on the debate stage, John Heckler approached his lectern. Margaret could see the ambition in this young man with the crew cut hair and bushy eyebrows. His hunger shone in his piercing blue eyes. Margaret knew ambition. She had it, too.

John flashed her a smile, but she refused to let his charm distract her from the competition at hand. The debate centered on whether the United States should have entered the Korean War. In her opening statement, Margaret mercilessly tore into John's argument, showing her adversary little compassion. Although John Heckler was a senior and came prepared, he was no equal to her. Margaret won both of her two rounds of debates against John, impressing him greatly. She had debated him and won.

John studied her more closely. He had not noticed it at first, but Miss O'Shaughnessy was more than an adversary. With her stylish short hair and sparkling eyes, she was a potential date.

Soon afterward, at a party at Fairfield University, the two met again—and this time, John shifted from opponent to suitor. "Well, hello, Miss O'Shaughnessy," he said, his voice smooth. "Our debate a few weeks ago was the first time we've lost since I joined the team."

Margaret winked. "I'm sorry to break your record."[6]

It took a lot to impress John Heckler. The eldest of three sons, John had grown up in the country in Meriden, Connecticut, developing a strong sense of self-importance and turning into a bit of a showoff. With his strong jawline and lean, muscular physique, he was a real looker. Attention from young ladies was the norm for him, but he was drawn in by Margaret's cosmopolitan flair. This was different. She was petite and feminine, not flashy or frivolous. Margaret possessed an intellect that rivaled John's. It was intoxicating.

For their first date, John took her to an expensive seafood restaurant in downtown Hartford. She ordered swordfish, a dish she had never tasted before. As much as John was smitten with her, Margaret was also taken by John. Five years her senior, he had served in World War II and had a worldly allure. Over a bottle of wine, they talked about their shared Irish Catholic backgrounds and love of politics. For John, there was no comparison between Margaret and the flirtatious, light-hearted girls he had dated before. He knew he had met his match.

John's parents, George and May Heckler, brought up their sons in a devout Catholic home. May was a third-grade teacher and was very strict, keeping tight reins on her three boys. She taught them the importance of godliness and honesty—but her eldest son always tested the limit. In his high school yearbook, classmate Carrie Lee wrote, "To a handsome brute, lots of success. You deserve the best. Go and get it."

As a child, John built model airplanes, entering them into competitions. Soon, he was saving his hard-earned dollars to take flight lessons. He earned his pilot's license before his driver's license.

In 1945, prior to finishing high school, John applied to the Coast Guard Academy. Local commercial fishermen volunteered their sailing vessels to provide the coast guard with boats that would be undetected by German U-boats. The coast guard's mission was to find German subs and bomb them using depth charges. The academy offered free education, time on boats, and a chance to avoid the draft, all of which appealed to John.

During his second year, John grew disenchanted. The white glove inspections were "a lot of chicken shit,"[7] and he had little interest in becoming a marine engineer like most of the other cadets. Applying to Fairfield University and Yale with his veteran tuition benefits, John was accepted into both. He chose the newly founded Fairfield, a Catholic all-men's college, where he would become a member of the first class to graduate.

When Margaret and John met, she had relatively little dating experience. In contrast, John was a ladies' man. He often rented a plane and took her on flights over Meriden, needing the extra flying hours. John's sense of adventure made Margaret yearn for a life with him. His carefree, playful nature balanced out her seriousness, allowing her to relax, and let go. He introduced her to fun in a way no one else had.

According to John's brother, George, John was always looking for the "brass ring"—just like a carousel rider reaching out to snag a ring as the brightly painted horses went around in circles. For John, Margaret was the "brass ring"—a girl who had talent and ability that he could not dismiss. John was smart, but Margaret was smarter. "She's so smart, I think I'll have to marry her," he confided to George.

In June 1952, John graduated magna cum laude from Fairfield, also earning the title of class salutatorian. After hearing John's graduation speech, the governor of Connecticut approached him and said, "Young man, if there is anything I can do to help you in the future, please do not hesitate to reach out to me."[8]

Margaret, meanwhile, was headed to a summer program at the University of Leiden in the Netherlands. Intent upon getting to Europe so he could see her over the summer, John found a job as a purser on the premier transatlantic cruise liner, the SS *America*.

Margaret traveled with her two closest friends from Albertus, both of whom came from upper-crust families. The girls boarded a Dutch ship, the SS *Waterman*, on July 10, 1952. They were quite the traveling troupe:

Oobie Butler, beautiful and stylish; Anne Gilbert, the wealthy, tall brunette; and Margaret, the petite auburn fireball, full of brains and passion. Once in Europe, Margaret took the fast train from the Netherlands to Bremerhaven, Germany, to meet John at his ship and wrote in her journal:

In ten hours I'll see John! It was quite an ordeal, but infinitely worth it. It's been four weeks since I saw him. I'm dying to see him.

When Margaret arrived, on July 21, 1952, the SS *America* was in its berth. She made her way through the crowds and spotted John:

John's nonchalance as he walked down the gangplank never betrayed this— the way his arms closed about me. I had been dulled by traveling alone and the exhaustive train ride. Thus, John's enthusiasm jolted me. How can he remain so in love with life? I hope his love for me will endure as thrillingly.

John had arranged a short rendezvous with Margaret aboard the SS *America* where they ate stolen caviar and toasted with champagne. He never took his eyes off her. For Margaret, John represented capability, "savoir faire" and—most of all—the security she'd never received from her parents.

In Holland, Margaret took a class titled "Eastern and Western World," which was taught in English. The course provided her with the chance to represent the United States at an East-West conference between students from both sides of the Iron Curtain, opening her eyes to a political boundary she had not experienced before.

When the summer study abroad program ended, Anne Gilbert invited Margaret to stay with her at the home of Anne's aunt and uncle, Anne and Henry Klouse. Henry Klouse was the CEO of Chase Manhattan Bank and the wealthiest financier in New York City. Mrs. Klouse was so taken with Margaret that she offered to arrange a private audience with the Pope for her niece and Margaret.

On the day of the audience, Margaret and Anne, wearing classic black dresses and lace veils, arrived at the Vatican where they would meet Pope Pius XII at St. Peter's Basilica.

Pope Pius XII was a tall, slender man with large eyes that looked even bigger through his round spectacles. He spoke seven languages, including English. Dressed in his white robes, he blessed the girls and said prayers for them. Asking about their future plans, the pope first turned to Margaret. She was prepared, replying, "I'm going back to the States to finish college. Then I plan to go on to law school. I'm also thinking about running for public office."[9]

Hearing these words, Pope Pius XII lit up. He said Margaret's idea sounded like "a worthwhile endeavor." He finished by saying, "*Be a lawyer, but serve.*"

For the rest of her life, Margaret believed she had received a papal blessing not just to pursue a law degree and a career in politics, but also to serve. The pope had sanctified her path, and she was headed home.

• 4 •

Speaker of the House

From Margaret's 1953 college yearbook.
Albertus Magnus College.

⊘n November 4, 1952, just thirty-two years after American women won the right to vote, Margaret stepped into a voting booth for the first time in her life. At twenty-one, wearing an "I Like Ike" button on her lapel, she was thrilled to pull the lever in support of Dwight D. Eisenhower, the Republican candidate for US president. She had spent the past several months, the beginning of her senior year at Albertus Magnus, volunteering for the League of Women Voters. Margaret recruited her classmates, who were mostly Democrats, to help write postcards for Eisenhower in his race against Adlai Stevenson. Her senior-year roommate, Phyllis Mays, recounted that Margaret was "popular with all the other students, a very good speaker. She believed in the Republican party."[1]

Margaret was inspired by Eisenhower and would remain so throughout the years. Eisenhower, with Richard Nixon as vice president, won a landslide victory in 1952, becoming the first Republican president in twenty years. Shortly before she graduated from college, Margaret had her own landslide political victory.

During Margaret's final year at Albertus Magnus, John was enrolled at Fordham Law School. Settled into his dorm one winter night, he wrote to her, expressing his feelings.

Now the day is the 20th of February, 1953, but only 12:30AM and I write again reclining and very much alone in my room:

My Darling Peggy,

You are almost constantly with me, my Darling and it was with you today that I discovered, or should I say completely thought, about the "why" I am here—you are not only the wonderful being that makes these days bearable, but also the prime motivation. It is all very true, very good and very blessed . . . let us say that the more I have come to know you, the more deeply in love I have fallen. . . . You're perfect—honestly Peggy, in most every possible way. . . .

For some of Margaret's college girlfriends, a marriage proposal would mark the end of their academic and professional aspirations. Margaret did receive her "ring by spring," which she gladly accepted, but her final months of college were defined by something else entirely: a run for elected office. For three years, Margaret had dominated at speech and debate tournaments, but now her attention turned toward something bigger: the Connecticut Intercollegiate Student Legislature (CISL).

The CISL was comprised of students from seventeen colleges and universities across the state. Taking over the State Capitol for a week while the Connecticut State Legislature took a spring break and the statehouse was empty, the CISL practiced parliamentary procedure and voted on mock bills. In preparation, students researched topics for bills they wanted to present and plotted positions to pursue. The top positions were the elected offices of Speaker of the House and President of the Senate. To win one of those spots, candidates had to campaign at participating college campuses.

After several years of being very outspoken on the debate team, Margaret was encouraged by her female teammates to run for CISL Speaker of the House, a position never before held by a woman. As Phyllis Mays explained, "We learned to be aggressive because we didn't have men. There weren't that many schools that were all-women. Peggy was able to assume her leadership because there were not any male competitors."[2]

Margaret wasn't concerned about running for a position that no woman had held before. She understood she would need to work twice as hard to fight stereotypes of female incapability. She spent countless hours in the library studying and memorizing Robert's Rules of Order and Parliamentary procedure. Margaret believed if you were going to compete, you should compete to win.

When John came up from Fordham to visit, she asked him what he thought of her bid for Speaker of the House. He enthusiastically lent his support as her campaign manager. Her passion became his obsession. John arranged meetings with fraternities, starting with his existing connections at Fairfield and Yale. The fraternity audience was the exact demographic Margaret needed to win, since most of the voters would be men. A determined, strategic man who was also "just one of the guys," John had the skills to help break Margaret into the old boys' clubs.

On a frosty afternoon in January, John picked her up in his black Chevrolet Bel Air to kick off the campaign trail at Yale—at that time, an all-men's university. They visited Yale fraternities, where Margaret shook hands and delivered a short speech. This formula became the model for every college she visited during her campaign.

The meetings at Yale stretched late into the night—the hours when most college students thrived. It was after 11:00 p.m. when John and Margaret arrived back on the Albertus Magnus campus. Margaret's dorm was locked. She had violated curfew, for which she received a warning.

Realizing she and John would need to return late from campaigning in the future, Margaret decided to ask for temporary leniency from the Dean of Students, Sister Francis DeSales, the Mother Superior. Margaret requested a meeting with Mother Superior and John came along to help present her case. They opened with an apology for breaking curfew, assuring the dean that Margaret was campaigning. John explained that he was assisting as her campaign manager and that if Margaret was to have a chance of winning, they needed to visit as many participating colleges as possible. Because of the distance they'd need to travel, there would be some evenings when they would return to Albertus Magnus after Margaret's 10:30 p.m. curfew. They stressed that the race was significant because Margaret was the first female to ever run for CISL Speaker of the House.

Mother Superior ran a college where young women were taught that they could do anything—even if some of them would never enter a "man's world" post-graduation. When she inquired about Margaret maintaining her grades and academic club involvement between campaign trail trips, Margaret assured her that she would do so. After a long pause, Mother Superior, in her full black habit, stood up from her desk and fixed her gaze on Margaret.

"Miss O'Shaughnessy," she said. "You may do this under one condition—*WIN!*"[3]

In the months before the session, Margaret whistle-stopped at thirteen of the seventeen member colleges. John, now a licensed pilot, flew Margaret to many speaking engagements as the March deadline for the vote approached.

A CISL dinner dance at the Hotel Bond in Hartford, arranged for all the students, attended also by the governor of Connecticut, preceded the vote for Speaker of the House and President of the Senate. It was Margaret's last opportunity to campaign. She shook hands with nearly three hundred guests to ask for their vote.

The big week finally arrived. As Margaret's classmate, Maureen McManus O'Donnell described it years later, she "could still picture Margaret on the steps of Mohan Hall in a plaid suit holding a briefcase. Her face was so serious, her hair perfectly coiffed. She was ready to go to the mock Connecticut student legislature like it was the real thing."[4]

The Connecticut State House's plush blue-and-gold carpet and three-story vaulted ceilings felt grand. On the first day of CISL week, a flurry of student lobbyists and attorneys flooded the room. Taking her seat in the same chair a state representative had occupied while debating and enacting laws, Margaret experienced her first magical taste of legislature in action.

The next day, the two candidates for Speaker of the House presided over the room. Based on his lack of preparation, Margaret's male opponent clearly expected that since he was a man, he had an edge. Then it was Margaret's turn. As she stood before the microphone, the entire room was still talking among themselves. Mustering all the strength behind her full five-foot, two-inch height, she laid the gavel down hard. "Good morning, ladies and gentlemen. It is 9:15 on March thirteenth, and this meeting is now called to order!"

The room fell silent. As her time at the podium went on, Margaret's hours of memorizing Robert's Rules of Order immediately set her apart from her opponent.

The final vote was scheduled during the Friday legislative session. The students would be voting for positions of President of the Senate and the Speaker of the House. Before the election, Governor Lodge gave an introductory speech. The first vote included all the candidates on the ballot, including Margaret. After tallying the initial vote, a second vote followed—and her name was still on the ballot. Finally, Margaret was named Speaker of the House, winning in a landslide: 163 to 97. It was both the largest majority ever received, and the first time the CISL elected a woman as Speaker of the House. While Margaret had held many leadership positions at her all-girls schools, this was by far the grandest stage—and the first one consisting of a male opponent and a male majority of voters.

In the 1953 Albertus Magnus yearbook, the school's collective pride over Margaret's achievement was evident, as her election was called "the biggest news on campus this year." A picture of Margaret, gavel in hand and a young man leaning over her desk was captioned, "Peggy O'Shaughnessy receives the congratulations of the minority leader."[5]

That year's Connecticut Student Legislature included a gentleman from Yale named Edwin Meese. When Margaret became Speaker of the House, neither he nor Margaret could have predicted that thirty years later, they would sit side-by-side in President Ronald Reagan's cabinet—he as counselor to the president and US attorney general and she as secretary of health and human services.

In May 1953, Margaret's schooling at Albertus Magnus ended. In her senior yearbook, the student experience was commemorated with these words: "We conversed with the world's great men. We met Homer and Dante and Shakespeare. We met Cicero and we asked ourselves about friendship and art. We met Plato and we asked of love and immortality. . . . Above all we have found a philosophy of life. . . . We have been given a vision of eternity so that no lesser directives can dominate our lives."[6]

For the eight years of Margaret's all-girl's Catholic education, female students and nuns had surrounded and challenged her to

Margaret's first elected position as Speaker of the House of the Connecticut Intercollegiate Student Legislature, 1953. *Albertus Magnus College.*

pursue excellence, regardless of the gender bias that prevailed in 1950s society. She received not only a degree in political science, but also a foundation in theology. Albertus Magnus set her on a path of steadfastness, philanthropy, and a desire to serve.

Following graduation, Margaret's summer was filled with wedding preparations. John's affection toward her provided a comfort that in the past she'd only received from Mrs. West. She trusted John and her love for him was certain.

August 28, 1953, was a blazingly hot day in New York City, but the marble interior of St. Patrick's Cathedral on Fifth Avenue was cool and comfortable. Sacredly grand and opulent, the historic landmark occupied a full block, giving Margaret and John's wedding the appearance of a royal occasion. The wedding Mass would not have been possible without the generosity of Margaret's friend Anne Gilbert's Aunt Anne and Uncle Henry Klouse, who were among the largest contributors to the Catholic Church in New York City.

Dressed in a tailcoat, a boutonniere affixed to his lapel, a pensive Jack O'Shaughnessy waited in the nave until the time when he would walk his daughter down the aisle and give her in marriage to John Heckler. Margaret had, by all standards, exceeded Jack's expectation. Today he would be giving his daughter away and yet, in a sense, she was never really his to give away.

Margaret's mother, Bridget O'Shaughnessy, sat beneath the flying buttresses in the front pew next to Belinda West, who was now in her nineties. These two women built a wall of faith around Margaret, which had brought her to this auspicious moment.

The afternoon sun embraced the city sky as John Heckler zipped onto Fifth Avenue in his convertible. In front of the bronze cathedral doors, John met his brother Charlie, his best man. His other brother, George, was in India serving as an aide to an admiral and could not make it back for the wedding.

In a back room, Margaret waited with her six bridesmaids in their rose-colored, chiffon gowns and white gloves. As the 2,500 pipes of the organ echoed throughout the cavernous sanctuary, the bridesmaids began their procession. Jack took Margaret's arm in his and they made their way down the long aisle. As Margaret approached John, he flashed his winning smile, putting her at ease. At the altar, her father kissed her and handed her over to her groom. The Mass was performed by Father Alban, John's first cousin. When they said their vows, Margaret was profoundly

At Margaret and John's wedding, St. Patrick's Cathedral, New York City, 1953.
Family collection.

moved. "I am my beloved's, and he is mine," was precisely how she felt about John.

In attendance was Margaret's friend, Oobie Butler, who remembered how the whole event, "was all very formal, very dignified." She said that while Margaret "had been deprived of many things in her life, her wedding was first class."[7] Margaret had invited her entire class from Albertus Magnus, who arrived on buses from all over New England.

When it came to the reception, Jack knew there was one thing he could do for his daughter, whom he had emotionally failed over the years. As a long-established doorman at The Pierre, Jack O'Shaughnessy had reserved a luxurious banquet room in the grand hotel, providing Margaret and John with a reception in one of the most sought-after wedding venues in New York City. The white marble double staircase, hand-painted frescoes on the ceilings, and magnificent ambiance of The Pierre completed a perfect wedding day. John's mother, May Heckler, commented that Father Alban had "tied a good knot."

• 5 •

Love and Law

Boston College Law School graduating class of 1956. *Boston College.*

On a breezy Sunday afternoon in early September 1953, soon after their wedding, John and Margaret sailed from the craggy coast of Marblehead, Massachusetts, on a twenty-two-foot catboat. As former captain of the coast guard sailing team, John managed the boat on his own while Margaret relaxed, bundled up to protect her Irish skin, enjoying the smell of saltwater in the cool fall air and admiring her husband's confidence at the helm. Whether it was sailing, flying, or race-car driving, she loved his adventurousness. Their personalities complemented one another: John provided fun and excitement, while Margaret laid the guardrails for their ambitions.

Finally, Margaret felt like she belonged to someone. Still, during that idyllic afternoon on the water, she was preoccupied with thoughts about what lay ahead. That week, she and John were scheduled to meet with the dean of Harvard Law.

Marblehead, a shore town north of Boston, was the ideal location for the newlyweds to begin their life together. They rented a one-bedroom cottage, allowing them to live on a tight budget while both attended law school. Margaret's childhood dream of pursuing a law degree, fostered by her East Elmhurst neighbor, Judge Farrell, felt within reach. During her senior year at Albertus Magnus, she had written a paper that won her a single-year scholarship for law school. She was accepted at Harvard Law School—the premiere law school in the country and her first choice.

Margaret's Harvard Law acceptance determined the newly married couple's decision to settle in the Boston area, so John applied there, as well. Remembering the offer of future assistance from the governor of Connecticut at his graduation from Fairfield University, John wrote to the governor, asking for a letter of recommendation. Belinda West also generously offered to pay for John's first semester at Harvard Law. Now, both Margaret and John were slated to begin there in the fall of 1953.

The incoming five-hundred-member class consisted of only a handful of women. Margaret had applied and been admitted using the name Margaret O'Shaughnessy. But mere weeks before classes would begin, the school's administration became aware of her marriage, and Margaret and John were called in to meet with the dean of Harvard Law School.

Arriving on the northwest corner of Harvard Yard, they faced the Romanesque façade of the Harvard Law Library. Above ten pillars were inscribed the Latin words, "*Non Sub Homine sed Sub Deo et Lege.*" In English: "Not Under Man but Under God and Law."

Margaret and John were ushered into Dean Irwin Griswold's office. After formalities, the dean, an imposing man in a three-piece suit, said, "We have never had a husband and wife in the same class. It is not advisable. It would put a terrible strain on your marriage."

Harvard had begun accepting women only three years prior, so the dean's theory was largely untested. Nonetheless, his opinion went unquestioned. Founded in 1636, Harvard was the first school of higher learning in the United States, but its law school was one of the last in the country to admit women. Dean Griswold felt that female law students would, at best, attend part-time because they would marry, get pregnant, and take time off to raise children. When women were first admitted to Harvard Law, the dean ignored their presence. According to Harvard historian

Daniel Coquillette, Dean Griswold stated, "Of the woman we admit, half will probably drop out or not practice law. Thus, we have admitted extra men to the class."[1]

When Margaret was accepted into Harvard Law in 1953, the GI Bill was less than a decade old. The bill, which offered college education funds to veterans, created an increased demand among men to pursue higher degrees of all sorts, including law degrees—thus pushing women back into domestic life. "Griswold did not like the idea of women taking a man's place at the school," Coquillette said.[2]

A pettier fear also drove Harvard's prejudice against women: that female students could surpass their male counterparts in the classroom. "Women were admitted to Harvard for the first time in 1950, and there were only a very few," Coquillette noted. "Harvard was a harsh environment for women during these early years. Harvard was very much an old boys' club. Some of the faculty and male students either encouraged women or were simply indifferent to their presence. At the end of their first year in June 1951, the women's grade distribution on the anonymously graded final exams matched closely to that of the men."[3] Coquillette recounted the story of Elizabeth Bartholet, a Harvard Law graduate. In 1963, Elizabeth Bartholet (LLB, 1965) and her husband were enrolled in the same course, and Elizabeth did better on the final exam. This outcome distressed "the course's professor, who feared it would be a crisis if a woman did better than her husband, because it could ruin her marriage." The professor confided in two other faculty members, who later relayed the incident to Bartholet. She recalled, even at "this ultimate meritocratic place, as Harvard Law School sees itself, there was a professor . . . [who] actually wondered what he should do . . . as if lowering my grade or raising my husband's was a possibility."[4] In the end, her grades were left alone.

Harvard was a new frontier for Margaret and other women her age. Three more years would pass before Ruth Bader Ginsberg, in 1956, walked underneath those Latin words inscribed on the Harvard Law Library. Margaret Heckler and Ruth Bader Ginsberg were not aware of it, but they were leading parallel lives, pushing against barriers of rampant sexual discrimination at a time when few women pursued a legal career. Both women were raised in New York, Ginsberg in Brooklyn and Heckler on Long Island; and they both married men who supported their quest to become lawyers. Both women trailblazed paths to the highest judicial and political appointments attainable in the United States. But because Margaret arrived first, she endured the worst of Dean Griswold's discrimination. The dean's attitude may have softened a bit by the time Ruth Bader Ginsburg successfully pushed through to attain a Harvard Law education.

In Dean Griswold's office, Margaret fell silent. The situation caused her to backpedal, thinking about all the years and hard work leading to this moment. She looked at John.

Turning toward her, John said, "Peggy, you plan to pursue politics. I'm the one who will most likely practice law. I should probably be the one to attend Harvard."[5]

As newlyweds, they didn't want to do anything that would put a strain on their marriage. Both John and Margaret agreed that it would be better for John to have the spot. She deferred to her husband, relinquishing a prized Harvard Law education. "I just accepted it," she later said.[6] If not for the obstacle that Dean Griswold placed in her path, Margaret likely would have been one of the first women to graduate from Harvard Law School.

Facing the dean, she said, "Well, tell me about the other surrounding law schools." Dean Griswold mentioned Boston College and Boston University. Margaret chose Boston College Law School.[7] After the couple left his office, Dean Griswold phoned the dean at Boston College Law School and requested Margaret be transferred out of Harvard Law and into Boston College. The dean at Boston College agreed to honor Margaret's scholarship, and Margaret prepared herself to be the only woman in a law class of 120 men.

In their Marblehead cottage one evening, sitting down to dinner, John said to Margaret, "You'll never guess what the largest organization at Harvard Law is."

Removing her apron, Margaret asked, "What is it?"

"The Harvard Wives' Club. It's a club that teaches women how to support a husband's law career. You're an automatic member because you're married to me."

Margaret laughed. "Ha! They discouraged me as a law student, but they're quick to embrace me as a wife."

Meanwhile, within the first semester at Harvard, John made a friend named John Chungus, an ambitious, entrepreneurial classmate. During class, they would say to each other, "What are we doing here? We could be making money." By the time spring rolled around, John had become part of a well-known Harvard statistic, flunking out with a third of the class by the first semester. Moreover, money was indeed tight. According to John's brother, George, "John and Margaret didn't have two nickels to rub together."

In the fall of 1954, while Margaret continued at Boston College Law, John Heckler and his Harvard colleague John Chungas bought into a company called National Homes, a manufacturer of prefabricated houses. Jack O'Shaughnessy gave John a loan for business seed money. On weekends, Margaret did the legal work for them, drawing up contracts. She encouraged John, telling him that if he kept at it, he would succeed. Early on, the two Johns received a federal contract for certain sections of New England, and they started assembling homes in Massachusetts and Rhode Island. They hired a small team, including John Heckler's brother Charlie.

At a time when most women's only concern was the upkeep of home and family, Margaret also represented the 3 percent of American women in law school. In addition to her studies, she ran the household, cleaned, cooked, and did the grocery shopping. After a full day of classes, Margaret arrived home exhausted but nonetheless obligated to perform the duties expected of any 1950s wife. Her male colleagues stayed late at the Boston College Law library, studying with no distractions. Meanwhile, it was not uncommon to find Margaret ironing John's shirts late into the evening, with her law books propped on top of the ironing board, surviving on very little sleep.

Well into her second year of law school, Margaret had been asking Mrs. West to move in with them. At ninety-two, she needed extra care and attention. She decided to sell her Long Island house and with the proceeds from the sale, Margaret and John hoped they would soon be able to buy their first home. At the same time, Margaret announced she was pregnant. The baby was added confirmation that it was time for Mrs. West to move in with them. Before the fall semester was underway, the couple and Mrs. West moved into a house they rented in Arlington, Massachusetts, a Boston suburb. Being closer to the city was beneficial both for John's business and Margaret's school.

Sadly, the days with Mrs. West were cut too short. Only six months into her time with the Hecklers, she passed away in Margaret's arms. She was as generous in death as she'd been in life, bequeathing Margaret her entire estate.

The passing of Belinda West closed a critical chapter in Margaret's life. Without the cornerstone of Mrs. West's love, Margaret would have had nothing. The benevolent, devoted woman was Margaret's "Nina"— her grandmother—and so much more. Mrs. West was the only person who fully understood the ache of Margaret's abandonment by her parents. Throughout her life, Margaret would credit Mrs. West with teaching her the work ethic that defined her own life. From Mrs. West, she learned that a woman could be feminine and refined, as well as strong and determined. But one of the great lessons Margaret learned from Mrs. West was witnessing her deep compassion for others.

Scarcely a week after Mrs. West's death, Margaret suffered a miscarriage. The dual loss hit hard. Adding to that pain, money remained tight.

At law school, however, Margaret flourished. Senator Ed Markey (D-MA), who would attend Boston College Law School in the 1970s, said about her, "While there was a small handful of women at Harvard, there was only going to be one at Boston College Law School [in the graduating law class of 1956]."[8]

Margaret said later, "I went from all women in high school and college to all men in law school." Yet she received full respect from her male colleagues and professors. "The professors called on me all the time," she recalled. "They would ask me, 'What are the facts of this case?' I knew I would be called on and got ready for that, and so I had a very active involvement with the class."[9]

Larry Fagan, a Boston College Law friend, noted that "Margaret was one of the guys. She was well accepted."[10] In her favor was the fact that, unlike Harvard, Boston College was welcoming and collegial because its students predominantly came from hardworking immigrant families.

Despite being the only woman in her class, Margaret recalled only experiencing derisive comments once or twice from her male classmates while there. One of them, Vincent Marzilli, made the following confession: "She sat behind me and between classes, for some strange reason, she would always pepper me with questions. Finally, one day I was feeling out of sorts, and I blurted out, 'Why don't you go home and cook for your husband?' I regretted it shortly after I said it. I felt very inadequate to answer her questions. And I thought if I was a big man, I would have apologized to her. I was amazed that anyone would ask me any questions. I regretted it for years."[11]

Among her classmates, Margaret's inner circle included Frank Privitera and John Brebbia. Privitera remembered Margaret this way:

> She didn't have to study as hard as I did. She wasn't a whiner. She was very popular. Everyone knew she was married. The relationship with the other students was strictly scholastic. She had to take care of her family. She was not studying in the library as I was. She was a quick learner and might have used some of my notes, but in the end, I finished up in the top five, and she finished sixth in our class out

of 120 men. . . . She became very comfortable with men. She always encouraged me and told me how smart I was, just like my mother did. I needed that encouragement, after my teachers for years told my mother while I was in grammar school that I would never amount to anything. Today, I'm a billionaire![12]

John Brebbia painted a similar portrait, saying, "Margaret had a very strong personality. Women had to fight their way up in those days. She was smart and tough. We were a close-knit group of revolutionaries. It was very clear that no one was going to get in Margaret's way. She didn't take any nonsense from anybody. . . . Then the administration at BC tried to weed out the students and only about forty graduated. Margaret won the moot court competition three years in a row."[13]

Between her wins at the moot court competition and becoming one of the first female editors of the *Boston College Law Review*, known in the 1950s as the *Annual Survey of Massachusetts Law*, Margaret was admired and respected by her male peers.[14]

To her great joy, in April 1956, at the end of her third year of law school, she learned she was pregnant again. Her days remained long, with a heavy load of classes as well as studying for the bar exam.

After graduating in the spring of 1956 and passing the bar exam, Margaret began looking for a job. She wanted nothing more than to use her education to become a Boston lawyer. However, within months, all of her male classmates landed jobs as attorneys with law firms; she did not. History had not changed yet toward female lawyers, no matter how successful they were in school. Most law offices simply did not hire women lawyers.

Margaret remembered her experience:

As a woman searching for a job at a Boston law firm in that era, I found that having been on the *Law Review* was simply not an acceptable credential for consideration. Once, I spent the whole day in a firm's waiting room. I was persistent enough to think, I must wait this out. Then, at the end of the day, the secretary said, "The hiring partner has just left," and she added sternly, "We would never hire a woman in this firm!" I knew that part of my problem was that secretary. The receptionist refused, I think, to even consider working for a woman lawyer.[15]

Margaret went on to describe a later experience:

When my children were young, I answered an advertisement for a part-time legal opportunity and was interviewed by the hiring partner. I was told, "Your credentials are excellent, but we would never hire you. You're a mother. You can't be serious about being a lawyer." Ironically, some sixteen years later, after I became a member of Congress, I received a letter from this same man, asking for my endorsement of his candidacy for a judgeship. I replied that anyone who had exhibited that kind of attitude toward women should not be sitting on the bench, and I couldn't possibly take his candidacy seriously.[16]

While refusing to endorse the man in later years would certainly be satisfying, during that summer of 1956, Margaret was trapped, all of her efforts produced the same negative outcome, a firmly closed door. As she recalled during her childhood being surrounded by law books in Judge Farrell's library, her enthusiasm to practice law never waned—but the resistance she encountered as a woman in what was considered a man's field, no matter her credentials, left a searing mark.

Both Sandra Day O'Connor and Ruth Bader Ginsburg would face the same scenario when they graduated from law school. Law offices balked at their audacity as they applied for positions they were beyond qualified to fill, and they were redirected to secretarial roles instead. Like O'Connor and Ginsberg, Margaret Heckler was told over and over, "This firm will never hire a woman attorney. You will only be considered as a secretary." Up until this point, she was able to compete and advance, and now the gates had been slammed shut to a seemingly all boys' club. After all of her painstaking sacrifices and her high academic achievements, Margaret was blindsided, with no promise of a job as a lawyer. But the pervasive sexism that existed in the 1950s for women in law wouldn't dissuade her from her course. She wouldn't take "no" for an answer.

It became clear to Margaret that to practice law, she needed to be more strategic. A job would have to come from those who knew her capabilities and bore witness to her strength. When three of her law school colleagues—Joseph Collins, Albert Boyle, and Richard Bennett—opened their own firm on State Street in downtown Boston, she asked if she could join them. With no question regarding her academic and professional abilities or whether she was committed to practicing law, Collins, Boyle, and Bennett gladly accepted her into their practice.

Margaret joined the firm practicing criminal law and family law. Relating one of her early cases, she recounted, "I went to a jail in Cambridge, Massachusetts, from a Republican women's luncheon, dressed à la 1950s, with a suit and stole, and the gatekeeper said, 'I'm sorry ma'am, visiting hours are over.' So, I drew myself up to my full five-foot-two-inches and told him, 'I hope you don't consider this a social visit. I am an attorney, and I want to see my client.' With that, I was ushered into the jail. The guards were all snickering. I guess I never looked like a lawyer."[17]

Her growing law career parallelled her growing family. On January 25, 1957, Margaret and John's first child was born. She later described it as "one of the happiest days of my life!"[18] They named the baby Belinda West Heckler after her beloved Belinda West.

After Margaret returned to work, she went to the bank with the proceeds from her inheritance to acquire a housing loan to purchase their rental home in Arlington, Massachusetts. What transpired was an experience that was imprinted on her memory. Because she was a woman and did not have her husband or father as a cosigner, the bank rejected her loan application. It did not matter that Margaret's financial standing was better than John's at that point because she was the sole beneficiary of Belinda West's estate and an employed lawyer. At that time banks did not extend credit to women, for fear that they wouldn't pay their bills. A woman could not apply for a department store credit card or any other "charge card" in her own name, either. For women in the 1950s, access to financial credit in any form was simply not an option.

For John, his company, National Homes, which had initially looked promising, was beginning to falter. Plumbing parts continually disappeared, and John could not keep up with the price of replacing missing supplies. He knew people were stealing from the company but didn't know how to stop the theft. That year, the business fell apart, and he lost everything. The Hecklers nearly went broke.

John needed to direct his frustration at someone, and Margaret was the only one nearby to absorb his failure and fear. Although she did all she could to support him, the failed business venture took a toll on their young marriage. Ironically, Jack O'Shaughnessy was the person who offered the best advice. With his own longtime experience trading in the stock market, Jack suggested that John look for work as a stockbroker. John decided to follow his counsel and took a job with Harris Upham & Company in Boston.

In 1959, Margaret had another little girl, named Alison Anne Heckler. Pink bows and matching dresses became Margaret's passion. Then, in 1960, Margaret gave birth to a son, John Maguire Heckler Jr. Margaret and John were delighted to have a boy who would carry on the Heckler name.

Things had come full circle. All her life, Margaret longed to have a family of her own. Growing up never living with her parents and without the support of siblings, her days of being alone were finally over. With satisfying work, beautiful children, and a stable marriage, Margaret felt fulfilled.

And yet politics called out to her. In 1958, the Heckler family moved to Wellesley, Massachusetts, a Boston suburb. They purchased an old, rambling colonial-style home that suited their growing family. Margaret began volunteering in local Republican campaigns, and she joined the Wellesley Republican Town Committee. Over the next few years, she became vice president of the Women's Republican Club of Massachusetts, a member of the Wellesley Town Meeting, and the legislative chairwoman of the Women's Republican Club of Wellesley.

Still, she itched for more. In 1960, she signed on to campaign for Brad Morse's election to the House of Representatives for Massachusetts's Fifth District. A fellow Republican in a mostly Democratic state, Morse was a candidate Margaret could eagerly support. She put her campaign experience to use, rallying a team of women to canvas door-to-door for him. They passed out fliers and took turns answering phones. On top of her law work and raising a trio of children under the age of three, Margaret dedicated a significant number of volunteer hours to Morse's campaign.

It thrilled Margaret to be involved in politics again, and she began to consider running for office herself. But she was stretched to the limit. In a time when most women stayed home raising their children, and their outside activities mainly consisted of volunteer service in their community, church, or children's school, Margaret was a wife, mother, and practicing lawyer. Could she truly add "political candidate" to that list?

II

ELECTED OFFICE 1961–1982

Snow White and the Seven Dwarves

With Congressman Joseph W. Martin (left) and John at a
fundraiser in her honor for her Massachusetts Governor's
Council seat, 1964. *Family collection.*

*I*n October 1961, Margaret sat in the office of her obstetrician Dr.
Bartlett Stone. Having delivered all three of her children, he had become
a confidant. She trusted him. "How are you doing, Peggy?" he asked.

His question provided an opportunity to confess something she had
not shared with anyone else. "Dr. Stone," she said, "three little ones are
keeping me very busy at home, but I'm torn between being a full-time
mom and being in the professional world. When I'm working, I feel guilty
about the time away from my children."

The elderly man leveled with her. "You have so much energy and
drive. With your personality, you need to do the work you're called to

do. Cutting off your professional aspirations would be a disservice to your children. If you put all your energy into your children, it would be too intense for them. Don't feel guilty—you're a better mother with something to occupy you besides your household duties. Your professional pursuits actually do your family a huge favor."[1]

Dr. Stone's words were groundbreaking. No one had ever given Margaret that kind of permission, and in 1960, hearing such words spoken by her doctor made her believe them.

It was not surprising that Margaret felt conflicted about her desire for a professional life. In the late 1950s and early 1960s, television shows like *I Love Lucy* and *Father Knows Best* depicted caricatures of perfect (albeit sometimes endearingly ditzy) housewives, crafting a culturally cohesive vision for how the postwar world should operate—and what a woman's primary role should be. In the shows, a white-collar husband arrived home from his desk job to a manicured housewife in pumps and pearls. Many women, even those who were college educated, aspired to this image of femininity portrayed on TV, and there were few alternative depictions of a woman's role in society to persuade anyone otherwise.

The emergence of these television shows in the 1950s encouraged women to re-embrace their domestic roles. During World War II, women had entered the workforce to fill the labor gap created when men became soldiers. Some women kept factories running to support the war effort, others went into the Central Intelligence Agency and became code-breakers, some became nurses and learned foreign languages.[2] However, following the war, as male veterans returned to the civilian workforce, women were expected to return to their homes, regardless of their education or experience level.

Margaret bucked these trends, but it wasn't necessarily a conscious rebellion. Rather, her peculiar upbringing allowed her to freely express herself beyond female stereotypes. Due to her childhood in the West household, which lacked a traditional family structure, Margaret knew that real-life women were stronger and more capable than their mid-century TV counterparts. Because Margaret had been a boarder, and her father paid her way, Belinda West did not expect her to do any housekeeping; instead, Margaret's schoolwork and piano practice took precedence—thus rendering her efficient in cerebral activities at the loss of domesticity. Margaret was feminine, but prior to running a household of her own, she was seldom seen in the kitchen or cleaning the bathroom.

Set apart from the latest cultural trends, Margaret had already broken social conventions by being the only female in her law school class, then becoming an attorney in a private law practice when only 3 percent of American lawyers were women. She had few comrades. In those years, only small numbers of women chose work outside the home over domesticity. Politics, in particular, was a new frontier for them. And of course, no woman had yet held a position such as Speaker of the House, Supreme Court justice, or vice president.

Campaigning for Brad Morse's successful 1960 election to the House of Representatives, Margaret learned important lessons from her volunteer work, which contributed to her thoughts of seriously considering her own turn in politics. She later stated:

> I contributed considerable amounts of my time . . . campaigning for the Republican party . . . and I realized that the candidates were not involving as much of themselves in their campaigns as I was. I'd have a whole team of women, taking all the abuse that one receives . . . at a railway station with commuters, about three days before the election, when all the worst things come out, right at the end . . . and he would have been at home with his feet up by the fire, sipping a cocktail. And that really annoyed me, and it happened repeatedly. After putting in all that effort for someone else's campaign, I realized that I should consider running myself.[3]

These remarks related to her later decision to run for Congress, but they also rang true in the earliest days of her political career. Margaret had the confidence and courage to continue her important vocations of wife, mother, lawyer—and soon, she hoped, politician.

It's important to note that at the same time Margaret began to be involved in Massachusetts politics, the Kennedy political power era was at its peak. In 1960, John F. Kennedy was elected president of the United States. Robert Kennedy was appointed US attorney general in 1961, and the following year, Ted Kennedy was sworn in as a new US senator from Massachusetts. In Boston, politics were dominated by the Kennedy name. While not directly in the Kennedy sphere because she was a Republican, Margaret would find herself on the periphery of the Kennedy dynasty for the next two decades as she herself rose in political prominence.

In 1962, Margaret launched her first political campaign, running for the Governor's Council. Also known as the Executive Council, the Governor's Council exists nowhere in the United States except Massachusetts. In 1629, nine years after the *Mayflower*'s arrival, the Governor's Council was formed by John Winthrop, then Massachusetts Bay Colony governor. Designed to provide counsel to the governor, the Governor's

Council still exists today as one of the few remnants of colonial-styled governance. The Council meets weekly to give advice and consent to the governor or lieutenant governor. It includes eight members, elected every two years from each of the state's eight districts, with the governor or lieutenant governor presiding.

Given the nature of the role, Margaret felt that "this was the office where there was a need for someone competent in the law and with no particular political entanglement."[4] She ran as a Republican. Margaret's former press secretary, Linda Bilmes, shared, "Here she was a trailblazer. She had become a Republican at first because at the time the Democrats in Massachusetts had so many people, old men, who wanted to run for office, and the Republicans didn't have much of a bench. . . . It was a strategy that John Heckler came up with, 'Run as a Republican.'"[5]

Because of her experience in criminal law, Margaret believed she understood the feelings of prisoners who sought pardons and paroles, an area upon which the council frequently advised the governor. She also felt there was a need for councilors who would take the time to investigate government payouts before they approved expenditures using taxpayers' money. This is something she pledged to do if she was elected. Margaret wrote about why she was running for the Governor's Council:

> Today, Massachusetts has a deplorable stature in the eyes of the nation and is notorious for its corruption in government. Public funds are being grossly misused, and this has sapped the financial strength of the state. The Governor's Council is supposed to be the watchdog over the use of public funds involved in state contracts. The house was robbed . . . and the watchdogs did not bark! I believe that only a woman would be willing and able to make the sacrifices of time and energy necessary to promote a thorough, dedicated, enthusiastic organization upon which the success of this campaign rests.[6]

In many ways, Margaret's run for the Governor's Council became a test for her congressional race that would follow four years later. She made a few effective campaign decisions that she effectively recycled throughout the entirety of her time as an elected official. First and foremost, she accepted John's offer to be her campaign manager. Working together, the couple quickly built forward momentum.

A second key decision was using the friendly and approachable "Peggy" for her campaign name, instead of the more formal "Margaret"— "Peggy" sounded like she could be your friend from down the street. Brochures read, "Vote for Peggy Heckler for the Governor's Council," but what Margaret really needed was a catchy slogan. Here, John made the best contribution, suggesting, "We Need a Heckler in the Governor's Council."

Another stroke of creativity helped distinguish her from the opposition. Margaret had a friend who worked for the New England Dairy Council. Her friend knew the owner of a dairy farm in her campaign district. In the early 1960s, milk was delivered in glass bottles to the doorsteps of homes. Margaret's friend thought attaching flyers to the milk bottles would be an instantaneous and efficient way for people in the district to become acquainted with Margaret's name and face. Margaret brought thousands of brochures to her friend, who in turn took them to the dairy farmer. Over several days, homes were blanketed with flyers that included an image of Margaret's pretty, smiling face.

Margaret remembered one woman who "let her cat out first thing in the morning. At the crack of dawn, there were her milk bottles and with the milk, there was my flyer. She figured if Margaret Heckler was up that early, she must be a very hard worker and just the type of person she would want in government representing her. She told many friends the story."[7]

There was a buzz around town about the woman running for Governor's Council. In the 333 years since the Council was created, only one other woman had served on it. Overnight, Margaret became a sensation.

Massachusetts's Second District included four Boston wards and thirty-one cities and towns. Margaret's main opponent was the incumbent Democratic Councilor Alvin C. Tamkin, from Dorchester. Two years prior, Tamkin had been elected to fill a vacancy on the Council after another member's death. An experienced thirty-eight-year-old attorney who had also served four terms in the Massachusetts State House of Representatives, Tamkin nonetheless was not prepared for the full force of his fiery female opponent.

With the support of the women of Wellesley who went door-to-door, the creativity of the milk bottle flyers, and Margaret's own relentless energy, she won the Second Councilor District by about seven thousand votes. In the words of one local paper, "A petite Wellesley mother is slated to be the first woman to sit on the Executive Council in 35 years."[8] Margaret "credited her win to the stalwart efforts of the women of Wellesley, a group that came out in droves to support her."[9] These Wellesley women, many of them college educated, were committed to seeing more women serve in government positions. Afternoon teas and bridge games had been put on hold as the women helped get their friend Peggy elected.

At the Swan Boats in Boston with Alison, John Jr., Belinda, and Oiget, their au pair, 1964. *Family collection.*

Margaret's victory over a Democratic incumbent in a mostly Democratic state caused a stir among the press. With the whole Heckler family now in the spotlight, one newspaper wrote, "Yesterday in her home at 30 Colburn Road—wearing a green frock and three-strand pearls—she sat beside her husband, John Heckler, at a victory news conference."[10] Among the questions asked, the most common was about her role as mother to Belinda, five; Alison, three; and John Jr., two. The press wondered who would take care of the children.

Knowing her constituents would also be fixated on her role as a mother, Margaret explained, "Time with the children was always my daily concern. I tried to be there every afternoon when they finished their naps. If being a councilor meant sacrificing anything then it was going to be my law practice."[11]

There also seemed to be a concern about how Margaret would work with the seven men on the Council. The *Boston Herald* asked Margaret if she was scared, pointing out that "Mrs. Heckler is now the second lady to serve on the council in its history. At the council table she will be the lone lady among seven other councilors and the lieutenant governor."

Her prompt response was "No." She thought for a moment, then added, "I don't expect to be cowed by any means."[12] When another paper asked Margaret how she planned to work with the men, she said, "I'm not trying to compete with them. . . . I will speak out, and fight for what I believe in—for all the people of Massachusetts regardless of party."[13] The best descriptor for the new makeup of the Governor's Council was a newspaper's title: "Snow White and the Seven Dwarves."[14]

The *Boston Herald* asked John how he felt having a Governor's Councilor in the family. Grinning, he said, "I feel that my wife is probably the finest wife, the finest mother, the finest lawyer, and now one of the finest people we have in government. In fact, I'll qualify that and say she is the finest."[15]

While John was all-in on Margaret's budding political career, he now found himself in the supporting spouse role, a sharp contrast to most political couples, where the husband was the official and the wife the supporter. John's first test was a Governor's Council dinner party hosted by Governor Endicott Peabody and his wife, Toni. Six of the other seven Councilors were there with their wives. Margaret arrived à la Jackie Kennedy, in a black cocktail dress, pearls and a matching black purse, with John on her arm. It was reported that there was such camaraderie among the group that no one even made a bad political joke.[16]

A reporter, James G. Colbert, said that

> in her first term in the Governor's Council, Margaret impressed her constituents by serving public notice that she really meant the things she said in her campaign about being against political wheeling, dealing and trading. It was like a breath of fresh air suddenly blowing through a smoke-filled room. Governor's Councilor Margaret Heckler, it seemed, was cut from a different bolt of political cloth.[17]

The year Margaret took her seat on the Governor's Council, Betty Friedan's *The Feminine Mystique* was published. In the book, Friedan urged women to question their identities and the social norms that told them how to behave or what they could do. To shock her audience with a provocative comparison, Friedan, a Jewish American and early modern feminist, declared, "The women who 'adjust' as housewives, who grow up wanting to be 'just a housewife,' are in as much danger as the millions who walked to their own death in the concentration camps."[18] A wake-up call for many American women and a book that was on the recommended-reading list for many colleges and universities, *The Feminine Mystique* was released during the second wave of feminism, which changed how women viewed themselves. Friedan, a Smith College graduate, found herself wanting more. She wrote about the dissatisfaction of women at home not having higher ambitions.

Although Margaret epitomized the professional woman Betty Friedan spoke about in her book, the way the two women built their case for the advancement of women was very different.

That spring, Margaret was asked to speak at the commencement for the Union Hospital School of Nursing in Fall River, Massachusetts. A popular vocation for women in the 1960s, nursing was one of the three most common "female" professions (the other two being teaching and secretarial work).

In front of the all-female graduates in their caps and gowns, Margaret opened her address with a discussion about *The Feminine Mystique*, saying, "I decry the influence of *The Feminine Mystique*," referring to the tone of Friedan's book. Margaret added, "Women have a unique contribution only they can make." She encouraged the graduates to honor the feminine role and put family above profession.

Although Betty Friedan enlightened millions of women about working outside the home, she believed that the culture systematically kept women at home even if they were unfulfilled there. Margaret felt that being a wife and mother was the highest calling, and that family should always come before career—while also maintaining that women should pursue other passions outside the home. She told the future nurses that their duty was not to conquer men but rather to work with them. The very things that make women distinct were part of a woman's superpower.

In May 1964, she announced her bid for a second term on the Council. For her reelection campaign, the Committee to Elect Margaret Heckler to the Governor's Council came up with a way to get all the male politicians in Boston to gather for a fundraiser: They secured the attendance of the voluptuous actress Tina Louise, better known as Ginger on the 1960s sitcom *Gilligan's Island*. Governor John Volpe, Attorney General Ed Brooke, and senior Congressman Joseph Martin practically lined up at the door.

Tina Louise wore a black evening gown that set off her shiny red hair and light brown eyes. Margaret arrived in a gauzy, sleeveless blue gown, white gloves, and a brown mink stole. Tina Louise represented the traditional Hollywood dream—but her equally redheaded political counterpart represented a new era: In addition to being beautiful, women could also be models of leadership, intelligence, and courage. Margaret easily won a second term.

Under Governor Volpe's leadership, Margaret thrived on the Council, but midway through her second term she began to find the role stale and her colleagues disreputable. Half of her cocouncilors were in legal battles or in jail for taking bribes. Because the Governor's Council had power over how people got paid, its members were often the target of bribes. On October 14, 1964, the *New York Times* reported, "Bribe Jury Names Ex-Gov. Furcolo; He and 4 Are Indicted in Boston for Conspiracy: The three councilors indicted today are Ernest Stasiun of Fairhaven, Raymond Sullivan of Springfield, and Joseph R. Crimmins of Worcester. All are Democrats."[19]

Margaret was not a councilor to earn side money from Italian Boston mob bosses. "Snow White and the Seven Dwarves" now seemed symbolic of Margaret's innocence in contrast to the shady business of several of her cocouncilors.

In April 1965, Margaret headed to Washington, DC, to attend the Thirteenth Annual Republican Women's Conference. She had also been invited by Representative Joe Martin, her congressman, to be his guest at the Capitol and observe proceedings on the House floor. After landing in Washington, she headed to the Capitol to call on him. Martin enthusiastically greeted her and signed her visitor pass to sit in the gallery in the US House of Representatives chamber. Martin shuffled slowly using a cane, walking her over to the House chamber. Occasionally, he held Margaret's arm for extra support. It was evident his health and age were affecting his ability to perform his duties. In fact, Joe Martin had only cast 53 percent of roll call votes in the last session of Congress, which was the second-lowest voting participation record among House Republicans.[20]

In the evening, Margaret joined the rows of women in three-piece skirt suits and heels at the Republican Women's Conference. A mélange of lipstick and perfume was like stained-glass windows and incense in the otherwise stale conference ballroom at the Sheraton-Park Hotel. The conference attendees heard from Representative Robert Dole (R-KS), Senator Barry Goldwater (R-AZ), and other prominent Republican leaders.

The Republican Party had recently realized that women, making up half of the population, were a largely untapped constituency. At a time when the vast majority of US homes had heat, electricity, and running water, and most were equipped with modern appliances, stay-at-home mothers had more time to cultivate interests and hobbies outside of the home, including political activism. The message to the women at the Republican Women's Conference was clear: they might want to move past political hobbyism and consider their own political potential.

Listening to Bob Dole's speech, Margaret interpreted his last line as a personal calling: "We must then bring new people into the party—organize—work—organize—work—and make the needed gains in 1966."[21] It was just the invitation Margaret needed to act on what she had already considered: a congressional bid against Representative Joe Martin.

When she returned home, she confidentially asked her assistant at the law office to run the numbers and hypothetically determine what it would take for her to win her congressional district. When the results were in, she carefully studied them.

In 1964, the Massachusetts Tenth District broke down as follows:

Republicans—70,230
Democrats—73,076
Independents—75,438[22]

Looking at the numbers, Margaret realized the odds were not entirely against her. Although she was a Republican in a largely Democratic state, about two-thirds of Joe Martin's congressional district were people she had already won over twice in her Councilor elections.

The situation sparked a new fire in Margaret to continue pushing the limits set before her. The primary barrier she would need to overcome was the culturally ingrained view of women. Most people believed that if a family had the means, a woman's place was in the home. If she were to be thrown into the public's scrutiny, success would only come if she had John's full support.

One Saturday morning shortly thereafter, Margaret sat with a cup of coffee in the red leatherette booth of her kitchen nook at home. The three Heckler children, aged six through nine, were nestled together under a blanket in the living room, watching cartoons.

When John joined Margaret, she looked up from her newspaper and said, "I think I can beat him."

"Peggy, if you are talking about Martin, I knew from the moment I shook his feeble hand at your last fundraiser that his days were numbered," John replied. "He is barely getting around anymore."

"When I saw him in Washington, he was so much older than the other congressmen," she agreed. "He's almost fifty years older than me!"

"It will be an uphill battle," John replied. "Being a woman breaking into a male-dominated Congress will be tough enough. And there's no setting Joe Martin aside. You know you'll basically have to win two separate elections. First, you'll have to defeat Martin, a beloved incumbent of more than forty years. And then you'll have to beat a Democratic opponent in the general election. But now is the time when no one else would oppose him. I know you can do it. Plus, you have me to back you up the whole way."

"But what about the children? They are so young."

"The kids will be fine," John assured her.

Instinctively, she knew he was right. She just needed to hear it from him. Then he added, encouragingly, "You're looking at your new campaign manager. Now let's go take down the giant!"[23]

Giant Killer

Campaigning at a Fall River factory. *Family collection.*

In the summer of 1966, deep into Margaret's campaign for a congressional seat representing Massachusetts's Tenth District, she slit open an envelope that had been mailed to her. Inside was a yellowed newspaper clipping sent by the administrative assistant of a former political opponent of Joe Martin. Dated July 23, 1924, the *Fall River Herald* clipping provided Joe Martin's campaign letter to prospective voters. It was then forty-year-old Martin's first election, and he was running against an elderly incumbent, William S. Green. In Joe Martin's own words, a congressional seat "is a position for one in vigorous health if the people are to be adequately served."[1]

Reading these words, Margaret smiled. Joe Martin would go on to win the seat in 1924 and in every subsequent election for over four decades. But in 1966, he would have his own words used against him when Margaret Heckler—a petite, Debbie Reynolds–lookalike and thirty-five-year-old mother of three—rose to challenge him.

By then, Martin had a long history in the House. He had represented the Tenth District for forty-two years and served as Speaker of the House twice (1947–1949 and 1953–1955). Even more significantly, he was the only Republican Speaker between 1931 and 1995, when Newt Gingrich assumed the role. Notably opposed to Franklin D. Roosevelt's New Deal, Martin had earned inclusion in President Roosevelt's condemnation of "Martin, Barton and Fish." But in general, Joe Martin was a moderate Republican, well-liked by those on the left and the right. Martin's House colleagues awarded him a "suite of offices in the Capitol and a chauffeur-driven limousine . . . as a token of their esteem, but even with these comforts the old warhorse's sight and hearing failed him. In recent years he took to a cane and could not walk alone."[2]

Despite his age, Martin's likability and longstanding status in the House made him a formidable rival for Margaret. The political risk of challenging an incumbent from your own party was bold, but to challenge a forty-two-year incumbent and two-time Speaker of the House would seem like political suicide. Nonetheless, Margaret was undeterred.

From her youthful days campaigning door-to-door for Judge Farrell to her groundbreaking college campaign to become the first female CISL Speaker of the House, Margaret had honed her natural political talents and then went on to polish them as a lawyer, campaign volunteer, and Councilor. She would later say it was "very good preparation for what I would need to win in my district. All of this happened by accident. It wasn't preplanned, but one step led to another."[3]

Margaret and her husband routinely talked strategy around the dinner table after Margaret decided to run for Congress and John agreed to be her campaign manager. Margaret's take was that Joe Martin could be a successful Republican in a majority Democratic state because he had maintained popularity in industrial cities like Fall River and Taunton, even if they were predominantly Democratic. But over the last few years, the district shifted to the left.

This shift was causing Martin's hold to slowly slip.[4] This was good news for Margaret, because she had already proven her ability to win heavily Democratic areas. Plus, most of the Tenth District was already part of her Governor's Council district. When she first ran for the Governor's Council seat in 1962, she beat a Democratic incumbent in a district even more Democratic than the Tenth Congressional District.[5] Because of this, she was more concerned about the primary race against Joe Martin than about the general election.[6]

Not wanting to prematurely alert Martin and the other Massachusetts Republican kingmakers about her intention to run, Margaret and John decided to first consult with a few trusted advisors and friends about their campaign strategy. Jim Angevine, a political strategist, and Brad Morse, the Massachusetts congressman Margaret had helped get elected, were among the first to advise and support her. They recommended she poll the district before announcing her candidacy, to ensure there was a real chance of success. John reached out to Edward Noonan, who ran a marketing and opinion research firm that did phone interviews.

The Tenth District stretched through thirty-four towns. Margaret planned to focus on four of them: her hometown of Wellesley, about thirty minutes west of Boston and a predominately Republican town that would feel loyal to Joe Martin; Fall River, which her supporters thought would be the most difficult for Margaret to win; the very blue and union-based Taunton; and Newton, home of Boston College and Lasell University and an area that was predominately middle to upper class and mostly Jewish. Joe Martin's North Attleboro, where he'd been born and raised, would be a special kind of hurdle.

Secretly, Margaret was not overly worried about Fall River. The town had a large Catholic Portuguese community and shared faith allowed her to relate to voters genuinely and deeply. She also had a close first-generation Portuguese American friend whose mother coached Margaret with some Portuguese phrases before the summer campaign season took off.

Noonan's firm created a survey broken into seven ethnic groups in the district: French, Italian, Irish, Polish, Jewish, Portuguese and Yankee (Americans born in the northern states). When asked if she would vote for Heckler, one Portuguese Republican said, "Yes, women tend to be more honest than men." Another voter, a female Yankee Republican, said, "I come from Wellesley, and I know she has all that you could ask for." And a male Portuguese Democrat said, "Yes. She's been informative."[7] Although the poll revealed that many people did not really know her, despite her years on the Governor's Council, a considerable number said they were open to voting against Joe Martin and many said they would vote for a woman. Based on the polls, Margaret decided there were adequate indicators to move forward.[8]

She reached out to Frank Privitera, her friend from Boston College Law, to tell him of her intent to run for Congress. He said, "Margaret, that is a Democratic district. I'll contribute to you, but it's close to impossible to win as a Republican in a Democratic district. In my hometown of Somerville, if you weren't a Democrat, you couldn't get elected."[9] Despite Frank's warning, all Margaret heard was that she had his support. Unbeknownst to Joe Martin, in the fall of 1965 the foot race had begun. It would become a race where he never quite got off the starting block.

At eighty-two years old, Joe Martin had struck a deal with Governor John Volpe (R-MA) and other Republican leaders: Martin would serve one last term before retiring and making way for the Republican favorite, state Republican chairman, John Parker. The former mayor of Taunton, Parker had joined the Massachusetts state legislature as a senator in 1953. Reported to have "kept a close eye on higher political positions,"[10] Parker was an obvious party choice to replace Joe Martin.

Out of deference to Joe Martin, John Parker never entered the race. But Margaret made the long game calculation: If Joe Martin was re-elected, she would have a much tougher candidate in John Parker in 1968. Plus, she would not have the element of shock to the old boy's network when she announced her bid, the way she would in 1966.

Margaret had until the Massachusetts primary on September 13, 1966, to demonstrate that Joe Martin was negligent and out of touch with his voters—and that despite being a woman, she was the stronger alternative. After the primary, she would have almost two months to flip her campaign and focus on the November 8 general election.

Her husband John was indispensable for fundraising, calling his closest business partners for initial campaign contributions. He caught the attention of David Babson, a member of the affluent Babson family that founded Babson College, who became a key fundraiser for Margaret.[11] David Babson and his wife were some of Margaret's biggest supporters, helping draw in any Republican willing to part from Joe Martin. Thanks to John and other volunteers, Margaret was able to raise the money needed to fund the campaign from start to finish.

Early on, Margaret also consulted with several key women in Wellesley who had helped her get elected to the Governor's Council, as well as Anita Vickers, a Boston socialite who could organize parties and events to attract both donors and voters. It did not take long for Margaret and John to create a dynamic core group of funders and volunteers. Their neighbors volunteered to host meet-and-greets and go door-to-door. The women of Wellesley organized. The newly minted campaign staff rallied. The phone lines started to buzz.

Doc Lombardi, a gifted musician and businessman, managed the Heckler campaign advertising. He suggested using Margaret's old slogan from college, "A Woman's Place Is in the House." His other essential suggestion was to include Margaret's maiden name, O'Shaughnessy, whenever the advertisement space permitted, as it would attract the Irish vote. Margaret's contribution was to use "Peg" as her campaign name. "You know Peg," she would say, "your good friend."

As Margaret would be the first woman from Massachusetts to run for Congress in her own right, rather than as the widow of a former congressman, she employed an initial campaign strategy designed to appeal to female voters. One of her first stops was to visit the women's group at the Wellesley Hills Country Club, where she pitched her candidacy to ladies who had the ears of their wealthy husbands.

Margaret elicited the attention of all social classes of women, from the socialite to the middle-class homemaker to the factory worker. She was relatable but also embodied a vision of the future they wanted for their own daughters. At last, mothers could point to a model of what a well-educated woman with career aspirations could accomplish outside of the home while also being a wife and mother of three young children.

From some women, she encountered a tepid response. Many still had little political interest or involvement and Margaret lamented that they would not attend Republican conventions or cookouts, which would have helped them better understand her own interest. Older women were especially taken aback by Margaret's candidacy, asking pointed questions about why she was running for office rather than staying home and caring for her family. Margaret's response was to ask, "Don't you think we should have more women in Congress?" She later said this strategy "worked very well and believe it or not, I think that in general, the younger women of my generation were more open to my candidacy."[12] She might not have been able to influence large numbers of older women, but she was able to attract suburban wives' attention, helping women her own age discover their political voice.

From there, she spoke to the Wellesley Republican Town Committee, where she had been a member for seven years. To her surprise, the committee was split between those who supported her and those loyal to old Joe Martin. Some members, horrified that she had the audacity to run against Martin, publicly insulted her.[13]

As the Massachusetts snow melted, Margaret and her team spent their time recruiting volunteers, preparing for TV appearances and debates, and creating flyers and posters. The arrival of spring would mark the start of long days and late nights leading up to the primary in early September.

The Massachusetts Republican establishment was not at all pleased about Margaret's decision to run. Governor John Volpe voiced his displeasure early on. He respected Margaret, but his support only extended as far as the Governor's Council. Unlike some establishment Republicans, Volpe knew from his close work with Margaret that she posed a serious threat to Joe Martin's race. While others were dismissive, Volpe attempted to pressure Margaret out of the race. He dropped hints of his disapproval during Governor's Council meetings and advised that she would have a better shot if she ran at some future time. Her unequivocal response: "*I'm not waiting.*"

"Be a Republican team player," Volpe admonished her—meaning, let Joe Martin finish out one more term, then let Volpe's friend John Parker take the seat.[14]

As Margaret showed no signs that she would back out of the contest, Volpe became more direct, notifying her that there would be no support from her own party if she continued. Although she was hurt by Volpe's reaction, Margaret decided she did not need the establishment Republicans if she had the voters.

As told in *Clout: Womanpower and Politics*, a book about women's ascension in politics, the prevailing mood of Republican leaders regarding Margaret's candidacy was, "What is that impertinent, pushy young woman doing? She doesn't have a chance."[15] But the voters to whom she appealed personally were much more sympathetic. When it came down to voting day, Margaret knew what wins elections—the people.

Margaret's campaign strategy focused on how she merged suburban motherhood and down-to-earth neighborliness with an attention to detail and work ethic of a lawyer. Grassroots door-to-door and supermarket saturation campaigning at the start of the summer proved effective in the towns already familiar with Margaret as a Councilor. What she needed now was to break into the towns not yet familiar with her.

On the Fourth of July, the town of Needham hosted a parade that would draw hundreds of voters from the surrounding towns who had little-to-no name recognition for Margaret Heckler. The entire week prior, a team of volunteers worked diligently to prepare brochures, listing Margaret's achievements as a lawyer, as well as flyers with "Vote for Peg Heckler for Congress." Margaret's friend Robert Greeley offered his 1960 white Plymouth convertible and his teenage twin daughters volunteered to walk alongside the car dressed patriotically in red, white, and blue.

Monday, July 4, 1966, was a perfect summer day in the Boston suburb of Needham, with sunny skies and highs in the upper eighties predicted. At 8:30 a.m., spectators began lining the parade route, complete with strollers, children on bikes, and dogs on leashes. As the parade commenced, families clapped and cheered. Children went wild collecting the candy scattered onto the pavement from the floats.

Amid antique cars, fire engines, and high school marching bands, Margaret made her congressional campaign debut. She was perched atop the back seat of Robert Greely's convertible wearing a white suit and wide-brimmed hat with a red ribbon. The signs on the car read, "Elect Peg Heckler for Congress." Her volunteers moved up and down the parade route, passing out the brochures, flyers, and buttons. "Vote for Peg Heckler!" they told spectators. Women proudly giggled when they saw her slogan, "A Woman's Place Is in the House."

Margaret made a splash. Afterward, the *Boston Herald* announced Mrs. Heckler as "the most attractive and articulate politician the state has enjoyed in years."[16]

While Margaret was waving to constituents from the back of a convertible and her volunteers were handing out campaign materials, Joe Martin was relaxing at his vacation home on Cape Cod. For the most part, he had written off Margaret as only a vague threat, giving little energy to his challenger and only expressing his disapproval about her candidacy to close friends.

That changed after the Fourth of July. Margaret's hard work had resulted in campaign momentum and her name spread throughout the Tenth District. As the summer's heat pressed onto the state, people began asking Martin about his campaign strategy against Margaret. Still, he dismissed her as irrelevant. Margaret held her own. She would later describe the tight line she had to walk:

> Sometimes appearing with Joe Martin got a little awkward, such as when I was at a very big Republican picnic. He was at one end of the line, and I would be at the other. I tried to stay out of his way and let him stay out of mine, but the end result was that I learned how to cope because I could never be harsh to him. I respected the man deeply. It was a little awkward because his brother was on the Republican Town Committee with me and the brothers naturally stood together, but his brother was very fond of me. So, I know that I was to *go gently but carry a big stick.*[17]

It was not until August 3, 1966, with just over a month left until the primary race, that Joe Martin awakened to the realization that Margaret could possibly unseat him. Out of concern, he penned a letter to his constituents, trying to combat Margaret's narrative that he was too old to run:

Dear Fellow Republican,

After consultation with my physicians, who have assured me that I am in excellent health, I have decided to run for a final term in Congress. Having devoted my life to the public services and to the Republican Party, I believe that after one more term, I should be entitled to some rest and leisure. This will be the last time I shall run for office. . . . During my nearly 42 years in the House of Representatives, I was privileged to serve two terms as Speaker and 20 years as Republican Leader. My stature in Congress has enabled me to perform many outstanding and valuable services for the people of Massachusetts.

An additional reason for running for a final term is my desire to keep the 10th District safely Republican. My demonstrated ability in many elections to attract thousands of Democratic and Independent voters in such Democratic strongholds as Fall River and Taunton offers conclusive proof that I am the candidate who is sure to win in the November election.[18]

Martin's words simply reiterated to his constituents what Margaret had heard from the Republican Party all along—step aside, do not trifle with Joe Martin's dynasty. She ignored the letter.

Martin showed that he was politically asleep at the wheel by being blind to her most easily exploitable weakness: *her sex*. In 1966, many people believed that the US Congress was no place for a woman, especially the mother of three young children. Instead of capitalizing on this, Martin bragged that he had previously beaten a woman candidate who had run against him years prior.

Margaret would later say of Martin that "his frequent remark was that if you had beaten one woman, you have beaten them all. This did, of course, add extra strength to the election campaign on my part and there is no reason to hide the fact that the remark was an added inspiration."[19]

Despite Martin's low blow to Margaret and to women, she did not respond in kind. She described her campaign against Joe Martin as "soft-spoken," with an emphasis on "the district's need for full-time representation," using "a staunch corps of women workers" to carry out "the strategy of treating Martin with utmost deference."[20]

With few women running for elected positions in the 1960s, Margaret was an easy target for the press. A constant stream of articles reported voters saying, "I would never vote for a woman." Media pundits posed incisive questions about whether it was appropriate for a woman to be a politician, and they speculated about whether Margaret was neglecting her family responsibilities. Reporters continually asked Margaret why she was not at home taking care of her children. Margaret responded that her children were well cared for by herself, the family, and a beloved Norwegian nanny, Oiget.

Early in her race, an editor at the *West Roxbury Transcript* advised Margaret, "You need to get in a man's world. You need to dress like them." Heeding this prudent political advice, Margaret most often chose to wear a gray women's suit. She found that wearing gray pinstripes neutralized the public's response to a female candidate. When she wore a gray suit, questions about her being a wife and mother diminished.

Flummoxed when Margaret suddenly traded in her typically bright and stylish outfits, her assistant, Jan Edmonds, asked her, "What gives?" Margaret responded, "It's a costume designed to help me to blend into the gray Massachusetts sky and into the equally gray male political arena, so the voters are forced to unconsciously identify me with the issues and to forget about the fact that I'm a woman."[21]

The summer and early fall campaign season was a frenzy. The Heckler home's fully enclosed side porch was the northern campaign headquarters. Papers, envelopes, and stamps littered tables and chairs, volunteers overflowed into the kitchen, dining room, and living room, and phones rang throughout the day. As campaign manager, John lived on coffee and cigarettes. As for Margaret, it seemed as if she never slept.

The election was John's project almost as much as it was Margaret's. He asked for leniency at Harris Upham & Company in Boston to dedicate time to Margaret's campaign. All evening, he was on the phone, ringing up old classmates, new business contacts, and friends, raising money to keep the campaign financed. Meanwhile, Margaret did the face-to-face grassroots work with the voters.

For the Heckler children, the pink boxes tied with string and filled with donuts from Hazel's bakery made up for living in a house full of volunteers. Belinda, Margaret's nine-year-old daughter, designed a blue heart-shaped "Peg" bumper sticker. Alison and John were rarely underfoot, choosing to spend their free time at the Brown School playground until dark. Nonetheless, Margaret was careful to keep her children out of the public eye.

Margaret had observed that traveling with a team was helpful not only for in-the-moment assistance, but also because it gave the impression that she already held the office she sought. Her team moved as a single, well-practiced entity from one place to the next.

A typical campaign day began with Margaret ensuring that her children were off to school with everything they needed. Then she moved to a neighborhood coffee hour appearance. Pat Howard-Johnson, Margaret's closest neighbor, hosted several of these coffees. Before guests arrived at 8:00 a.m., Pat set up a playpen for women with toddlers in tow. She brewed coffee and arranged trays of pastries before removing her apron to receive her guests. The women scurried up the front steps—anxious to hear what their good friend and neighbor Peg Heckler had to say.

"Thank you, women of Wellesley. I wouldn't be here today without your loyalty and support. It is time for a change in the Tenth District," Margaret said. Her voice heightening, she added, "And as you may have heard me say before, a woman's place is in the house—the House of Representatives!" The tightly packed audience burst into applause.

These coffees not only promoted Margaret but also empowered the suburban housewives to view themselves as active political participants. For many of them, it was a first-time realization. Soon, a gaggle of hardworking housewives and their husbands would do the footwork for her.

Margaret hit the pavement running. "I was like a gazelle running through the precincts," she said. On weekends, she could be found at area A&P supermarkets, handing out brochures to people with their arms full of groceries. With a twinkle in her eye and an honest smile, Margaret asked for their vote.

At the train stations in each of her townships, Margaret caught the Boston business commuters. As a train rolled in and lurched to a stop, with hundreds of people rushing in and out, Margaret was there meeting the voters. Some nights she'd be on her feet for hours. On any given day on the campaign trail, Margaret shook over a thousand hands.

In the southernmost reaches of the Tenth District, Margaret headed to the Fall River factories for scheduled visits. Each factory served an important role in Margaret's campaign strategy. To beat Joe Martin, Margaret needed votes from not only Republicans but also Independents, even those who leaned left—and the Portuguese community, many of them factory workers, predominately leaned that way. Because of the dangerous work environment, which could easily take a finger or worse from a worker operating the machinery, Margaret's team had to convince the factory owners to grant her special permission to tour the facilities. The stylish candidate stepped into industrial warehouses that clamored with noisy machinery. "Hi, I'm Margaret Heckler," she would say, flashing her

Irish grin at women in garment shops or men entering factories for the 5:00 a.m. shift. Threads and swaths of fabric littered the floor. Portuguese workers bent over their tables or bustled between stations, earning their modest wages by each piece they made.

With the help of her friend's mother, Margaret practiced Portuguese and developed some level of proficiency in the language. She stopped at every bench to shake a worker's hand, and say "*Olá, como vai?*" or "*Obrigado por seu trabalho.*" ("Hello, how are you?" and "Thank you for your work.") Smiles lit up the workers' faces.

With each factory tour, Margaret fell more in love with the Catholic Portuguese community in Fall River. It was, in part, because of such communities, that she worked superhuman hours to earn a seat in Congress. "If elected, I will protect your rights and help craft equitable labor laws to ensure the system does not take advantage of you,"[22] she told the workers. She explained that as the daughter of an immigrant herself, she did not want any American immigrant to ever be without an advocate, especially among the families she represented.

Once the factory tour was over, the team would sweep Margaret into a television interview or preparation for a debate later in the evening. As frequently as possible, she appeared as a guest on television during the news hour. Television ads were expensive, but local news coverage through interviews and events was free. On television, she shared what she intended to accomplish in Congress, keeping away from controversial subjects such as the current administration's handling of the war in Vietnam. She made the case that she was a fresh alternative to the "smoke-filled, back-room, party-dominated brand of politics."[23]

By the end of the day, when most people were getting ready for bed, Margaret appeared at cocktail parties and campaign events. For many of these public functions, John was by her side, enticing women and men alike with his charm. The Hecklers played off each other, cracking Irish jokes and entertaining prospective donors and voters with often told stories. Together, they were magnetic—and it was all too clear to Margaret's volunteers and team that she was determined to win both the primary and the general election.

After a late-summer campaign sprint, the primary election was held on September 13, 1966. The Hecklers, volunteers, and team gathered at the Heckler home to watch the votes come in. Sidney Hill Country Club was reserved for either outcome—victory or defeat. Both Margaret and John had uncertainty about the outcome of the election, but each felt confident they had put in their full effort. Running on fumes, they had not fully slept in weeks.

At 9:00 p.m., the group made their way to the country club, where cocktails and hors d'oeuvres were prepared. Over the course of the evening, additional volunteers and supporters arrived, until over a hundred anxious adults filled the room. At 11:15 p.m., the news broke: Margaret had won by 3,103 votes.

Joyous cheers rose up throughout the room. John planted a kiss on Margaret's cheek. Margaret stepped up to the microphone, still stunned at the outcome and spoke to the crowd, thanking them for all their support over the last few months. Early on September 14, 1966, Margaret Heckler claimed victory over the patriarch of Republican congressmen, Joseph Martin.

It was one of the biggest Republican incumbent upsets in the last one hundred years. The upstart candidate Heckler received 14,912 votes to the incumbent Martin's 11,809.[24] Margaret also managed to turn out thousands of voters who were usually apathetic about the primary race: That year, eight thousand more Republicans voted than in the 1964 primary. Joe Martin was reported to say that he had "mixed feelings about his primary defeat by a Wellesley housewife."[25]

The victory celebration was short-lived. Now there were less than two months to shift the focus to her next opponent, a handsome, silver-haired Democratic labor lawyer and captain of the Naval Reserve, Patrick Harrington.[26] He had the support of President Johnson, along with other top Democratic names, including Vice President Hubert Humphrey and Senator Robert Kennedy (D-NY) along with his brother Senator Edward "Ted" Kennedy (D-MA). As Margaret later explained, "I didn't want anyone to campaign for me. That way I wouldn't owe any favors when I got to Washington." She would not have the benefit of any big-name Republicans supporting her.

Margaret's team had to put in the same level of effort they had maintained over the summer. Bitter that Margaret had defeated Joe Martin, the Republican Party gave lackluster support in the general election. Harrington was a less popular contender than Martin, but as a female candidate in a man's world, Margaret was still at a disadvantage. Harrington put out a red, white, and blue flier with the words, "Elect a man of experience to work for you in Congress." In a telephone poll, a male Jewish independent voter from Newton told the pollster he'd be voting for Patrick Harrington, saying, "I have heard fine things about the woman, but I do not believe a woman belongs in politics."

In order to become the first woman from Massachusetts elected to Congress without succeeding a deceased husband, Margaret needed 51 percent of the vote. "The men kept saying I couldn't make it," she recalled, "but the women convinced them that a woman, even if she was the underdog, deserved their backing."[27]

In a final push, John raised enough money to attract the attention of the Republicans. His team had raised $30,000 for the primary race and was close to doubling the amount for the general election. Begrudgingly, the National Republican Congressional Committee (NRCC) contributed just $5,000 to hold the seat.[28]

On November 1, 1966—at the last minute—Margaret decided to send a letter to all Democratic voters in the Tenth District. The letterhead featured Margaret's headshot, followed by her final case for why Democrats should vote for a Republican:

Dear Democratic Voter:

You might be surprised to hear from me, a Republican Candidate for Congress. But I am writing to you and other Democratic voters . . . in the Tenth Congressional District, where I am now the nominee for Congress. . . . I am sending this letter even though I suppose it isn't exactly conventional, because so many Democrats in these communities supported me in 1962 and 1964 and helped elect and re-elect me to the Governor's Council from your District.

I have enjoyed serving you in the Council and have always earnestly tried to represent all the people—Democrats, Independents and Republicans. Now I would like the high honor of serving you in Congress, where I would practice the same principles of faithful service to all regardless of party that I have stood by in the years of serving you in the Council.

If you feel that dedicated, full-time representation of your interests in Congress is more important than having a particular party label, then I hope you will elect me as your Member of Congress on Tuesday, November 8.

Faithfully yours,
Margaret M. Heckler
Present Governor's Councilor
Candidate for Congress[29]

On Election Day 1966, Republican watchdogs and inspired young women across the country, Republican and Democrat alike, turned their attention toward the unprecedented race in Massachusetts. At Wellesley College, only a few miles from Margaret's campaign headquarters, the head of the Young Republicans Club, Hillary Rodham, must have watched to see if Margaret Heckler would become the first woman elected to Congress from Massachusetts in her own right.

Similar to the primary race, pollsters projected it would be a close finish. Some showed Margaret as the favored candidate and others Harrington. Democratic VIPs poured into the area to campaign for Harrington, and Margaret watched her opponent chip away at her lead. In a final push, Ted Kennedy wooed votes for Harrington, stumping for him by helicopter.[30]

When the votes were tallied, Margaret won, with 51.1 percent, the winning margin: 4,159 votes.[31] This occurred "despite a last-minute underground campaign by Harrington to exploit *the mother vote* of people who thought Mrs. Heckler ought to be tending her home and 3 children instead of romping around on Capitol Hill."[32] Against all odds, Margaret achieved a miraculous victory: a Republican in a Democratic state, a

Victory kiss from John for her wins over
Representative Joseph Martin and Patrick Harrington in her first bid for Congress, 1966.
Family collection.

woman and a mother, facing a man who had become an institution in the primary and having received little support from the Republican Party.

The ballroom crowd commenced celebrating. Once again, Margaret thanked her supporters and volunteers. Then she gave John an affectionate gaze and he kissed her. She said, "If not for my husband's confidence in me to run and his ceaseless hours of dedication to the campaign, I would not be standing here before you as the next Massachusetts Congresswoman."[33]

In the freshman class of 1967, forty-eight Republicans entered the House and the Senate for the Ninetieth Congress. Forty-seven of them were men, including George H. W. Bush, who would be elected president twenty-two years later, as well as the new Massachusetts senator Edward Brooke, who also made history that year as the first Black US senator.

Then there was Margaret Heckler, who said she was prepared to "think like a man, look like a girl, and work like a dog."[34]

Margaret thought back to her trip to visit Joe Martin in his congressional office only nineteen months earlier. In a prophetic moment, Martin had given her a visitor's pass stamped with his official signature—almost as if he was handing over his seat to her. It was later playfully said that Margaret visited the Capitol the year before she ran because she wanted to measure Martin's office for drapes.

· 8 ·

A Woman's Place Is in the House

With President Lyndon Johnson and the Republican freshmen congressmen in the Cabinet Room, 1967. *Yoichi Okamoto.*

Wearing a dark, tailored dress, Margaret stood on the plush royal blue carpet and looked around at her freshman colleagues—72 men in black and navy suits—and at the other 352 congressmen and 10 congresswomen scattered across the room. The *Congressional Quarterly* recorded that the *lone* victorious nonincumbent woman in the Ninetieth Congress was Margaret Heckler. It was January 1967 and Margaret fixed her gaze at the front of the chamber, where House Speaker John McCormack (D-MA) stood before the large American flag on the wall above their seats.

Over her shoulder, Margaret heard a congressman snicker, "What is that secretary doing on the floor of the House?"

"Don't you know?" a New England–based congressman responded, his tone low and reverent. "She's the one who beat Joe Martin."

As the only new woman to enter Congress that year, Margaret tilted up her chin and pressed her shoulders back. She appreciated her fellow New Englander's support, but she also knew it would be a long, tiresome process to change attitudes about women in Congress. Between the Senate and the House, the Ninetieth US Congress was composed of 523 men and 12 women, which meant women filled only 2 percent of the 535 available seats. Margaret was one of 11 women in the House—6 Democrats and 5 Republicans.

Years later, she reflected on what she had overheard, saying, "When I became Secretary of Health and Human Services, I was officially called 'Madam Secretary' and I must admit I was tempted more than once to contact my former House colleague to underline the irony. I wanted to tell him, 'The Secretary is back—*Madame* Secretary.'"[1]

Despite the negative comment, Margaret turned heads as she was escorted by Representative Bradford Morse (R-MA) to a seat toward the front of the chamber. As one newspaper put it, "There was a stream of traffic as male colleagues introduced themselves and paid their respects to the attractive Wellesley housewife."[2]

Immediately after taking the oath of office, Margaret was swept into the political game. The day before, she had decided to take the minority stance to oppose repeal of the "21-day rule," a policy that required bills to be taken to the floor after twenty-one days had passed so they would not be stuck indefinitely in the Rules Committee. For hours, Margaret remained either directly on the House floor or nearby, taking a stand for her own party. The negotiations meant Margaret missed a reception in her office in the Longworth Office Building. A group from Massachusetts wishing to offer their congratulations had gathered, but duty called.[3]

That evening when the phone rang, it was the same crusty old news editor from the *West Roxbury Transcript* who had given her wardrobe advice before. "What are you doing?" he asked. "Why are you wearing those outfits?"[4]

Margaret replied, "You told me to dress like a man. You said this was what I needed to do to blend in."

"Ditch those things! You need to be seen now. I looked for you on TV and I couldn't even see you."

Margaret took this advice to heart, changing her attire from the dull days of campaigning to the bright days of being a standout woman in Congress. From then on, Margaret wore pinks, purples, and reds. This grabbed the attention of the media, which reported, "On her second day, the color had changed to a bright raspberry. . . . The third day of the session found her outfitted in a reddish-pink dress."[5] She appeared to be in constant motion. With her high heels clicking, Margaret talked fast and walked faster.[6]

Freshmen in Congress typically did not garner such attention, but because she was a Republican in a Democratic state, had waged an unorthodox race against Joe Martin, and quickly embraced a bright, colorful wardrobe that had not yet been seen in Congress, the media was taken with her. She was an immediate sensation.

In Margaret's first few days, some of the older Republican congressmen—bitter that she had defeated Joe Martin—gave her the cold shoulder. She attempted to strike up conversations with the senior congresswomen in her party but was met with half smiles and few words. It became clear to Margaret that the senior congresswomen played to the likes and dislikes of the men around them.[7]

Nonetheless, there were bright spots. On her first day, Margaret was intercepted by a barrel of a man who stood six-foot-four, weighed 260 pounds, and was topped by a shock of white hair. Congressman Thomas "Tip" O'Neill Jr. (D-MA) wanted to introduce himself.

Two decades Margaret's senior, O'Neill was also a member of the Massachusetts delegation and a Boston College graduate. But she knew they shared something even more significant. As he leaned down, welcoming her to Congress, Margaret said, "Did you know, Mr. O'Neill, that on the surface I'm a Heckler, but underneath I'm much more than that?" Then she revealed her full Irish name.

His blue eyes sparkling, O'Neill threw his head back and laughed. "Why, of all things—is Margaret Mary Catherine O'Shaughnessy Heckler a Republican?" From this brief exchange, a friendship was formed.

Through the lens of the twenty-first century, the bipartisan congressional friendships of the 1960s and 1970s might be difficult to imagine. But during this era, moderate Republicanism thrived. It was not uncommon to see Republicans and Democrats breaking bread together after a long day on Capitol Hill. Most set store by the politics of civility. For her part, Margaret deeply believed in the power of the two-party system and in later years she shared with her children that she had chosen to be a Republican in a mostly Democratic state in order to maintain the two-party spirit of compromise and deliberation.

Her relationships in Congress exemplified her love for the democratic process and her skillfulness working across the aisle. Describing Margaret's interactions with her states' politicians and congressmen, Senator Ed Markey (D-MA) said she "fit in perfectly with the Republican party from Massachusetts. Margaret was 'the Woman,' John Volpe [governor] was 'the Italian,' Elliott Richardson [attorney general] was 'the Wasp' and Ed Brooke [US senator] was 'the African American.'"[8] As one newspaper reported, they were all young Republicans who hoped to "rebuild the image of the party in Massachusetts so that it [could] compete successfully with the Democrats for all offices and return the Commonwealth to a two-party system of government."[9] From the start, Margaret worked cooperatively with Tip O'Neill (D-MA), Eddie Boland (D-MA), and Silvio Conte (R-MA)—three men of the same generation who had a history of working efficiently together on behalf of their constituents.

Not all men in the House welcomed women serving in Congress. One day, Congressman Strom Thurmond, a senator from South Carolina who was infamous for his blatantly racist and sexist beliefs, passed Margaret in the hall. He made it clear that he believed she should be home in her kitchen and *not in this house*. After that, she tried to avoid Thurmond, but whenever she encountered him, he glared at her. Margaret wasn't the only female in Congress Thurmond pestered. In the 1980s and 1990s, he earned a spot on a list shared among female Senate staffers of senators known for frequently harassing women.[10]

While some did not welcome her presence on the House floor, Margaret also grappled with the opposite issue: congressmen who took notice of her youth and femininity. At the Women's National Press Club dinner on January 13, 1967, the elder statesman and Minority Leader Everett Dirksen (R-IL), a widower, approached Margaret, took her in his grasp and kissed her hard. She was caught off guard by his advance. The next day the press's photo made the news in all the major media papers.[11]

Senate Minority Leader Everett M. Dirksen (R-IL) steals a kiss, 1967.
AP Photo/Charles P. Gorry.

Such behavior from a few of her male colleagues continued to surprise Margaret, but what really shocked her was the lukewarm reception from some of her fellow congresswomen. Most astounding to Margaret was the atmosphere in the Congressional Ladies' Reading Room. An expanded suite in the Old House Chamber, the room served as a powder room, kitchen, and sitting area for congresswomen. The three-tiered chandelier, marble fireplace, heavy crown molding, and pleated jabot curtains gave the room an air of stiff refinement. One of the more notable pieces of furniture in the room was the couch upon which John Quincy Adams died in 1848 after giving an impassioned speech about abolition.

When Margaret entered the Congressional Ladies' Reading Room it was mostly silent. The women were not chatty. There were congress-women who were surviving spouses and those who were elected in their own right. Because of this, there were several cross-current issues.[12] Margaret had anticipated that a private room for women would facilitate friendship and female ingenuity, especially among herself and the other Republican congresswomen: Frances Bolton (R-OH), Catherine May (R-WA), Florence Dwyer (R-NJ), and Charlotte Reid (R-IL). What she found was that she was decades younger than the others. The closest woman to her age was fifty-two-year-old Catherine May, seventeen years Margaret's senior.

To Margaret's astonishment, there was little solidarity among con-gresswomen of either party. The stalwart congresswomen, both Democrat and Republican, who broke barriers to get elected during the 1950s and early 1960s had spent their entire careers operating within a man's world. They extended few favors to each other, much less to the new generation of women entering Congress. During Margaret's early years, an unsympa-thetic competitiveness distanced congresswomen from one another. Mak-ing matters worse, Margaret was an outlier because she was a Republican (the minority party), a moderate, and a young mother.

As a woman who had been raised on the tenets of female alliance and cooperation, Margaret longed for collaboration with her fellow congress-women. She knew collaboration was the key to women reaching the upper echelons of power, where there was room for change. A few years later, in the mid-1970s, when the old guard was voted out and female unity began to rise, she would not forget her early desire for female camaraderie.

Other than dodging the wrong kind of attention from congressmen, Margaret's first week was a blur. It was difficult not to get lost in the halls and tunnels, going from her office in the Longworth Office Building to the House floor. When a vote was scheduled in the next fifteen minutes, a bell in her office rang, initially making Margaret jump. Pumped with adrenaline and anxious to not miss a vote, she speed-walked in her heels, sometimes almost breaking into a run. There was also the ladies' room dilemma: There were no restrooms for women anywhere near the House floor. Several seasoned congresswomen advised her that if she was unsure whether she had enough time to use the restroom between votes, she should stay put to avoid missing a vote. Congress used a teller vote, which meant congressmembers were required to walk physically through a line to be counted. In an interview, she said her first few days in office were "monumental and quickly sobering."[13]

She discovered an unforeseen haven: her personal congressional office. She kept a sign on her desk with a quote from Charlotte Whitton that said, "Whatever women do, they must do twice as well as men to be thought half as good. Luckily, this is not difficult." In no small part, this humming space reassured her because she had appointed skilled women to help run it.

With little mentorship and guidance for how to navigate the complex web of spoken and unspoken House rules, regulations, and decorum, Margaret asked questions of just about anyone—the elevator operator, the Capitol police, veteran secretaries, and any senators or representatives willing to take her seriously. As a member from the opposite party, Tip O'Neill could offer only limited assistance. As for her own party, the Joe Martin grudge placed her firmly on the fringes. Over time, this led to Margaret's belief that she didn't owe the Republican Party the loyalty they expected.

Margaret learned as she went and adjusted when a barrier presented itself. Her mix of independence and can-do spirit led her to make one of her first major personal decisions as a congresswoman: pursuing a position on the highly sought-after Judiciary Committee. She had two reasons for this. First, for women, representation on a powerful committee mattered. Secondly, Margaret was motivated to write equality for women into law.

Her qualifications—ten years as an attorney, four years on the Governor's Council, presenter of a case in front of the Massachusetts Supreme Court, and service on the *Law Review*—were exemplary. Regardless of rumors that she would be blocked from the committee because she broke party ranks by running against Joe Martin, Margaret persevered. In interviews with reporters, she was outspoken about her plans to join the Judiciary Committee; the press responded with confidence that she would get the position. One newspaper article read, "Mrs. Heckler, a lawyer, is seeking a position on the House Judiciary Committee. An informed House source said it appears highly likely she will get her wish."[14]

Although the Judiciary Committee was all male, it did not cross her mind that being a woman would be cause for concern, especially because the media made even her believe her request would be granted. She followed procedures to join the committee, but almost immediately the committee's chairman, Emanuel Celler (D-NY), notified her that no opportunities were available. Margaret knew there was an open spot, but Celler was not about to admit a woman.

The outright rejection was devastating. She later said, "Even though I was surrounded by men at Boston College Law and didn't experience discrimination from my classmates or professors, I couldn't even get on the right committee in the Congress."[15]

Rejection from the Judiciary Committee became a defining moment of Margaret's congressional career. As in the past, the sexism that pervaded American institutions, even well into the 1960s, proved a frustrating barrier. Not to be deterred, Margaret instead resolved to use her position to help other women move ahead in male-dominated fields. She promised herself that the next time she faced opposition, she wouldn't back down so easily—especially if it was because she was a woman. Unbeknownst to the hundreds of men in Congress, the tectonic plates of power were beginning to shift beneath their feet.

Determined to move forward, Margaret pivoted her attention to the House Committee on Veterans' Affairs. It was common practice for new members to choose committees upon which former members from their state had served. Edith Nourse Rogers, the first elected female representative from Massachusetts, had previously chaired that committee, leaving office in 1960. For that reason, it was deemed acceptable that Margaret pursued a position on this committee. However, Margaret also had a personal interest. Inspired by her father's service in the navy, she had an affinity for veterans' affairs. Tip O'Neill advised her to instead select a committee that would advance her career; nonetheless, she joined the House Committee on Veterans' Affairs as the sole female member. She would serve on this committee for sixteen years, diligently seeking policy reform in Congress and beyond.

During this time, Margaret attempted to make an appeal to Congress on behalf of an American citizen detained overseas, pleading for his release. The Czech government had detained one of Margaret's constituents, Vladimir J. Kazan-Kormarek, when a Soviet airliner on which he was a passenger made an unplanned stop in Prague. Making the appeal on the House floor, Margaret was immediately reprimanded by her party leadership for speaking up as a newly elected freshman.

Decades later, House historian Matt Wasniewski noted how this event was impressive because Margaret's "first speech was on behalf of a constituent immediately."[16]

At the time, the scolding left Margaret feeling embarrassed and frustrated. She carved time out of her day to retreat to the chapel in the Capitol. There, she found her grounding and strength. Over the course of her congressional service, she would return to the chapel in search of solace whenever she hit a low point. In her own words: "One of the great political resources of my career was my faith. At very difficult times I would go to a little chapel in the Capitol or a church across the street. That is your strength, and it was my strength during the most difficult moments. A woman's spirituality is tied to her integrity. The integrity of a candidate is the most important quality of all, and it's supported by one's faith. Don't ever think you're alone. You have not only your constituents and your family; you have a divine source of support."[17]

After the challenges of her first weeks, she didn't have to wait long to receive a flurry of attention for several major successes. A reporter named William H. Young, discussing whether "women are handicapped in the predominantly male world of politics,"[18] shared two of Margaret's significant accomplishments from her first two months in office. The first was that she was elected by her Republican colleagues as vice president of the 90th Club, an established group for the fifty-nine Republican freshmen in the House. The position was mostly an honorary recognition but one that demonstrated Margaret's future leadership potential.

The second achievement was even sweeter. Unwilling to relent in her advocacy for Vladimir J. Kazan-Komarek, she soon prevailed in securing his freedom. In newspapers across the country, Margaret was pictured at the airport celebrating the reunion of Kazan-Komarek and his wife.

Young concludes his piece by writing, "But being a woman appears to have helped rather than hindered Mrs. Heckler in overcoming what is perhaps the major problem of all freshman members of the House—obscurity."[19] With her passion, determination, and spirit, Margaret ensured she was anything but obscure.

If Margaret had concerns about relocating her family to the Washington, DC, area they were allayed during a family dinner before the move. Around the kitchen table, Margaret asked John Jr. what he wanted to be when he grew up.

Her seven-year-old son replied, "I wanna be president."

"You can't do that," quipped eight-year-old Alison. "You're not a girl."[20]

In a South Boston St. Patrick's Day parade, 1967. *Family collection.*

In 1967, Margaret was the only congresswoman with young children. To facilitate their new lifestyle, John and Margaret purchased a New England–style stone and clapboard house in McLean, Virginia, a Washington suburb. The house on Rocky Run Road, situated on ten acres along a quiet country lane, featured a pool, terrace, a barn, and mature trees.

While their children were adjusting to the move, the Heckler marriage was less adaptable. John retained his stockbroker position at Harris Upham & Company in Boston, splitting his time between Massachusetts and Virginia. He spent his weekdays alone at their Wellesley home and flew to Virginia for the weekends. The time apart made John distant, pulling him away from his family. While physically present on the weekends, he had a short fuse and was easily ready for a fight. It didn't help that he drank too much. Although he loved and supported Margaret's career, there were unspoken, competitive tensions underlying their relationship. He had enjoyed being the center of attention, and without that, he would get irritable and jealous. Recognizing John's needs, Margaret frequently ceded the floor to him inside their home and in public.

Despite their marital challenges, when John was in Virginia, he was able to throw himself into the Washington social and political scenes.

John joined the Congressional Wives Club as the only husband in the group. His reputation as charismatic and witty preceded him and he easily charmed the women in the group. While they embraced him, the downside was that John soon became involved in the particulars of female pettiness. Betty Ford, wife of House Minority Leader Representative Gerald Ford (R-MI), was in charge of the club. At a club meeting, some members were being disrespectful toward their leader. John, proved to be Mrs. Ford's ally by scolding the other ladies saying, "Why don't you straighten out! We'll do what Betty tells us. That's it!"[21]

From the outside, John and Margaret's partnership appeared electric; however, John struggled to accept his wife's growing popularity on a much bigger Washington stage. Dinner parties, birthday parties, and fundraisers at beautiful homes off Rock Creek Parkway and in upper Georgetown kept Margaret and John in a constant social swirl. They still wooed entire rooms with their Irish humor, playing to one another's strengths. From across a jam-packed ballroom or a congressman's living room, John could hear his wife tooting his horn while he smooth-talked her colleagues. Compared with Margaret's time on the Governor's Council, the bar had been raised in terms of their public and social demands—but the Hecklers naturally fell into step.

With a frenetic professional life and active social schedule, Margaret couldn't manage her time without the assistance of in-house help. Rita from Norway, lived with the Hecklers in Massachusetts and then in Washington, DC. She cared for the children, cooked, and kept house. When Rita moved on, Margaret sought out a housekeeper in Washington who had been recommended to her and who had previously served President Lyndon B. Johnson's family. Elsie moved in and subsequentially ran the Hecklers' McLean household.

Margaret wanted to maintain an active motherly role, especially since John was absent during the week for much of their day-to-day

Waving goodbye with John. *Family collection.*

lives, so she tried to have breakfast with the children and kissed them as she left for the day. Then, during her forty-minute drive in rush hour traffic down the winding Georgetown Parkway, she had to mentally transition from mother to congresswoman.

That summer, heat intensified the daily Vietnam War protests outside the White House. Signs read "LBJ Must Go," "Hey, hey, LBJ, how many kids did you kill today?" and "Children are not Born to Burn: Stop the War Now!" American casualties in Vietnam reached nearly seventy thousand. Although the war was unpopular among political leaders and the public alike, President Johnson increased troops by 55,000, for a total of 525,000 men in combat. Johnson drew relentless criticism from both the Left and the Right. The Vietnam War cut him down to the knees.

Gerald Ford, Minority Leader of the House, was asked by the freshman class of Republican congressmen to request a meeting for them with President Johnson. The sheer size of the class warranted a meeting, and President Johnson agreed to it. According to former congressman Jim Gardner (R-NC),

> Johnson hated Republicans with a passion. We were not quite sure why we were able to meet with him. It must have been because Johnson felt he had to pay a little bit of attention to the new Republicans. He ran the Senate with an iron hand. He was a hard ass. But for whatever reason, he invited forty-six of the newly elected Republican congressmen and Margaret, the one congresswoman, to the White House after the first few months of their first term. We were the youngest group of Republican congressmen ever elected. And one of the largest groups ever elected. Most of us were in our thirties.[22]

Representative George H. W. Bush (R-TX), president of the freshman class in Congress, led the group into the Cabinet Room in the West Wing of the White House. A mahogany table stretched the length of the room, lined with nail-studded black leather chairs. After welcoming the freshmen Republicans, he opened the room for questions. Margaret bravely raised her hand.

"Alright, little lady," Johnson said. "What's on your mind?"

"Mr. President, how much longer is this war going to go on? Why are we not getting truthful information?"

Johnson exploded. He yelled and cursed about the protestors outside his window and the pundits who endlessly criticized his every decision.

When he finished his tirade, Margaret held her own, saying, "Mr. President, you still didn't answer my question."

"Why are you questioning me about what we're doing?" was the only answer she received.

Congressman Jim Gardner (R-NC) was charged up. His younger brother was in Vietnam currently serving in the war and had told his brother that he "felt like he was fighting with his hands tied behind his back."[23] Gardner then asked the president, "Why aren't we bombing their combat missions, their major seaports where their missiles are stored?"

Jumping up, Johnson yelled, "What do you know of this damned war?"

It was evident that President Johnson had his own plan for how to advocate for troops currently serving in the war, as well as veterans who had returned to the United States with injuries and PTSD. Margaret's thoughts turned to the House Committee on Veterans' Affairs. *What,* she wondered, *might a committee member be able to do for those currently serving and those who had served in Vietnam?*

Unlike President Johnson's evasive approach regarding Vietnam, Margaret wanted to be transparent with her constituents. Furthermore, as a member of the House Veterans' Affairs Committee, her responsibilities encompassed veterans and their after-service care. So, in the summer of 1967, Margaret sought to arrange a congressional fact-finding trip to Vietnam. She was told of the risks associated with such a tour, but she packed her bags and flew over the Pacific.

In Saigon, while the war was going on, Margaret met with the president of South Vietnam, Nguyễn Văn Thiệu; the American ambassador to South Vietnam, Ellsworth Bunker; and US Army general Creighton Williams Abrams Jr. The general arranged a helicopter tour for her of the battlefields. On the ground, Margaret bounced along in military vehicles to war-torn villages. It was a dangerous mission. In fact, the same helicopter that took her to the war zone, was shot down by enemy forces the next day.

When asked why she felt a trip to Vietnam was necessary, Margaret shared:

> To be a great leader, one must see for themselves with their own eyes. I wanted an accurate picture of what was going on during the war in Vietnam so I could come back home and vote on defense appropriation.
>
> At that time, I couldn't believe the White House or the Pentagon. I was skeptical of some media coverage about Vietnam as they were not thorough and had their own slant. Not only had the Johnson Administration lied to the people regarding matters in Vietnam, but

they had frustrated the Congress with bewildering and contradictory statements. While I initially took the position that the US could not withdraw militarily from Vietnam, I chastised the manner in which the Administration was conducting the war.[24]

At home, Americans watched *CBS Evening News* anchor Walter Cronkite, seen and trusted by millions, showing actual footage of Vietnam and sharing death-toll figures. After she visited Vietnam and saw soldiers in hospitals with missing limbs, Margaret had an inside view into the horrors of the war. As the only woman on the Veterans' Affairs Committee and a mother of a young son, Margaret's views on the Vietnam War changed. She was no longer in support of the war.

As the war dragged on, the American public continued to boo and spit on homecoming Vietnam veterans. In most cases, no military bands announced their safe return to the States. But Margaret was determined to be the Vietnam veterans' biggest advocate. She began drafting legislation to assist them and to flip the narrative about their service to their country. Margaret believed that troops returning home from an unpopular war 8,500 miles away still deserved the same respect and comprehensive care that any veteran of the US armed services would receive.

November 10, 1967, started out like any typical day for Margaret. She watched her children board the bus for school and patted the heads of the family's three dogs. Margaret started on her twisty morning commute to Capitol Hill in her blue Chevy station wagon. She turned onto Old Dominion Drive, which had no rails protecting motorists from the steep cliffs that dropped fifty feet.

Halfway to the Washington Beltway, the car's steering locked, forcing Margaret to drive straight off the road. She plunged forty feet down the side of a ravine, until a large tree blocked her fall. Margaret's knee was crushed against the steering column. Upon impact, two studded snow tires stowed in the back seat flew forward toward Margaret, knocking her out and pinning her against the steering wheel. When she regained consciousness, she was terrified. No one could hear her cries for help. She pounded the horn and silently prayed, *God, if there's more for me to do, let me live.*

Finally, her blaring horn caught the attention of a passing truck driver. Ambulances and fire engines soon arrived, stopping miles of traffic on the two-lane road. The emergency team later stated that it was a miracle Margaret survived the crash.

John was flying into Washington for the weekend when he heard the news. The family rushed to Margaret's bedside at Arlington Hospital. Her right knee was mangled, and her hip was injured. She received a call and flowers from President Johnson, and a few days later he sent out a memorandum on White House stationary: "Congresswoman Margaret Heckler (R-Mass) was injured in a car accident last Friday morning, when her car went out of control near her home and plunged into a ravine. She has painful injuries which will keep her in the hospital about ten days and on crutches about two months."[25]

Members of Congress flooded her hospital room with flowers and notes of condolences and wishes for a speedy recovery. One note from a colleague read, "We miss your smiling face. Hope to see you back in the hallowed halls of Congress. You haven't missed anything. Get well soon." She was surprised by a visit from House Minority Leader Everett Dirksen (R-IL), from whom she had garnered a great deal of respect. When her friend George H. W. Bush sent her flowers and placed a personal call to her in the hospital, it was a kindness for which she was especially grateful.

Margaret also wrote a note to the president.

Dear President and Mrs. Johnson,

Despite being a member of "the loyal opposition" I know of nothing more uplifting to the spirits of a rather uncomfortable Congresswoman than the receipt of a beautiful bouquet from the president of the United States and our charming First Lady.

My family and I deeply appreciate your kindness at a very trying time. Please accept my heartfelt thanks.

Gratefully,
Margaret Heckler
Member of Congress[26]

An assessment of the crash revealed that a mechanical problem with the Chevrolet caused the steering to lock. After months of rehabilitation for hip and leg injuries, which would affect her for the rest of her life, Margaret was able to walk unassisted. The shake-up and extended aftermath of the accident slowed her down physically but not mentally. Margaret's ambitions were only reinforced by her close encounter with death.

While she was recovering, she savored a political victory. On November 8, two days before the accident, President Johnson had signed HR 5894, a bill "Providing Equal Opportunity in Promotions for Women in the Armed Forces." In his remarks, he noted that women in the military received less pay than their male counterparts for the same positions. They had only a 10 percent chance for promotion to the status of major, and zero opportunity to be promoted to colonel. The new bill removed all barriers for women to rise through the military ranks.[27] A month into her recovery, Margaret received a note from the White House:

December 5, 1967

Dear Mrs. Heckler:

The President wants you to have the attached [a personalized, signed copy of the Act] as a memento of that historic day—November 8, 1967—when the president signed H.R. 5894, an Act removing restrictions on the careers of female officers in the Army, Navy, Air Force and Marine Corps.

Sincerely,
Juanita D. Roberts
Personal Secretary to the President[28]

On Margaret's first day back to the Capitol, December 13, 1967, the press caught Representative Donald Riegle (R-MI) on camera assisting Margaret up the stairs into the House. She was headed inside to cast a vote on a bill to increase Social Security benefits. Margaret was ready to join the "Congressional Track Team—albeit on crutches."[29] Her fellow freshmen congressmen circled the wagons around her. She stood out now more than ever—not just for being the only woman newly elected to Congress that year, but for persevering through a near-death tragedy.

· 9 ·

Nixon and the Republican Feminists

With President Richard Nixon and best-selling author from Massachusetts James Fahey and his wife, 1969. *White House Photographer.*

$\mathcal{M}$argaret's second year in office was overshadowed by dual assassinations. First, Martin Luther King Jr. was killed on April 4, 1968, in Memphis, Tennessee, and his assassination threw Washington, DC, into chaos. Cities throughout the United States experienced riots in the days immediately following King's death, but the nation's capital was hit the hardest, with fighting in the streets and death and destruction all around. The city was under siege and burned for four long days.

Three days after the fires and protesting in Washington started, the Heckler family had just finished their usual 10:00 a.m. Mass. Afterward, Margaret impulsively decided that she wanted to take the family to Washington to view the unrest that had occurred. She wanted to see for herself what was going on. She felt secure because she had her husband John by her side. They drove straight to downtown Washington.

As a freshman congresswoman, Margaret was granted permission to drive into what, earlier that morning, had been a riot zone but was now secured by troops. As they approached a security checkpoint on Fourteenth Street, John was motioned to a stop. A National Guard soldier leaned into the Plymouth convertible, saying, "This area is closed sir."

Margaret quickly spoke up. "I'm Margaret Heckler, congresswoman from Massachusetts. I was told I could come." After verifying her license plate and ID, the officer let their car through. As Margaret viewed the mass destruction, she wondered, "What else can I do to help?"

The Heckler family observed looted storefronts and fires burning. Police and troops stood on guard by smoldering buildings throughout the area. Margaret had just voted for the soon-to-be-enacted 1968 Civil Rights Act. Viewing the rubble, Margaret recalled Martin Luther King Jr.'s well-quoted line, "Darkness cannot drive out darkness; only light can do that. Hate cannot drive out hate; only love can do that." It seemed distant and unachievable, but she hoped that from this tragedy, change would come.

On their way out of the city, the Heckler children, aged eleven, ten, and seven, observed the Capitol. Although they understood little of what they saw or the historical context of Martin Luther King's assassination, they sensed what it meant to work at the core of the nation's power and what that danger and threat posed for their mother.

After four days of riots in the nation's capital alone, 13 people were dead, over 1,000 were injured, and 6,100 were arrested.[1] President Johnson had declared martial law, and 13,000 armed soldiers were sent in to restore peace.[2]

There was also political turmoil. President Johnson announced he would not seek a second term, fearing a loss of support over the Vietnam War. Just a few months later on June 6, 1968, Senator Robert F. Kennedy was assassinated in Los Angeles after winning the California primary. Amid continued division about the Vietnam War, the country was rocked with grief over the loss of these two towering public figures. In the November general election, former vice president under Eisenhower, Richard M. Nixon (R-CA), defeated incumbent Vice President Hubert H. Humphrey (D-MN) and became the thirty-seventh US president.

For Margaret, Nixon's election provided an opportunity to make progress with the support of a Republican president. The Democrat-controlled House allowed little room for Republicans to set the legislative agenda or accomplish their own goals, but with a Republican president, Margaret knew she and her party could capitalize on having an "in" with the White House, and her background as a lawyer gave her an edge. Her initial focus would be policies geared toward the advancement of women in the federal government.

Although women had served in Congress since 1917, minimal accommodations had been made to welcome their increasing presence. It took a decade for a single women's lavatory to be designated (in 1927) and it wasn't until 1962 that the initial lavatory was refurbished and expanded into a suite in the Old House Chamber, later renamed the Lindy Claiborne Boggs Congressional Women's Reading Room. In between votes, congresswomen scurried, ten minutes' round trip, past tourists in Statuary Hall, requiring a mad dash back to the House floor lest they miss a vote. Nearly five decades later, in 2011, a women's restroom was finally provided directly off the House Floor—a luxury that congressmen had never lived without.

As more women joined Congress, exclusionary rules were also developed. The west balcony and the House's gym and pool were only open to congresswomen from 8:30–9:30 a.m. because some congressmen liked to swim in the nude. On February 6, 1967, Congresswomen Patsy Mink (D-HI), Charlotte Reid (R-IL), and Catherine May (R-WA) protested the policy by marching through the halls of Congress to the gym's entrance. Although she fully supported her fellow congresswomen, Margaret couldn't join the march as she had an event in her district.[3]

At the same time, the profile of a US congresswoman was changing. From the 1920s to the 1960s, many women landed their positions in Congress through the deaths of their husbands who were congressmen. Between 1955 and 1976, twenty-seven of the thirty-nine women who entered Congress were elected outright.[4] This shift, toward women attaining their own seats in Congress, occurred as a result of changing perceptions during the civil rights movement, the Vietnam War, and the sexual revolution. Margaret was the second Massachusetts congresswoman, but the first woman to be elected from the state in her own right.

The "first wave of feminism," which took place in the early twentieth century, was propelled by suffragettes fighting for women to be allowed to vote. Their efforts resulted in women earning that right in 1920. In 1969, during her first term in Congress, Margaret found herself in the midst of a massive new women's movement, referred to as the "second wave of feminism." Suddenly, she was able to help address some of the most pressing issues facing women at that time.

Fortunately, Margaret and her fellow Republican congresswomen—Florence Dwyer (R-NJ), Catherine May (R-WA), and Charlotte Reid (R-IL)—all recognized the newfound opportunity presented by a president from their party and were eager to make their voices heard.

Almost immediately upon Nixon taking office, Dwyer, the most senior Republican congresswoman, wrote the president a letter on behalf of the four Republican congresswomen, requesting a meeting to discuss sex discrimination and the specific details of women's treatment in government.

Dear Mr. President,

We, the Republican women members of the House of Representatives, respectfully request an early opportunity to meet with you for the purpose of discussing a number of matters of direct and immediate concern to women generally.

We believe that we can provide you with information and ideas which should be of value in the opportunity to cooperate with you and your administration.

If you could suggest a date and time convenient for you to meet with us, we should be deeply grateful.

Signed,
Florence P. Dwyer, Catherine May,
Charlotte Reid, Margaret Heckler

In response, the women received silence. Undeterred, the women continued submitting appeals to meet with the president. On June 23, 1969, Bryce Harlow, counsel to the president, sent a memo to Dwight Chapin, special assistant to the president, regarding the letters: "See attached letter from the four G.O.P. ladies of the House. They request a visit with the president 'On matters of direct and immediate concern to women generally.' They are glinty about it. . . . One of the major concerns is the paucity of Federal appointments for women. . . . Their concern is vibrant and real. I strongly recommend that they be given a visit with the president. The meeting should not be scheduled in the Congressional half-hour as the discussion will obviously be substantive."

These congresswomen were not the stereotypical bra-burning feminists often associated with the 1960s, but they passionately cared about the ways in which sexism was institutionalized in the nation's laws and the consequential social and cultural behaviors that made unequal treatment of women permissible. Representative Dwyer and Representative Heckler were the most moderate Republicans. Representative Reid was more conservative, and Representative May was center right. Margaret was the youngest and newest congresswoman. Of the four, all but Charlotte Reid had entered politics on their own and not through their husbands.

Similar to Heckler, over the course of their careers each of the other three women had made advancements for women's equality. In 1952, while Florence Dwyer was a New Jersey assemblywoman, she championed a law for women to receive equal pay. Dwyer would go on to pursue, alongside Catherine May, the national Equal Pay Act of 1963. In heated congressional discussions about the Civil Rights Act of 1964, Representatives Dwyer, May, and Reid ensured that, alongside race, color, religion, and national origin, Title VII included no employment discrimination based on sex. Margaret Heckler, who had defied gender barriers for decades, was in good company as the four of them pursued an invitation to the White House. Historian Susan Hartmann referred to the formidable group as "tiny but mighty" and said, "They were indispensable to the feminist policy transformation."[5]

Although Nixon detested face-to-face meetings, he knew he couldn't continue to put the congresswomen off.[6] Congresswomen Dwyer, Heckler, May, and Reid finally were summoned to a meeting with President Nixon in the Oval Office on July 8, 1969.

To make serious inroads in toppling institutionalized sexism, the four congresswomen knew their meeting with the president would have to be memorable. Acting on a cunningly devised plan, just before the meeting they released a memo to the press about the purpose of their visit with Nixon. They accused the administration of having a dismal record on women's rights and even went so far as to say that some administration officials were "positively anti-women."[7] The involvement of the press meant Nixon could not ignore their agenda.

The meeting was scheduled for a Tuesday afternoon. All four women walked into the Oval Office as if they were going into battle. Despite the heat and humidity of a typical Washington, DC, summer, they wore suits, pearls, and pumps, an embodiment of the new feminine power that had begun to break into male-dominated arenas. They were directed to sit on two gold sofas facing each other, which were positioned on a bright blue carpet designed by First Lady Patricia Nixon, and in view of long, gold curtains framing the windows. Members of the press anxiously waited outside.

President Nixon strode into the room, greeted the women with a polite smile, and took a seat in a chair between the two couches. While Nixon was known to think that women were more "erratic" and "emotional" than men, he said, "It's an honor to have you here this afternoon."[8] As his eyes scanned the notes he was holding, he lifted his head and asked, "What can I do for you ladies?"

The women exchanged quick glances, then opened by expressing their concern regarding civil rights as they applied to women, including appointments in the Nixon administration. The "tiny but mighty" group emphasized to the president that if modern American women didn't see themselves represented within their government, there was a risk that women would begin to distrust that government.

The only reason Nixon had agreed to meet with this group was because they were the only Republican women in Congress in 1969, making their requests a bit more persuasive. He pointed out that there had been more appointments of women in his administration than most people realized. Still, he admitted, "We have not done enough. Although, I am not interested in 'tokenism' but rather want to make appointments of women who would earn those appointments by virtue of their outstanding qualifications and abilities. This is one of America's untapped human resources."[9]

Even though Nixon was not a pro-woman advocate and could have cared less about their demands for change, attention from the press was not the only motivator for the president to act; there was also the next election cycle to consider. Having only received 43.4 percent of the female vote in 1968, he was already concerned about the 1972 election.[10] The female vote could help him secure reelection.

The four congresswomen agreed to act as a congressional task force to bring Nixon's administration the names of qualified women. Three months later, the Task Force on Women's Rights and Responsibilities, appointed by Nixon, submitted their first report to the president. One position that was discussed was that of Federal Maritime chairman. Nixon had already promised to appoint maritime reporter and journalist Helen Delich Bentley as a Federal Maritime commissioner. Bently told Margaret that the Nixon administration planned to name a "less knowledgeable" man as chairman of the Federal Maritime Commission. So Margaret told President Nixon that they would not applaud Helen's appointment unless *she* was made the chairman, a higher-ranking position than commissioner. Soon thereafter, Bentley's request was granted.[11]

The meeting with Nixon and the creation of the task force marked the start of some of the most productive gains for women's rights in the immediate years to follow.[12] A new era had dawned for women with government and political aspirations.

Viewed from a present-day lens, Richard M. Nixon was an unlikely ally for women. But in 1971, in the buildup to the 1972 election, Nixon made his first major move related to the Task Force on Women's Rights and Responsibilities, hiring Barbara Hackman Franklin, a former New York business executive, as staff assistant to recruit top-level female talent for full-time, policy-making positions in his administration. Remarkably, the number of women in policy-related positions tripled, from 36 to 105 in just one year. By the following year, the number rose to 130. More than half of these positions had never been held by a woman. In addition to helping women receive appointments to prominent positions, Franklin also curated a list of women for potential openings. Despite a 5 percent reduction in federal employment between April 1971 and April 1972, Franklin assisted more than a thousand women into mid-tier government roles.[13] Her work was a tremendous success, and for the first time, a pipeline opened for well-educated and skilled women to compete for government jobs for which they were qualified.

Nixon went on to appoint Jayne Baker as the first woman in ten years to be commissioner and vice chairman of the Civil Service Commission. He asked her to do everything possible to see that women in the career civil service would be guaranteed equal opportunity for employment and advancement. Additionally, Nixon nominated five women to the rank of general in the armed forces and the first female naval officer to the rank of rear admiral. During this time, the first female sky marshals, secret service agents, air traffic controllers, narcotics agents, and tugboat captains were also appointed.[14]

Another dramatic outcome of the Nixon-appointed task force of Dwyer, Heckler, May, and Reid was the influence it had on the legislative work of the four women themselves. During the Nixon administration, more legislation was passed to promote female equality than at any point in US history, and it was predominantly led by Republican women.[15] They took advantage of the shifting culture and the Republican administration to apply pressure on Nixon to make real, lasting changes, such as the Equal Rights Amendment and Title IX.

While Republican women led the charge with Nixon, they enjoyed full bipartisan support in Congress thanks to the growing belief in equal rights for women. During this historic political shift, Margaret was an instrumental architect and advocate for early 1970s legislation regarding women. According to Dee Wedemeyer, "At the 1972 Republican National Convention, Margaret was applauded for her persistence in getting the party to adopt a women's rights plank in its platform for the first time in history."[16]

Bolstered by the success of the Task Force on Women's Rights and Responsibilities, Margaret next turned her attention to the Comprehensive Child Development Act of 1971. This bill was designed to provide federally funded access to daycare for thousands of American families either headed by a single parent or living below the poverty line and thus relying on both parents to work.

The need for daycare was a new concept for parents in middle- and upper-class, two-parent households, easily living on a single-source income. Still, because so many women in this demographic were choosing to enter the workforce, the need for affordable childcare was growing. As the only congresswoman with young children, Margaret felt alone in this fight and was acutely aware that childcare was a necessity for women working outside the home.

After the Comprehensive Child Development Act passed the Senate, Margaret hosted a town hall meeting in Fall River. She directly asked her constituents whether they wanted her to support the bill in the House. The working factory women of Fall River showed up in droves. They reported a lack of affordable, quality daycare, saying they often had to select facilities that didn't meet their standards for their children. Their message to Margaret was "loud and clear—daycare is a must in our society."[17] Margaret worked over a staggering total of ninety-six drafts of childcare legislation. In Washington, the bill began to lose Republican support even among moderate Republicans. During committee meetings, Margaret went on the record citing her survey of the Fall River community's desire for more and better childcare options. As she explained, "I believe that the people of Fall River speak for America; because of this I am continuing my efforts to provide Federal assistance for daycare."[18]

Margaret was successful in getting the bill to pass the House, only to see it vetoed by President Nixon. Margaret was furious. Nixon insinuated that the bill would "Sovietize" American children. Despite women's strides in the 1960s, American culture in the early 1970s still primarily valued a "homemaker" model. In fact, Nixon relied on his advisor Daniel Patrick Moynihan's belief that the bill would damage the American family.[19] Margaret called President Nixon's veto "a serious setback to the concept of child development."[20]

While federally funded childcare was already available for low-income, at-risk families, it remained an elusive dream for other families with working mothers.

On a brighter note, during this time the Equal Rights Amendment (ERA) finally seemed like it had a chance of passing. First proposed in Congress in 1923 by Republican Congressman Daniel R. Anthony (nephew of Susan B. Anthony), the ERA failed to gain traction due to criticisms and fears that it would harm labor and health protections that were already in place, such as long working hours for impoverished working women. The amendment then floundered for five decades.

Representative Martha Griffiths (D-MI), elected in 1954, was one of the first congresswomen who sought to change how congresswomen interacted in the halls of Congress. She observed, "The error of most women was they were trying to make the men who sat in Congress not disapprove of them." Griffiths was a political tiger as she proclaimed, "I didn't give a damn whether the men approved or not."[21] Griffiths, along with many other congresswomen of the era, often had to fight to be heard by their male colleagues in Congress.

Although by the end of the 1960s the second wave of feminism brought renewed attention to the ERA, it remained stuck. Longtime House Judiciary Committee chairman, Representative Emanuel Celler (D-NY), the same man who had blocked Margaret from joining that committee, opposed the ERA on the grounds of the traditional belief that it would inhibit labor protections. Having been newly elected in 1923 when the ERA was first proposed, Celler was closing in on almost fifty years in Congress. Despite his opposition, women in the House would have their final say before Celler left office in 1973.

In 1971, Martha Griffiths and Margaret Heckler carried the hard copy version of the ERA to the House floor. The year prior, Margaret had testified to the Judiciary Committee about the ERA, arguing that the nation's creative and intellectual potential was harmed by women's unequal access to jobs and unequal pay. She cited astounding statistics, including that 40 percent of the labor force were women, but they accounted for only 3 to 9 percent of workers in professional positions like attorneys, doctors, and scientists. Moreover, there was an equal pay disparity. While women received 40 percent of all college degrees, when they were hired for professional jobs, their annual salary was the same as for a man with only an eighth-grade education. On average, college-educated women were paid $6,694, half the amount of an average college-educated man, who earned $11,795.

In one of her most well-known speeches on the ERA, Margaret poignantly stated:

> The average woman in America has no seething desire to smoke cigars or to burn the bra—but she does seek equal recognition of her status as a citizen before the courts of law and she does seek fair and just recognition of her qualifications in the employment market. The American working woman does not want to be limited in advancement by virtue of her sex. She does not want to be prohibited from the job she desires or from the overtime work she needs by 'protective' legislation. . . . In fact, I have heard it said quite often that the only discrimination that is still fashionable is discrimination against women. . . . Women are not requesting special privilege—but rather a full measure of responsibility, a fair share of the load in the effort to improve life in America. . . . The seventies mark an era of great promise if the untapped resource of womanpower is brought forth into the open and allowed to flourish so that women may take their rightful place in the mainstream of American life. Both men and women have a great deal to gain.[22]

As one of the key sponsors of the Equal Rights Amendment, Margaret Heckler worked both sides of the aisle to get it passed in both houses. Socially, she was seen with Joan Kennedy, Eunice Schriver, and Betty Ford—all rallying to support the ERA.

It was a great day for the congresswomen on October 12, 1971, when the ERA officially passed in the House. The final version of the amendment stated that "equal rights under the law shall not be abridged or denied . . . on account of sex."[23] It was approved by the Senate on March 22, 1972. The ERA's next hurdle would be ratification by thirty-eight states before March 22, 1979, but Congress would then extend the deadline to June 30, 1982.

Adding to the hope-filled passage of the ERA, Title IX, developed and defended by Patsy Mink (D-HI), was enacted as a part of the 1972 Education Act. Margaret cosponsored the measure. Another major reform against gender discrimination, Title IX protected women and girls in federally supported educational, vocational, and school-based athletic opportunities. Prior to its passage, the federal government only provided funding for boys' sports. When it was passed in 1972, Title IX was meant to not only give women opportunity in sports, but also to protect them. When her congressional friends asked Margaret, "Why are you supporting Title IX? Doesn't your son play football?" Her answer was, "I also have two daughters. Why should I deprive my daughters of the same athletic benefits?"[24] The passage of Title IX was a watershed moment for women's sports in the United States.

In 1973, Vice President Spiro Agnew (R-MD) resigned because of financial improprieties. When Nixon asked House members for recommendations for vice president, Margaret made the case for a woman to fill the role. In a letter to the president, she suggested Counsellor Anne Armstrong or Helen Delich Bentley, chairwoman of the Federal Maritime Commission, writing, "No woman in high public office has ever been tainted with a hint of scandal, and nomination of a woman as vice president would go far toward helping restore public confidence in our government."[25] In the end, House Minority Leader Representative Gerald Ford became vice president. It was nearly fifty years before America elected the first female vice president, Kamala Harris.

A budding political relationship was developing between Margaret and President Nixon. On a few occasions, Nixon invited Margaret and her family to attend formal church services on Sunday in the East Room of the White House.

In early 1971, President Nixon approached Margaret to ask if she would consider running for Senate in Massachusetts in 1972. Nixon was worried that Senator Ted Kennedy might run for president, which posed a serious threat to his 1972 reelection. So, Nixon promised Margaret that if she ran against Kennedy for his Senate seat and lost, he would appoint her to be the first female Supreme Court Justice. Margaret was tempted by the proposition, yet she felt loyal to her constituents. In addition, since the Kennedy family name was so big in Massachusetts, she reasoned, "That's annihilation, and why would I do those kinds of things?"[26]

She also did not trust Nixon to make good on his word. While he had done much for women during his first term, Margaret knew his support was tied to his reelection in 1972. As expected, Kennedy announced his bid for the presidency, but he eventually withdrew as a result of questions surrounding his involvement in the death of a campaign worker, Mary Jo Kopechne, at Chappaquiddick in 1969. Ultimately, it was Senator George McGovern (D-SD) who received his party's nomination to run against Nixon.

Margaret's instincts were correct. A year after Nixon asked her to run against Kennedy, the Watergate scandal erupted. On May 28, 1972, members of Nixon's Committee to Re-Elect the President (which was often mockingly known as CREEP) broke into the Democratic National Committee headquarters, located at the Watergate Hotel in Washington, DC. Burglars stole copies of top-secret documents and bugged the office's phones. Since the wiretaps failed to work properly, five burglars returned to the Watergate building and tried to break into the office with a new microphone, but were seen by a guard. The police were called, and the prowlers were caught.[27]

On June 23, 1972, the FBI seized tapes of Nixon ordering the FBI to minimize their investigation into the Watergate break-in. These tapes were the basis for President Nixon being investigated in relation to the incident and led to calls for Nixon to resign the presidency.

Despite the scandal, Nixon defeated McGovern in a landslide that November 1972. Significant for Margaret, the only state that McGovern carried, along with Washington, DC, was Massachusetts.

During his second term, calls for Nixon's resignation continued. The House Banking Committee was holding preliminary hearings about Watergate since it had been determined that the Committee to Re-elect the President had raised over $1.7 million in banks that had been deposited throughout the country and in Mexico.[28] However, the majority of the House Banking Committee members felt there was no need to move forward with an investigation of the president that early on.

The *Boston Globe* also published a story stating, "The House Banking Committee voted to prohibit an open public investigation into allegations of federal criminal misuses of substantial campaign funds, allegedly used to fund the breaking and entering in the Watergate scandal."[29] Soon the letters started pouring into Margaret's office, including a memo from a Cambridge, Massachusetts, resident, Paul Fisher, who was "VERY upset" with "her vote on the Committee on Banking and Currency to bury the Watergate incident." He went on to say that he never considered Heckler "a political hack," but that he was "disgusted and horrified."[30] His view was not uncommon in the overwhelmingly Democratic state of Massachusetts.

To assess the risk to her own political future, Margaret had her team conduct a poll of her constituents about whether Nixon should resign. According to Joe Byrnes, a former staffer, the results were a 50/50 split.[31] And then, as the Watergate crisis began to unfold, she was surprised to learn that in three majority-Republican towns in her district, the vote was 100–1 in favor of impeachment of the president. Shortly thereafter, Margaret supported the resolution to authorize and launch formal impeachment proceedings, with a little less fear that it would impact her own reelection in 1974. She wrote: "I was dismayed by the consistently amoral attitude expressed in conversations in the Oval Office. Now we are confronted by the President's own admission of involvement in cover-up activities, which is shocking beyond belief."[32]

Ahead of the vote that would kick off the impeachment hearings, President Nixon reportedly asked one of his confidants, "Who is on the House Banking Committee?" When Margaret's name was mentioned, Nixon confidently said, "Oh, she's easy. She'll do anything I ask." Margaret was furious. Not only was she disappointed in Nixon's behavior throughout the controversy, but she didn't like the fact that he thought he could push her around.[33] During a television appearance, Margaret did not hold back from acknowledging that she was surprised to learn how many people in her district felt Nixon should be impeached.[34]

After an intensive examination of the evidence, Margaret drafted the following telegram to President Nixon:

> I strongly urge your swift and unqualified compliance with the Supreme Court ruling that tape-recorded conversations and other evidence must be turned over to the special prosecutor. Failure to comply would indicate you hold yourself above the law and would, in my estimation, guarantee an overwhelming vote in the House for your impeachment. . . . Your apparent efforts to thwart a criminal investigation and bring those responsible for Watergate to justice has brought disrepute upon yourself and the office you hold, and this has served to weaken the presidency.
>
> For the good of the presidency, for the good of the nation, I ask you to comply with the Supreme Court's decision and meet any and all requests of the special prosecutor so that we can get Watergate behind us and unite our great nation.
>
> —Congresswoman Margaret Heckler[35]

President Nixon's efforts to obstruct the investigation into the break-in resulted in the House initiating impeachment proceedings against him. Margaret was saddened by the outcome stating, "A vote for impeachment of the president is a vote that is cast in sorrow."[36]

In the end, the House Judiciary Committee approved three articles of impeachment against the president. However, before the articles of impeachment reached the House floor, President Nixon resigned on August 9, 1974.

As the Watergate winds of change swept over Washington, it touched on Margaret's office too. After Vice President Gerald Ford assumed the presidency, Margaret's secretary, Glenda Leggitt Etchison, told her excitedly, "Mrs. Heckler, I think I want to go work for Gerald Ford. He's history in the making!" Shocked, Margaret reacted, "Glenda, *I'm* history in the making!"[37]

Margaret was serious, because after several terms in Congress, she had cultivated a cadre of female staffers who would be instrumental behind the scenes while Margaret fought for one of the most important pieces of legislation for women in over fifty years.

• *10* •

Women Finally Get Credit

In the Oval Office with President Gerald Ford.
White House Photographer.

While the Watergate drama enveloped most of Washington, Margaret was not distracted from her efforts to pass legislation giving women the ability to take charge of their own financial futures.

Women's suffrage was achieved by the ratification of the Nineteenth Amendment in 1920; however, the right to vote was only part of the women's rights movement. It also required the power of the purse, which needed to be achieved by legislation giving women the right to credit.

The early 1970s were a perfect storm for women's rights and Margaret was in the right place at the right time and in a position to make a difference. Her memories of being denied a mortgage in the 1950s—as a practicing female attorney in Boston—were seared into her mind. Margaret had joined the Committee on Banking and Currency (commonly known as the House Banking Committee) during her first term in Congress, determined to ensure women were granted economic justice and fair treatment under the law. She was one of only two women to serve on that male-dominated committee in 1968, and the House Banking Committee was where any legislation regarding women's credit would need to be discussed.

According to US law, women were simply not equal to men in areas of finance, and were unable to be granted credit in their own name. Quite simply, women were 100 percent dependent upon their husbands or fathers when it came to securing loans or credit, with no consideration given to their own earning power.

In a *Good Housekeeping* interview, Margaret noted, "I feel it is important for every woman to have at least her own economic identity established through a personal credit rating."[1] Well into the 1970s, banks were consistently denying women access to credit in their own names. Without credit reform, women's economic freedom was severely limited. Women could not open a credit account in their own name or take out a loan or qualify for a home mortgage without their husband's or father's signature. Although women were obtaining college degrees and now made up a growing share of the American workforce, they were barred from securing their own financial futures. The credit discrimination era was quickly forgotten in American collective memory.

For single women or women who were the primary breadwinners, credit discrimination was stifling, patronizing, and left them vulnerable. Life without credit was equally bleak for divorcees and widows; without credit, they had few financial options to provide for themselves and their children.

Due to the social and religious stigma surrounding divorce in the 1960s and 1970s, divorcees were especially vulnerable. If they had been full-time housewives, they were suddenly forced to enter the labor market—often without previous job experience and with no credit in their own names. What had been their most important job—raising children and being home—came back to bite them. If they wanted to buy a house or a car, start a business, make a large purchase or buy food, their options were generally limited to cash payments.

The urgent need to address financial discrimination against women stirred up some of Margaret's earliest memories. Belinda West and her widowed sisters had made financial decisions on a razor's edge—any move in the wrong direction could have resulted in all of them being penniless and losing their home. After her husband died, Belinda West had worked well into her eighties, relying on multiple sources of income. Her widowed sisters had no option but to move in with her after their husbands passed. Until the mid-1970s, many widowed women kept their deceased husbands' accounts open to retain credit. Opening new credit accounts was not an option for them.

Housewives and working women ended up being the driving force behind credit reform in the 1970s, for good reason; it was impractical and demeaning for women to have such constrained purchasing power when so many of them were now earning their own money, and they were also the primary shoppers for their homes and families.

Department stores were at the nexus of change in how Americans accumulated credit from the 1950s through the 1970s. In that era, if a woman wanted to purchase a new dress at Macy's, she would charge the expense to an account in her husband's name, accumulating credit at the store that he would then pay off at the end of the month. In those days, department stores also routinely denied credit account applications from single women.

As a member of the House Banking Committee, Margaret was inspired to author and sponsor The Equal Credit Opportunity Act of 1974, the law that would finally give women the right to credit in their own names and make it illegal for creditors to discriminate against credit applicants on the basis of race, color, religion, national origin, sex, marital status, or age. The legislation before her work omitted two categories, sex and marital status. In other words, "women."

While Heckler's devotion to financial equality for women was straightforward, the legislation that actually codified equal credit into law was anything but linear, with multiple drafts from multiple sources making the rounds in both the House and Senate.[2]

Representative Bella Abzug (D-NY) was the first to introduce legislation related to credit discrimination.[3] It was referred to the House Committee on Banking and Currency, but as Edmund Rice, Heckler's chief of staff explained, "Abzug was known for her loud, brash and activist-oriented political tactics, resulting in many Congressmen tuning her out whenever she pushed a new reform bill."[4] Additionally, unlike Heckler, Abzug did not prioritize bipartisan support regarding women's rights legislation, hampering Abzug's ability to sponsor and pass legislation. "If it was just Abzug, no Republicans would have supported the Equal Credit Opportunity Act. It took a bipartisan effort. It took Mrs. Heckler to get it through the House," emphasized Rice.

Heckler and Abzug were friendly colleagues but had polar opposite approaches to their congressional work. Opting for decorum and charm to woo members on both sides of the aisle, Heckler was poised to push the legislation the furthest because of her diplomatic tactics. She was also well positioned on the House Banking Committee, which had jurisdiction over that type of legislation and was responsible for addressing those exact issues. According to Rice, "The work in the Banking Committee, the work in the House, the work to find the allies—all of this Margaret Heckler had the lead on; others were there rhetorically. But all the hard work was Margaret Heckler."[5]

Her counterpart, Senator William E. Brock (R-TN), was working to pass a version of the Equal Credit Opportunity Act in the Senate. As soon as it passed there, it was turned over to the House—and Margaret dug her high heels in deeply.

In one of several addresses before Congress, Margaret introduced a bill on July 23, 1973, that was identical to the one passed in the Senate.[6] She went on to describe the credit discrimination that both single and married women encountered, citing the example of a female staffer on her team, the primary breadwinner in her home, who was denied credit independent from her husband, an unemployed graduate student. Margaret concluded with "the hope is that this legislation can be passed, in this session, so that this discrimination, a carryover from our economic past, can be eliminated once and for all."[7] Unfortunately, Heckler's hope and hard work did not result in the bill being passed in the House that summer. The fight was not going to be quick or easy.

A few months later, a band of congressmen and women, including primary sponsors Margaret Heckler, Ed Koch, Matt Rinaldo, and thirty-nine cosponsors, assembled in the House to support another version of the Equal Credit Opportunity Act. Margaret's statements before the Subcommittee on Consumer Affairs Hearings on Credit Discrimination, on November 13, 1973, mentioned that for over a year she'd worked tirelessly to "eliminate unwarranted discrimination in the issuance of mortgage credit,"[8] but that any bill that would accomplish the two most important cornerstones necessary to establish women as economic equals had her full support. The two foundational principles she identified were that "there should be only one set of criteria applied equally to all credit applicants. The only considerations that *should be* allowed are those which definitively affect *an individual's ability to pay,* and that marital status should not be taken as determining the economic relationship between husband and wife."[9]

During a floor speech in Congress, Margaret outlined the level of economic discrimination women endured—facts that may have been thought about, but were rarely spoken about:

—single women have more trouble than men obtaining mortgage credit;

—married women are generally required to have credit placed in their husband's name, even if they are in fact economically independent;

—divorced or widowed women have trouble establishing credit in their own names, even though they might have been the bill payers during the marriage;

—separated women find themselves without a credit record, despite the fact that they might have been the family breadwinner;

—a wife's income often is not counted in joint credit applications, without regard to the stability of her income."[10]

Margaret wasn't finished. Fired up, she cited studies proving these patterns of discrimination and their lasting effects on women and families. Then she added,

It is clear that different standards are applied to men and women applicants, the net effect of which is to make it more difficult, or impossible, for women to establish themselves as economically independent. . . . These traditional practices fly in the face of the new economic realities in this country. Too little account seems to be taken of the fact that over 40 percent of women are working, and that in 10 percent of all households, the wife is the breadwinner. Yet women still must face these inequities.

"It would be foolish," Margaret urged, "for the House to fail to act on a bill already halfway through the legislative process."

Heated discussion followed her remarks. "Legislation is not necessary," a congressman retorted, "because the pressure of competition will, in time, bring all credit grantors into line with the more 'enlightened' view of women."

Margaret shot back, "An open-minded timetable is unacceptable and unjust. Credit-worthy women will continue to be rejected in credit applications in many sections of the country where enlightenment is slow to emerge." Margaret ended her remarks by saying, "The important point to keep in mind is that we have been working to establish principles of economic justice for women, and justice delayed is justice denied."[11]

American women had long been viewed as financially irresponsible, an opinion that persisted in the 1970s. The primary objections to credit reform were based on these outdated fears and prejudices. Most women lived their day-to-day lives on an allowance, and if they were married, they required "permission" from their husbands or their fathers, to make the most basic purchases. They would receive funds for groceries, and perhaps, a little extra "mad money" for the pair of shoes glimpsed in a shop window. Single women faced an equally bleak situation: For example, if there was not a man in a woman's life to help her purchase an expensive item, she was generally given the option to put the item on layaway, a system by which the store held the item while the woman paid for it in installments. Only when the purchase price was fully paid off could she take the item home.

Credit discrimination was incredibly invasive. Creditors could ask any woman of childbearing age whether she was on birth control or planned to have children, making assumptions about the likelihood of her continued participation in the labor force and using that information to deny her access to credit.

For nearly a year after the November 1973 hearing, Margaret continued to drive the Equal Credit Opportunity Act forward as its primary author and sponsor, meeting opposition at every stage of the process. In one of her statements before the House, Margaret described how most people still thought of "the so-called little woman who kept her pin money in the sugar bowl, saving for a rainy day."[12]

Quite simply, the pushback women received was primarily cultural. As Rice put it, "The world was not ready for the change" and "it was still not established in the culture that women could stand on their own two feet individually from their spouses."[13]

Margaret disagreed, strongly. Deeply rooted cultural obstacles were no match for her conviction that women deserved equal treatment under the law. The world was changing, she fervently argued—regardless of whether that change was acknowledged. Women suddenly made up a sizable chunk of the workforce, and the number of women interested in careers outside the home showed no signs of slowing.[14] If passed, the Equal Credit Opportunity Act would mark the beginning of a new era.

Facing pushback in Congress, Margaret's next tactic was to arrange a meeting with CEOs of several major banks, such as J.P. Morgan, Chase, Wells Fargo, and others. She wanted to discuss their hesitancy to extending credit to women. Billy Mittendorf, the CEO of Boston Five Cents Savings Bank, was a close family friend of the Hecklers and the first to hear

Margaret's pitch. Overall, the banks' position was that women did not have jobs so they could not pay bills; but if they had jobs, they could become pregnant and then lose their jobs and not have the means to pay their bills. Margaret dispelled this fear of women not being credit worthy, assuring them they could approve and deny female applicants based on credit eligibility, just as they did with men.[15]

The final breakthrough came thanks to a female Mastercard executive, one of the few women with a leadership position in the financial industry at that time. She urged Margaret and her team to consider a more business-minded tactic: the growth side of the equation. By refusing to work with women, credit-granting authorities were missing out on half of their potential clientele. "Margaret started to use that argument in talking to representatives at the banks and credit card companies. No one wanted to miss a business opportunity." Margaret's chief of staff, Ed Rice, recalled, "We tried to play on that."[16] In the end, the CEOs saw the light and were unable to resist the opportunity to double their business.

During a district visit, Margaret joined a hearing for the Governor's Commission on the Status of Women at the Massachusetts State House. Margaret testified that it was absurd that women could not fully participate in the economy. She exclaimed, "Credit is more valuable than cash in this society."

Reflecting on this fact, Margaret recalled that women were the majority of the population and controlled the majority of the funds. Still, on credit, most credit-worthy women with good incomes were not extended the same credit opportunity as men, such as in home mortgages.[17] Margaret and the media continued to tap into the equal rights movement as a solid reason to pass the Equal Credit Opportunity Act, working to topple any and all excuses for financial discrimination.

Department stores were second only to banks in granting credit. Considering that women were their primary customers, department stores were obvious potential allies. Working this angle, Margaret arranged appointments with the presidents and CEOs of major department stores throughout the country. The president of Sears Roebuck and Co., the department store with a catalogue in almost every home, signaled his support for the Equal Credit Opportunity Act.[18]

As major financial companies and retailers came on board, Margaret appeared unstoppable. However, she still faced opposition—and it came from within her own committee. Moreover, it came from a woman.

Representative Leonor Sullivan (D-MO), a widow who had assumed her husband's seat in Congress (who insisted on being referred to as "Mrs.

John B. Sullivan"), was the only woman in Congress to vote against the Equal Rights Amendment. Mrs. John B. Sullivan, chairwoman of the House Banking Committee's Consumer Credit Subcommittee, was also rigidly opposed to the Equal Credit Opportunity Act. She was the biggest obstacle to the bill's success. Some described Sullivan's policy positions as "out of something from another century." Sullivan was opposed to the idea that there should be a law that women should be treated equally for commercial credit or bank loans. Presumably, her view mirrored the view of her husband and most men of that era.

Margaret was baffled, which led her to often feel like she was a committee of one. How could any woman not want her rights protected by law? Especially someone like Sullivan—a widow who without such protections had no economic rights, unless she was able to keep her dead husband's credit alive. Margaret's goal was twofold: She not only had to convince the thirty-seven men on the committee that women needed to have credit in their own name, but she would also have to convince Sullivan, a reluctant ally.

The bill bounced between the House and Senate for several rounds of amendments. In order to skirt around Mrs. John B. Sullivan, Margaret worked tirelessly, maintaining momentum, as well as the attention of other members of Congress, banks, and equal rights groups. Then, at long last, she got exactly what she needed to drive the bill home.

Representative Lindy Boggs (D-LA), who in March 1973 ascended to office after the death of her husband and asked Speaker Carl Albert (D-OK) for an assignment on the House Banking Committee because her husband, Hale Boggs, had joined the committee as a freshman. In order to accommodate Lindy Boggs, an additional seat was added.[19] It was difficult for Representative Leonor Sullivan or the other twenty-four congressmen on the committee to argue against Boggs's tears as she relayed the painful and unjust financial realities she'd endured in the aftermath of her husband's recent tragic death in a plane crash. Boggs's firsthand experience finally gave Margaret the leverage she desperately needed to pressure Sullivan and others to change their votes.

At the final committee meeting, Margaret stood displaying the same tenacity that got her into Congress in the first place and presented the revised printed version of the Equal Credit Opportunity Act of 1974. The force of bipartisan support and the arrival of Lindy Boggs on the committee had ultimately prevailed over Mrs. John B. Sullivan's objections, and the bill was on its way to the House floor for its final passage.

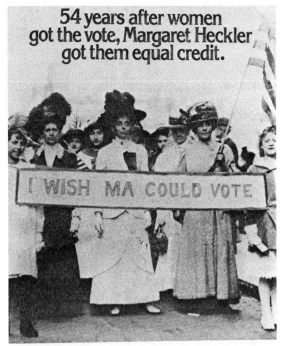

54 years after women got the vote, Margaret Heckler got them equal credit.

I WISH MA COULD VOTE

Over the years, Margaret Heckler has led the fight in Congress on many bills that are important to women.

For instance, she *wrote* the laws that let women get credit in their own names and qualify for a home mortgage regardless of sex or marital status.*

She co-sponsored the Women's Economic Equity Act to insure equality for women in pensions, taxes and tax credits.

She co-sponsored the legislation to eliminate

Social Security discrimination against women.

She co-sponsored the bill to provide federally funded child care facilities.

And ten years ago she was one of the original sponsors of the ERA.

That's why it's important that we send Margaret Heckler back to Congress next year.

So she can keep fighting for justice and equality for all the people of this district.

And all the people in this country.

Vote Margaret Heckler Nov. 2.

A campaign ad that highlights equal credit for women, 1977. *Family collection.*

The time for women to be granted access to credit in their own name was long overdue. Consider the sting of rejection Margaret felt as a newly minted lawyer in 1956 when she was denied a mortgage on her own. A popular ad campaign of the time claimed: *You've come a long way baby.*

When the bill was sent to the House for a vote, Margaret was seated in the front row, anxiously watching the votes come through the new electronic voting system. "The big board" was like a baseball scoreboard. The display showed congressmembers' names, how they voted, and the running vote tally. Representatives milled about, inserting their individual voting cards to select a button for yay or nay. The new system, which had been installed the prior year, cut the amount of time needed for a vote in half—from over thirty minutes to just fifteen minutes—so Margaret's anxious concern was relatively brief. The bill passed by an overwhelming majority in the House, on October 9, 1974, and was quickly approved by the Senate on October 10, 1974, where the final vote was 89–0. It was a turning point for women's rights, but it took more than seven years of discussions, hearings, and committee meetings to win the battle.

The bill was signed into law by President Ford on October 28, 1974. The Federal Reserve System Board of Governors was then tasked to implement the new law into federal monetary policy. On October 16, 1975, the Equal Credit Opportunity Act took effect. A year later, President Ford would sign the Women's Equality Day proclamation. Getting the presidential seal of approval demonstrated that he was an advocate for women's rights during the second wave of feminism.

The Equal Credit Opportunity Act made it unlawful to "discriminate against credit applicants on the basis of race, color, religion, national origin, *sex*, marital status, age, because an applicant receives income from a public assistance program, or because an applicant has in good faith exercised any right under the Consumer Credit Protection Act" (emphasis

President Gerald Ford signing a Women's Equality Day Proclamation with congresswomen looking on, 1976. *White House Photographer.*

mine).[20] This was not only an economic win for women, but also a major cultural breakthrough. It created a path for women's full financial participation in society, without the need for a male overseer or cosigner.

The "Article and Factual Information on Credit Discrimination" was a document that detailed the scope of the Equal Credit Opportunity Act. The document specified that women were legally granted access to credit from banks, finance companies, department stores, and credit card issuers. It also explicitly ended the invasive and discriminatory practice of creditors inquiring about women's birth control or childbearing capabilities. These presumptuous questions seem inconceivable in twentieth-century America.[21] The added clarifications, economic stereotypes, and views of women and other groups previously discriminated against were permanently shifted. Creditors could no longer merely view female applicants as irresponsible, jobless child bearers.

The Equal Credit Opportunity Act was a landmark win for women. While Margaret Heckler was a congresswoman working to ensure all women would be granted credit in their own names, Ruth Bader Ginsburg still almost twenty years away from being nominated to the Supreme Court, was an American Civil Liberties Union (ACLU) lawyer, representing individuals to overturn financial discrimination on a case-by-case basis.

In later years, Margaret considered the Equal Credit Opportunity Act as the crowning achievement of her congressional work.[22] Without her determination and tact, the bill may have had trouble gaining traction both inside and outside of Congress.

The year 2025 marks the fiftieth anniversary of the Equal Credit Opportunity Act's implementation. Women won the right to vote over a hundred years ago, but only in the last fifty years did they gain the financial freedom to receive credit in their own names.

On April 14, 2000, in a talk to college students, Margaret referenced the credit discrimination days as "those dark ages," which "many women listening to this today would not believe they ever existed, but they did."[23] It's ironic that such limitations were quickly forgotten.

In 1975, with the implementation of the Equal Credit Opportunity Act, Americans could not have predicted the ubiquitous use of credit in an increasingly cashless world. Credit cards and phone apps have replaced cash for nearly everything—parking meters, restaurant bills, and virtually every other purchase or transaction. Today, when women are flooded by credit card offers, they can remember Margaret Heckler, who served as the catalyst to provide credit worthiness to American women in their own names.

• 11 •

A Legislator at Home and Abroad

With veterans on the Capitol steps. *Public domain.*

*M*argaret's assistant, Jack Horner, parked his lime-green Datsun at Washington's Union Station on an autumn day in 1972. His mission was to meet a train from New York. Aboard were Jack and Bridget O'Shaughnessy, and it was Jack Horner's job to escort them to their daughter's congressional offices in the Rayburn Building. Margaret suspected Horner was the right person to meet her parents, as they would bond over their shared Irish heritage.

Horner had earned the trust of Congresswoman Heckler going from summer intern to a congressional staffer. His Irish wit, strong work ethic, and ability to keep the mood light on difficult days earned him the nickname of Margaret's "Boy Wonder." Horner sometimes picked up Margaret's kids from school, adding cohesiveness to her responsibilities between Washington and Virginia. The Heckler children grew attached to Horner, who allowed a young John Jr. to sit on his lap and drive the "Happy Pickle."

Jack Horner walked with the O'Shaughnessys down a long marble corridor through the Rayburn building with the two Jacks bantering and cracking jokes in the Irish way. When the O'Shaughnessys stepped into the suite of offices what her father noticed was a space humming with skilled women. At the front desk, Mary Anne Thadeu greeted them. She was a first-class caseworker as well as one who oversaw constituents' services. Carol Bauer, Margaret's Executive Assistant, oversaw everything related to the Washington office. Patti Tyson, Margaret's Legislative Assistant, functioned in the role of both "advance and organizer."

Jack O'Shaughnessy choked up with pride at the sight of Margaret sitting behind her large, double pedestal desk. The phones in the reception room rang off the hook and stacks of legislative drafts and memos were scattered across Margaret's desk. Jack became misty-eyed when he spotted documents labeled "Geriatric Centers for Veterans." He was moved knowing his daughter was working on issues that honored his own military service.

In a royal blue suit, Margaret stood, greeting her parents. "Please hold my calls for the next two hours," she told her assistant as they walked out of the office. She escorted them for lunch.

In the Congressional Dining Room, Jack and Bridget took in the linen tablecloths, gold-rimmed plates, and congressmembers sprinting between meetings and votes. As they finished their meal Jack lit up as Congressman Tip O'Neill approached the table.

As an Irishman and a Democrat, O'Neill was one of Jack's political heroes. The congressman put his hand on Jack's shoulder and said, "Your daughter is very special to me. And to the entire nation."

After O'Neill walked away, Jack enthused to Margaret, "I'm pleased to see the camaraderie among Irish Americans extends to the halls of power."[1] Margaret was at the top of her game and had become a woman of faith and purpose, fulfilling Jack and Bridget's greatest hopes in life for her. Her parents always followed their daughter's career from a far. Yet Margaret briefly felt wistful, because it could not make up for the decades-old feelings of parental abandonment. Her incessant drive to excel stemmed from her father's earliest expectations.

In these tumultuous times Margaret could not escape the reality that America was at war in Vietnam. As the only woman on the Veterans' Affairs Committee working alongside twenty-four congressmen, not a day went by when she did not feel the effects of war as she was briefed on war reports, visited vets and their families in military hospitals, and attended VFW local events.

Margaret's work on veteran's policies faced three challenges. The first was that there was public hostility toward the Vietnam War in the late 1960s and early 1970s regarding the military draft. Just a few miles from the Capitol, protesters and draft dodgers stationed themselves against the tall iron fencing around the White House, chanting, "Hell no, we won't go!"

The second challenge was that the returning Vietnam vets felt forgotten. Margaret had been influenced by one of her staff, Peter Saroka, a Vietnam vet who observed, "No one pays attention to us." Saroka and his fellow vets were shunned or even spit on when they returned home after their service. No bands played and no receiving lines formed for these soldiers. Instead, they were mostly met with disgust, because many Americans thought the United States shouldn't be involved in Vietnam.

The third challenge was that Margaret was bringing her female perspective to a committee dominated by men. Throughout her sixteen years in Congress Margaret remained the only female Republican on the Veterans' Affairs Committee. As a woman and mother of three she saw the consequences of battle with her own eyes in her trip to Vietnam and subsequent visits to veterans' hospitals.

Margaret also dedicated her veterans' committee work to bolster women's advancement in the military. She clearly saw the ways in which women were barred from military careers they were more than capable of handling. For most of US history, policies related to the military and veterans affected men, and the associated decision-makers were male. In the 1970s, only a slow trickle of women pursued military careers.

A deep motivation for Margaret's commitment to veterans was her father, Jack O'Shaughnessy, despite the pain he caused in her life. Margaret proudly remembered her work on the Veterans' Affairs Committee "as one of the best things I ever did in my life." She explained how her father's service gave her "a feeling for veterans" because their role in society "was so essential to the freedom of America. I just had a great sense of patriotism. . . . I was very aware of what it cost my parents to come to America."[2]

Margaret's work on Veterans' Affairs eventually reaped major legislative rewards. From 1967 to 1983, she sponsored or cosponsored 107 bills related to veterans, spanning concerns from education to housing to geriatric centers. She recalled, "I was committed to helping those who had the most to lose while defending our country."[3] She also uniquely combined women's interests and veteran policy in a way that forever reshaped the US military.

In her home district, Margaret became well-known for her veteran advocacy. Earl Blackwell, a supporter from Taunton, offered her the use of his red Cadillac convertible for local parades on Memorial Day. During one Veterans Day service, they were driving through a cemetery on an unpaved road designed for horse carts, anxiously attempting to avoid graves, when McCarthy accidentally rolled over a large tree root, causing Margaret to fall into the back seat of the Cadillac. Two veterans in uniform rushed over, scooped her up, and sat her back on her perch saying, "Here you go Peggy."[4]

According to her regular driver, Danny Converse, Margaret was immensely popular with veterans. During her reelection campaigns, World War II and Vietnam veterans would stand on bridges in Fall River waving flags and banners that read, "Re-elect Peg Heckler to Congress."[5]

Veteran respect for Margaret grew from her compassion and willingness to hone in on the lives of individual veterans. If a veteran with a medical issue or problems with eligibility called her office, Margaret's staff coordinated on their behalf with a VA office or hospital. On any given morning, Margaret might meet with Vietnam veterans who were paraplegics or a mother who had lost her son overseas. The former soldiers and their families would ask, "What can you do to help us?" After they left, Margaret would often close the door to her office, sit at her desk, and cry.

Her staff member and former Vietnam vet Peter Saroka asked for Margaret's help locating storefronts to be converted into outreach centers for Vietnam vets. At the ribbon-cutting ceremony for one center, a group of constituents gathered. While some celebrated the new facility, the returned Vietnam veterans were in the back of the room, glued to television news reports. Some of the men were experiencing flashbacks from their time in Vietnam. By the end of the week a veteran friend of Peter's, Mousy Burns, committed suicide—providing Margaret with a tragic window into the soldiers' all-too-common postservice struggles with battle fatigue (later referred to as post-traumatic stress disorder or PTSD).[6]

By 1975, when the United States finally decided to pull out of Vietnam, the numbers were staggering: 2,709,918 Americans had served, 58,148 were killed, 75,000 were severely disabled, 23,214 were 100 percent disabled, and 5,283 lost limbs. Over 60 percent of those killed were under twenty-one years of age. The grim facts haunted Margaret when she remembered what President Herbert Hoover once said: "Older men declare war, but it is the youth that must fight and die."

While the Vietnam War was at the center of national debate, Margaret

- ensured that veterans received their pensions in timely payments;
- requested funding for better medical care and increased compensation for disabled veterans;
- called for equal treatment of married female veterans; and
- drove an increase in payments for veteran funeral expenses and burials.[7]

She also sponsored legislation to give priority treatment to Vietnam veterans exposed to Agent Orange, a chemical herbicide and defoliant used by the US military in Vietnam from 1961 to 1971. The chemical caused significant health problems for those exposed, as well as for their offspring.

Securing adequate medical care was the most urgent and difficult challenge for veterans to face. Many required special accommodations, access to affordable medications, extended rehabilitation, and much more. Aging veterans of World War II and the Korean War also had extensive medical needs. Margaret described the veteran medical system as one of her "greatest interests."[8]

Margaret felt the graphic presentation during her first Veterans' Affairs Hospital Subcommittee meeting highlighted why veterans' medical care was so important to her. Margaret remembered:

I'll never forget the first meeting. They were presenting a movie on new procedures, new prosthetic devices that were used in the hospitals for amputees. Having never liked the sight of blood, I was appalled at that experience. I can remember my mental anguish, but I said to myself, "I've chosen to run for office. I said I could do the job. I must endure this. I must sit through the whole thing and watch it." And I did. It was the goriest experience of my whole life. . . . What was interesting was when the lights were turned on, all the men on the committee [had] left the room. I was the only one left.[9]

From then on, Margaret led a charge to increase the budget for VA medical programs, a number that is now more than $137.1 billion.[10] She introduced the Veteran Senior Citizen Health Care Act of 1979 (HR 4015). She thanked her colleagues for their unanimous support, marking the "passage of the first significant piece of legislation in this Congress which is designed to assist the veteran senior citizen."[11]

After her bill died in the Senate she tried to rally public support for veterans' senior health care. Margaret introduced the Veterans Health and Gerontological Health Services Act four times until it was eventually rolled into the Veterans' Administration Health Care Amendments of 1980. This public law expanded VA services for geriatric health and extended end-of-life care. Despite President Carter's veto of the bill, it was overridden by both chambers and became law. Margaret became the acknowledged leader of the VA's Geriatric Research Program, which established Geriatric Research Education and Clinical Centers (GRECCs) and made great strides in the treatment of traumatic brain injuries, psychiatric ailments, hypertension, cancer, and other diseases affecting the elderly. As a result, twenty GRECCs were established to provide better health care for older veterans.

From 1973 to 1983, Heckler introduced twenty-eight pieces of legislation related to veterans, most of them related to postservice career development and health care. In addition to her own authored legislation, Margaret cosponsored fifteen bills and supported and advocated for more than a hundred pieces of legislation that successfully became law, including seventeen compensation increases for veterans, fifteen increases in pensions for nonservice-related disability, as well as support for several GI education bills and support for the GI home loan program. The Vietnam section in the GI Bill was her workmanship, and it earned her an award from the American Association of Community and Junior Colleges.[12]

Margaret also showed a keen interested in international affairs during her sixteen years in Congress. So much so that she was invited on a congressional trip to China, a place where no American had set foot in more than twenty-five years until President Nixon visited in 1972.

President Nixon sought to improve relations with China in an effort to gain a strategic advantage over the Soviet Union during the Cold War. Chinese American relations had been strained since the Korean War in 1950, when the People's Republic of China (PRC) gave massive aid to their communist allies in North Korea and the Soviet Union. In retaliation, the United States placed a trade embargo on the PRC.

Two decades later, Mao Zedong, the longtime leader of the PRC grew weary of the Soviet Union and increasingly desired to expand China's economic and political will on the world stage. Nixon's efforts to thaw relations were well positioned. In February 1972, President Nixon and an accompanying delegation made the monumental trip to China. They were the first Americans to set foot on Chinese soil since World War II.

While there was well-placed criticism of the visit due to Mao Zedong's responsibility for forty to eighty million deaths throughout his rule (from 1949 until his death in 1976),[13] Nixon's historical visit is still considered one of the most important diplomatic visits of any US president. As Nixon later commented, it was "the week that changed the world."[14] Nixon in China indeed marked a turning point in the Cold War and China's introduction to the world economy. The trade embargo was lifted, and for the first time in decades, Americans saw images of mainland China.

After Nixon's visit, congressmembers were eager to pry open the slightly cracked door. In 1975, Senate Foreign Relations Committee chairman Senator Chuck Percy (R-IL) planned for a congressional delegation to visit China, inviting Senator Jacob Javits (R-NY) as well as House members Representative Paul Findley (R-IL), Representative Pete McCloskey (R-CA), and Representative Margaret Heckler (R-MA) to join him. The delegation numbered seventeen, including spouses. Although John Heckler sometimes grew weary of the trappings of being a congressional spouse, the trip to China was a happy exception.

What Margaret and John enjoyed was the comradery with their peers in the delegation, as they had a lot in common. Everyone was bright and had a love for politics and travel. From Margaret's perspective, the objective of the trip was "to gain a better understanding of China's governing system, to estimate its future directions and to try to perceive its external purposes and motives,"[15] as well as to meet with Chairman Mao Zedong at the great palace on Tiananmen Square.[16]

Cultural sensitivities abounded and in retrospect, held eerie foreshadowing. Congressman McCloskey remembered an old man with a whispering beard who approached their group and said, "We consider you Americans barbarians. Your civilization is three hundred years old; ours is four thousand. Someday, we will bury you."[17]

Throughout this visit the delegation was treated to elaborate nine-course banquets with fish as the main course. This seemed to be an honor aimed to impress the American delegation. On their final day, they visited a fish farm outside Beijing. The farm featured square, four-acre water ponds where thousands of fish leaped and tossed in the water before being sent to the markets. Looking across one of the ponds, the group observed buckets of human waste being dumped into it. In horror, they realized they had been "consuming shit-eating fish."[18]

As stomach-turning as it was to discover the origins of her food, Margaret nonetheless left China with the belief more members of Congress—particularly congresswomen—needed to see the country for themselves. In her remarks to the World Affairs Council of Boston, she perceptively shared that "China is our biggest threat once they modernize and industrialize."[19] Margaret noted that part of its strength stemmed from women and men having the same civic responsibilities, a type of communist equality that mobilized all citizens regardless of gender. She described Chinese gender roles as:

> "[A] two-in-one principle" between men and women. The equality of the sexes, as guaranteed by Chairman Mao, is evident both as a consciousness of women's rights and as a policy of equal job assignments, equal military service, and equal domestic responsibilities. In a country where, before the revolution, girl babies were sometimes left to die, the most significant signs of the Great Leap forward were young women installing high transmission wires, barefoot women doctors visiting rural patients, young and middle-aged women performing drills with the militia, and women working in the factories and fields alongside men. Within the context of communism—with its limitations on freedom of choice—women's options in building China seem to equal men's.[20]

Margaret had been the first congresswoman to visit China. The trip inspired her to lead a delegation of congresswomen to China as a part of International Women's Year. Due to her tenacity, China formally invited all seventeen US congresswomen for an official visit. Margaret was appointed leader and began organizing the visit, which took place December 27, 1975, to January 10, 1976.[21] The congresswomen who attended included Liz Holtzman (D-NY), Patricia Schroeder (D-CO), Bella Abzug (D-NY), Patsy T. Mink (D-HI), Lindy Boggs (D-LA), Yvonne B. Burke (D-CA), Cardiss Collins (D-IL), Helen S. Meyner (D-NJ), Virginia Smith (R-NE), Gladys N. Spellman (D-MD), and Millicent Fenwick (R-NJ). Many of the congresswomen sought to bring their husbands or other relatives.[22] Margaret's request to bring her daughter Belinda, who was eighteen at the time, was granted.

Before embarking on her trip Margaret released a statement saying in part, "We are going to the People's Republic of China. . . . We have much to learn from each other."[23] "I am hopeful that the knowledge we gain will enable us to function better as legislators when we are called upon to deal with matters of concern to the United States and China."[24]

Once again, Margaret, being a leader, saw with her own eyes. Margaret's vision for the visit also led to everyday Americans getting a firsthand view of a previously closed country. Accompanying the congresswomen were producer-director Tom Fleming, and reporter Lynne Joiner, who produced a syndicated sixty-minute documentary about the historic trip titled *Flowers from Horseback with Lynne Joiner,* which NBC aired.

China tightly censured what the delegation saw and experienced. However, their tour guides did not hide all features of the communist regime, including reeducation camps. Their Chinese hosts demonstrated with pride special schools for professional workers whom the state distrusted for possible bourgeois sentiments. In the end, as *Flowers from Horseback* concluded, "If [this documentary] only scratched the surface, that must be laid at the door of the Chinese themselves, who have been reluctant to allow foreign newsmen into the country. If the time comes when there is greater freedom to examine the place, this Group W [syndicated] documentary will serve as a valuable primer."[25]

The trip was considered a major success. Thanks to *Flowers from Horseback,* the congresswomen's delegation provided a window for Americans to learn more about a country that had been closed off for decades. But for the congresswomen, perhaps the most concrete benefit was how it unified them. What else, they must have wondered on the flight home, might they be capable of—if they worked together?

· *12* ·

The Sky's the Limit

Women Airforce Service Pilots (WASPs).
Texas Woman's University Libraries' Woman's Collection

One Sunday in the fall of 1975, seventeen-year-old Marene Nyberg, a high school senior from Kingston, Massachusetts, was reading the *Boston Globe* alongside her father. The newspaper featured a one-paragraph article that announced that women would be allowed to attend military academies and receive full scholarships. Marene's father, an air force veteran who had recently lost his civilian job, handed the newspaper to his daughter saying, "You should read this."

Although Marene had already applied to Wellesley College and a few other schools, the article made her consider the possibilities of an

Air Force Academy education. Soon after, a staff member at her high school—who also happened to intern for Margaret Heckler's office—told Marene, "I think you should apply to the military academies, now that they've opened their doors to women."[1]

President Gerald Ford was also an advocate for opening the academies to women. On October 7, 1975, he signed Public Law 94-106, requiring all-male military colleges to admit qualified female candidates. In fact, Margaret Heckler peered over the president's shoulder as he placed his signature on the new law. This was a culmination of eight years of Margaret working tirelessly to grant women access to military academies.

A lot of different pieces were pushing forward the rights for women. Most of the Ivy League colleges had gone co-ed by the time the military academies were opening to women. Another significant factor was the unpopularity of the Vietnam War. Although American troops had totally withdrawn from Vietnam by 1975, there was a residual effect: Men had a real lack of interest in entering the military academies because of Vietnam.

Marene was in the right place at the right time, watching a window of opportunity open before her eyes. Ultimately, she was able to pursue a military education thanks in large part to the legislative work done by her forward-thinking congresswoman.

When asked why women would want to attend one of these academies, Margaret's response was, "It represents a $100,000 scholarship." She believed women should have equal access to these prestigious academic institutions. She hadn't forgotten her own experience with Harvard Law, nearly two decades earlier. Margaret did not want young women to have experiences like her own.

Margaret expounded in a speech, "The military offers some of the best opportunities to learn marketable skills. . . . There are more than 300 nontraditional job areas open to women in service—jobs in high technology and professional fields. There are also career opportunities in complex industrial fields like computer sciences, aviation, and laboratory technology—career skills that can lead to high-paying jobs in the private sector. When I entered politics, I was determined to see women excel in all career areas, including the military. Today's Army has opportunities as never before, and I urge both men and women of the Tenth Congressional District to consider a military career."[2]

Applicants to military academies required sponsorship from their senator or member of Congress. Each academy is designated a single principal nomination and ten alternates from a congressional member's office. In the fall of 1975, Margaret's assistant, Jack Horner, was overseeing the screening of applicants when Marene Nyberg's application came across his desk.

Helping Jack sort through the applications was the intern who also worked at Marene's high school. Recognizing her application, the intern immediately spoke up on her behalf telling Margaret that Marene was a very bright and motivated student. After reviewing her application, Margaret proclaimed, "I want this one to go to West Point." Because of her work on the Veterans' Affairs Committee, Margaret knew the military academies well. Although West Point was a completely different academy than the one Marene had applied to, Margaret felt it was the best place for the young woman. This decision dramatically altered the course of Marene Nyberg's life. As Marene recounted, "The first person who sponsored me was Margaret Heckler. . . . She chose West Point for me. In 1976, I went to West Point, sight unseen."[3]

The following year, on July 7, 1976, West Point, the academy for the US Army, admitted 119 female cadets in an incoming class of 1,452. Marene Nyberg was one of these young women.

From the top brass on down, West Point was not prepared to welcome those women. West Point Superintendent Lieutenant General Sidney B. Berry was not in favor of accepting women. The academy lacked sufficient time and motivation to modify the all-men's institution for the practical, day-to-day needs of women. Women's restrooms still had urinals, uniforms were not designed for the female form, and misogynistic attitudes were unadjusted and ignored. The new women's uniforms had plastic zippers, and the pants easily split open.[4]

Even women's grooming was an issue. Platoon sergeants were flummoxed as to whether female cadets could keep their hair long or needed the same short cut of their male counterparts. Marene Nyberg recalled, "I had a platoon sergeant who decided that my hair should be as short as the guys and . . . by August of 1976, I had hair less than one inch long all over my head. The tactical officer said to me, 'Cadet Nyberg, don't get another haircut,' and then the platoon sergeant would say, 'Cadet Nyberg, go get another haircut,' so I just kept going to get haircuts."[5]

While it was typical for plebes to be hazed into the program, the women were "hazed" far beyond the norm. In describing the consequences of breaking through the figurative glass ceiling, Marene shared, "There's some shards of glass that may have been embedded in my shoulder now and then." It was not the strenuous academic or military requirements that drove the women to their breaking points; it was the reality that most of the men didn't want the women there.[6]

One day while Cadet Nyberg was walking up the mess hall steps, a guy yanked her by her skirt and pulled her off the steps, then yelled at her, saying she should not wear a skirt in his formation. When she got to her table, an officer said, "Miss, STOP. What happened?" Although reluctant because she wanted to avoid retaliation for reporting the action, she told the officer. The skirt-yanker was punished and did not repeat his actions. The event "crystallized" for Marene that she needed to make sure such treatment "never happens to women in this situation again."[7]

These first female cadets had the near-impossible task of carving their place and names into the stone of an all-men's world. Despite the trials and rigor, Marene and sixty-one other women managed to persevere, and were the first female West Point graduates, in May 1980. In an interview for the US Army, Marene recounted how she'd asked her roommate if it was all real—were they in a dream or did they make it to graduation? Her roommate assured her that they really had persisted through all four years.[8] At Marene's graduation party, Margaret was there to congratulate Marene in person. The two women stayed connected throughout their lives.

After graduation, Marene joined the military police in Fort Hood, Texas. Later, she and her husband joined the FBI as agents. Marene Nyberg Allison has since become vice president and chief information security officer for Johnson & Johnson.

Serving as president of the West Point female graduates' network, Marene began a speech at one of their gatherings by thanking former congresswoman Margaret Heckler who had symbolically yelled out to the West Point female cadets, "It must change." And change it did. To date, there are over 5,700 female West Point alumni, in addition to the thousands of other women who have graduated from military schools since 1977.

Echoing Margaret's oft-stated sentiments, Marene said, "Women should sponsor women more than they do."[9] "Heckler didn't take no for an answer. She helped move a whole class of women by pushing for women to be at the academies. I was one. What I couldn't see in myself at the age of seventeen, she saw in me. She was a catalyst for change, moving women forward at an accelerated rate. That's the power she had."[10]

Almost fifty years after Marene Nyberg entered the military academy, she would receive, in 2023, the Distinguished Graduate Award from West Point.

In the summer of 1976 another group of women, the Women Air Force Service Pilots (WASPs) had their own battle to fight. Fifty-five-year-old Bernice "Bee" Falk Haydu, who had been a WASP during World War II, came to the Capitol to meet Representative Heckler to share her story.[11] Haydu had waited over thirty years for military recognition for herself and her peers, and she was in search of an ally. As the only woman serving on the House Veterans' Affairs Committee, Margaret was eager to learn about the WASPs' service to our country. Although the WASPs had been promised full militarization, they were not recognized as veterans entitled to benefits.

The WASPs had bravely served their country at a critical moment in history. After the Japanese bombed Pearl Harbor on December 7, 1941, a woman who had already made a name for herself as an aviator, Jacqueline Cochran, approached First Lady Eleanor Roosevelt with a proposal for a program that would become known as the Women Airforce Service Pilots, or WASPs.[12] In order to launch the program as quickly as possible, WASPs would be classified as civilian employees.

From August 5, 1943, to December 20, 1944, Cochran served as the director of the WASP program. About 25,000 women applied for training, 1,879 were accepted, and 1,074 completed the program at Avenger Field in Sweetwater, Texas. The impressive 57 percent completion rate beat the "'wash-out' rate [of] fifty percent of male pilot cadets."[13] They were chorus girls to farmers' daughters. Some WASPs were as young as eighteen; some were mothers of young children. The WASPs lived in barracks, wore uniforms, and were subject to military discipline. They had to follow strict army regulations.

Because of their service, WASPs freed up time for male pilots to receive combat-related training. This was important since so many seasoned male pilots had gone overseas during the war. WASPs ferried newly built planes, towed targets for aerial combat training, and served as check pilots. Over the program's brief existence, WASPs flew twelve thousand aircraft, a total of sixty million miles.

At its outset, General Hap Arnold, chief of Army Air Corps and overseer of the WASP program, "was skeptical of women's ability to fly before he met the WASPs. By the end of their service, they had made General Arnold a believer."[14]

To that end, in an address to the WASPS, Arnold said, "I salute you. You and more than nine hundred of your sisters have shown that you can fly wingtip to wingtip with your brothers. . . . We of the Army Air Forces are proud of you. We will never forget our debt to you."[15]

That debt would not be repaid in the same way it was to male veterans and their families. Since the war ended in 1945, there was no further need for the WASP program. Both Cochran and General Arnold fiercely advocated for full militarization for WASPs, but their request to commission WASPs as service pilots was denied on January 13, 1944. Because of their status as civilians, not military personnel, the history of the WASPs became sticky. Attempting to go around air force procedure, Cochran and Arnold went to Congress to promote bill HR 4219, which would formally include the WASP program within the US Army Air Force. They fought hard lobbying for the WASPs, but on June 21, 1944, the bill was short nineteen votes.

As World War II was winding down, war planners concluded that the WASP program was no longer necessary, and it was disbanded on December 20, 1944. The cancellation of the program was a crushing blow, because WASPs had not received official militarization as promised. It was dubious it would ever occur.

As Representative Patricia Schroeder (D-CO) recalled decades later, "They put them in uniform; they were under military command, and they were told they would be treated like other military. Well, guess what? They weren't."[16]

The thirty-eight WASPs who died in service to their country received no respect. Lack of recognition for these women was especially hurtful to their families. Their legacies were treated differently than those of male pilots who were killed in similar and sometimes the same accidents. Bodies of WASPs were sent home in cheap pine boxes. No American flags draped their coffins. No gold stars were permitted in their parents' windows. Returning WASPs and the families of deceased WASPs received no G.I. benefits.[17]

The disparity of treatment of the WASPs was unjust especially for exceptional women like Bee Haydu. She was a twenty-three-year-old engineering student who took classes at night and worked as a secretary by day. On a whim, Haydu took an aviation course. Her first flight had her hooked and soon most of her secretarial pay was going toward flight school. When she saw an ad in a Newark, New Jersey, newspaper, placed by Cochran and calling for female pilots, Haydu applied. She was accepted in the 7th class of 1944.[18] Haydu believed the promise that, if the program was successful, the WASP program would be adopted into the Army Air Corps. Unfortunately, "they did not keep their promise."[19]

Over thirty years later, the promise remained unfulfilled, until on September 20, 1977, Congresswoman Margaret Heckler, in a hearing before a Select Subcommittee of the House Veterans' Affairs Committee, testified before the 95th Congress, stating, "I was the chief sponsor of H.R. 5087, a bill which provides that the service of the Women's Air Force Service Pilots during World War II be considered active duty in the Armed Services and that appropriate veterans' benefits be granted."[20] Then Margaret began the long campaign of generating congressional support for the bill.

The Congresswomen's Caucus, which included every woman serving in Congress in 1977, banned together as cosponsors for the bill in support of the WASP's military benefits. Representative Lindy Boggs (D-LA) was one of the most ardent advocates for justice in this situation. "This was a women's rights issue, and it would require hard work that needed to be done in the House Veterans' Affairs Committee, including that of changing male attitudes. I ultimately had to face down a member of the committee, the chairman," Margaret said, "who insisted that the women had not really served in hazardous duty and did not deserve veterans' benefits."[21]

Opposition to the bill was based on fear that granting veteran status to the WASPs would be a catalyst for other people who wanted to claim veteran ranking, thus lowering the status of veterans and putting a strain on veteran benefit resources.[22] The bill died in the House Veterans' Affairs Committee.

Margaret needed to sway twenty-seven men with whom she served on the House Veteran Affairs Committee to right this injustice. Although some of the men on the committee had been in the military, they were not easily convinced that the WASPs deserved veterans' benefits. Such was the case with her good friend Representative Olin "Tiger" Teague (D-TX) who had served in World War II. Fortunately, Senator Barry Goldwater (R-AZ), also served in World War II and flew with the WASPs and was on her side.

With the help of Representatives Lindy Boggs (D-LA) and James Quillen (R-TN) in the House, Margaret tried a different route. A version of HR 5087 was rolled into Title IV of the GI Bill Improvement Act of 1977 (P.L. 95-202), with a provision to extend active-duty service and military benefits to the WASPs.[23]

With a hearing scheduled for August and September 1977, Bee Haydu organized a grassroots telephone campaign to flood Capitol Hill offices. Katherine Sharp Landdeck, author of *The Women with Silver Wings* (2020), stated: "[T]elephones began ringing across the country as Haydu's captains dialed every number on their list [to get them to lobby members of Congress]. It was a red alert."[24] According to Landdeck, Bee Haydu also mobilized former WASPs, sending "Action Now" flyers and making an ardent plea that they attend the hearings in Washington. The WASPs lined up a strong list of testimonials: Senator Barry Goldwater, Congresswomen Margaret Heckler and Lindy Boggs, and retired Colonel Bruce Arnold, a tremendous advocate for the WASPs and the son of General Hap Arnold, who oversaw the program.[25]

Despite this support, there were painful reminders during the hearing of how men viewed the women in the WASP program. Representative G. V. "Sonny" Montgomery (D-MS) recounted visiting the WASP training facility because "they were the most attractive persons in that part of the country," then went on to introduce a woman providing a testimony with, "Besides being such an attractive person, she's also a very capable person."[26] According to Landdeck, "One WASP supporter later vented about the language the congressmen used, saying it 'symbolized to me . . . how these men feel about women. *No* ideas, *no* arguments will ever penetrate their attitudinal wall.'"[27]

However, the tide began to turn when Margaret prompted Assistant Secretary of the Air Force Antonia Handler Chayes to share her expert opinion. Chayes made a strong counterargument against the criticism that it would set a bad precedent for other civilians if the WASP request was granted. Landdeck summarized Chayes's brilliant insight: "Chayes, in another strategic move, suggested that the WASP story had in fact already set another, more troubling precedent. The promise to the WASP of militarization had not been kept: What did this say to present-day and future volunteers? Chayes insinuated that to deny the WASPs their recognition would risk losing the trust of all potential volunteer military personnel, particularly the greatest untapped pool for the new, post-Vietnam all-volunteer force: women."[28]

Calling into question the honor and honesty of the military was a hard blow to the skeptics and opponents in the room. As the ranking member of the House Veterans' Affairs Committee, Margaret acknowledged that the testimony stirred the conscience of the House of Representatives. She noted, "The bill to provide veterans' rights for the WASPs was the only piece of legislation in which all the Congresswomen concurred and that says something."[29]

To drive home the point, Margaret shared a story that changed the course of the hearing: "Thirty-eight WASPs lost their lives in service. They are the cause for the justice of the issue of veterans' benefits. Isn't it true that they paid the ultimate price? I happen to know of a case where four crewmen were together, a pilot, copilot, crewman, and a WASP, and on October 2, 1944, in Victorville, California, their B-25 crashed. The three men received military honors and veterans' benefits and the WASP and her family did not receive anything. All WASPs who lost their lives in service received the same treatment from their country."[30]

In a clear, direct conclusion, she said, "The incontestable facts of the WASPs' service are that they served as officers in the Army Air Force of the United States and were treated, paid, and decorated as such. The reasons why they were denied their due status and eligibility for benefits have never been answered. I strongly urge that justice and equity be provided for this gallant and courageous group of individuals."[31]

Despite compelling testimonials and statements, the supporters left the House chambers unsure of the final verdict. It was difficult to gauge if they had persuaded enough people to their cause.[32]

Having flown with WASPs during World War II, Senator Barry Goldwater had a personal interest in the matter. With Goldwater in the

WASP president Bee Haydu (second from the right) with Congresswomen Margaret Heckler (second from the left) and Lindy Boggs (D-LA) (fourth from the left) on the Capitol steps, celebrating the women pilots receiving their long-awaited veterans' benefits. *Texas Woman's University Libraries' Woman's Collection.*

Senate and Heckler and Boggs in the House, they were able to secure one final compromise to keep the amendment in the bill: The air force would have to certify that the WASPs were military personnel in World War II. Thankfully they did, and the bill passed. On November 23, 1977, President Carter signed the GI Bill Improvement Act of 1977 into law.[33]

Margaret celebrated justice for the WASPs but had to endure an irritating insult: following the signing of the GI Bill Improvement Act, the Veterans' Affairs Committee chairman, Herbert Roberts (D-TX), said that Lindy Boggs had acted like a lady, intentionally omitting mention of Margaret Heckler. Margaret said she "was so affronted. I had always been a lady, but you're not supposed to argue and assert and win. [Apparently, to her fellow committee members,] it was more lady-like to simply advocate and not necessarily fight to the draw."[34]

WASP Patricia Collins Hughes said that without Heckler's "daring debate there would have been no victory" and credited Heckler as having "rekindled our faith in Congressional leadership."[35] Bee Haydu stated, "Margaret Heckler was the voice that made the change happen. Ms. Heckler had the courage to stand up and speak up for all of the women pilots who served with me. My husband called Margaret a 'Spitfire,' the name of the British fighter plane used to help win the battle for Britain during WWII."[36]

The House Veterans' Affairs Committee Chairman Roberts reminded Margaret that now, more than ever, women in government needed to work together to fight the long history of sexism in all areas of US society. Strength in numbers, Margaret believed, was the key to true progress on women's issues.

· 13 ·

The Queen Bees Organize in Congress

In the Ladies' Reading Room of the Capitol prior to the formation of the Congresswomen's Caucus. From left to right: Representatives Marilyn Lloyd (D-TN), Martha Keys (D-KS), Patricia Schroeder (D-CO), Margaret Heckler (R-MA), Virginia Smith (D-NE), Helen Meyner (D-NJ), and Marjorie Holt (R-MD). *Public domain.*

From her first day in Congress in 1967, Margaret had hoped that congresswomen would be united in their efforts. As a woman and a Republican coming into a Democratic-run Congress, Margaret was a minority within a minority. After nearly five full terms in Congress, Margaret knew the importance of collegiality to achieve policy objectives in Congress as she experienced in her first congressional trip to China. Moreover, later during the International Women's Year in 1975, Margaret organized a trip of congresswomen to China. This showed how congresswomen banding together could highlight women's issues. So this led to Margaret hosting a dinner at her house to lay the foundation to create a Congress-women's Caucus.

Of the eighteen women in Congress, twelve had accepted Margaret's invitation. On a springtime evening in 1976, Joe Rayball, Margaret's chief of staff, met several of the congresswomen on Capitol Hill and ferried them in his station wagon to Margaret's home in McLean, Virginia, for a get together.

Before leaving the Hill, the group had to wait in the car in the Can-non parking garage for Representative Bella Abzug (D-NY). After a long wait, Representative Martha Griffiths (D-MI) stomped up to get Representative Abzug. When they returned, Griffiths chided her for "how inconsiderate she was in making the congresswomen wait in the car while she took her sweet time. 'You are not the only one with a lot to do,' Griffiths said. Then she proceeded to push Bella's head into the already packed car."[1] The other passengers were Congresswomen Patsy Mink (D-HI), Pat Schroeder (D-CO), and Millicent Fenwick (R-NJ).

It is not surprising that this lack of conviviality contributed to a lack of cooperation among congresswomen on Capitol Hill. Even getting this gaggle of girls to the party caused some henpecking. Patricia Schroeder noted, "The moment I walked in the door for the first time, I thought, *Of course the congresswomen got together.* I was very surprised to find that wasn't true."[2]

What soon became apparent was that each congresswoman tended to operate as a "Queen Bee" in charge of her own hive. These women had been elected to Congress because they were leaders, breaking glass ceilings in their own districts. At home, these women were stars—and few could reconcile the idea of becoming part of a constellation by joining forces with other congresswomen.[3]

Margaret believed women working together in a congressional women's caucus would pave the way for the next generation and see more women elected to Congress.[4] It would also help educate the public—and congressmen, most of whom sorely needed the education—on women's inequality.[5]

While Margaret knew that both Republican and Democratic con-gresswomen could gain a lot by sharing their thoughts, many of her fellow

Republican congresswomen were either retiring or were uninterested.[6] No women's group had been formed in Congress, and she wanted to create something entirely new. Unfortunately, she found that most of her fellow Republican congresswomen were either retiring or uninterested. Several were enthusiastic, but the more conservative women were "never happy" about the idea.[7]

Undaunted, Margaret tasked herself with selling the caucus idea to the House majority Democratic congresswomen. Initially, the Democrats were hesitant to join forces with the minority in the House, the Republican women.[8] Martha Griffiths (D-MI) was the senior congresswoman and already set in her ways.[9]

The congresswomen were surprised by the forty-five-minute trek to suburban McLean, Virginia. Many of them had apartments near Capitol Hill. They were baffled by Margaret's lifestyle with three children, a husband, two homes, three dogs—and a demanding job.[10] As the group enjoyed their meal, Margaret explained her idea: "There are many things that really apply to women in different ways and affect women differently than men. If we band together, our concerns will be heard. We are the minority, but we can have greater notice if we unite."[11]

Unfortunately, what transpired next was tremendously disappointing. Margaret had high hopes. She had been so optimistic, she had even invited a press secretary to secretly wait in her study, ready for the moment when she would announce the new congresswomen's caucus. With opinions echoing from all sides of the room, Margaret discerned that "the women had different views and they didn't want to be dominated by views that [were] not their own."[12]

Dissent occurred even within parties. Marjorie Holt (R-MD) was leery about joining forces with Margaret because Holt viewed her as too progressive. A baffled Margaret later said, "She thought I was too liberal for her, but I wasn't a real liberal, I was pretty moderate all along."[13]

The women's caucus would have to wait. For over a year following the strategic dinner, Margaret appealed to congresswomen to come together—with no success. Finally, in April 1977, Representative Elizabeth Holtzman (D-NY) agreed to join Representative Margaret Heckler as cofounder of the Congresswomen's Caucus. Heckler and Holtzman shared similar congressional origin stories, both starting as lawyers and unseating longtime incumbents to earn their seats.[14] They united around a common cause and remained friends in the process.

Holtzman viewed Heckler's commitment to women's rights as sincere. "Margaret was a very feisty, energetic woman and grass did not grow

At a news conference announcing the founding of the Congresswomen's Caucus, 1977.
From left to right: Representatives Elizabeth Holtzman (D-NY), Margaret Heckler (R-
MA), Lindy Boggs (D-LA), and Barbara Mikulski (D-MD). *Family collection.*

under her feet," she said.[15] Likewise, Heckler respected Holtzman's brav-
ery as the first Democrat to make a significant alliance across party lines.
Heckler hoped that with Holtzman's support for the Congresswomen's
Caucus, other Democratic congresswomen, who outnumbered Republican congresswomen almost three to one, would be less nervous about
the optics. Together, Heckler and Holtzman identified several legislative
priorities for the new caucus members to address, then convinced fifteen
of the eighteen women in the House to join them.[16]

The Heckler-Holtzman partnership was an essential ingredient for
success, but in numerous ways, the Congresswomen's Caucus remained
Margaret's child. Patricia Schroeder described how Heckler was "the
mother of it all. She was the one who wanted to do it and wanted it to be
bipartisan. She pushed for it more than anyone else."[17] Holtzman credited
Heckler with the structure of the caucus, including having two chairs, one
Republican and one Democrat, and attributed the strength of that structure to the caucus's survival over the decades.[18]

Individually, each of the congresswomen were ambitious, smart, and
independent, clearing their own paths through male-dominated rooms.

Of the caucus, Holtzman said, "The women were formally brought together and had much richer relationships because it was focused on issues and we got to know each other better. So, I think it helped us cement that relationship."[19]

Margaret Heckler arranged another carefully orchestrated dinner to celebrate the caucus's launch. She later said about that evening, "We had to learn to be friends, get out of the atmosphere, and so we had a big dinner and that started us on a very good note. Food always works. It's one of the big devices that makes people change their opinions quickly. We had a very lovely time, and we respected each other. We never talked about the other women; we just tried to find commonalities that we could work on."[20]

This new generation of women in Congress was ready to create unlikely alliances and push for bold legislation. The first official meeting of the caucus occurred on April 19, 1977, at the Capitol in the Ladies' Reading Room. Attendees included Representatives Lindy Boggs (D-LA), Yvonne Burke (D-CA), Shirley Chisholm (D-NY), Cardiss Collins (D-IL), Millicent Fenwick (R-NJ), Elizabeth Holtzman (D-NY), Barbara Jordan (D-TX), Barbara Mikulski (D-MD), Patricia Schroeder (D-CO), and Margaret Heckler (R-MA).

Representatives Burke, Chisholm, Collins, and Jordan were the sole Black women in the 95th Congress. According to Shirley Chisholm, at that moment in history, it was almost worse to be a woman than to be Black in Congress.[21] The Congressional Black Caucus was all-male and resisted supporting their Black female colleagues. These four congresswomen found unity and support among each other in the newly formed Congresswomen's Caucus.

As the Republican chair of the Congresswomen's Caucus, Heckler fostered cohesion by making sure all caucus members were in agreement about the issues that would officially make it into their platform.[22] According to Holtzman, this rule was implemented because "women were concerned how they would be perceived in their district and if the press would make fun of us, so we decided that we wouldn't do anything unless there was unanimity. If someone felt uncomfortable with a certain issue, we would go to the next one. . . . It gave us heft on substantive issues, but it also brought us together and we became much friendlier with each other. Everyone really respected Margaret. It was a good model on how to get things done working together, coming from both sides of the aisle."[23]

While consensus was an essential aspect of the caucus, it also meant that a particularly contentious topic never came to the table: abortion.

The Congresswomen's Caucus meeting a delegation of women from China. Front row from left to right: Margaret Heckler (R-MA), Shirley Chisholm (D-NY), Barbara Mikulski (D-MD), and Patricia Schroeder (D-CO). *Family collection.*

By the late 1970s, many of the women Margaret worked with in Congress were pro-choice. Margaret's Catholic faith guided her stance, but she remained on the fringes of the debate, saying, "Some people took it very strongly, I didn't."[24] By tabling the seemingly unsolvable debate and through her bipartisan outreach, Margaret was able to hold on to her convictions about the right to life, while also working alongside those with whom she had fundamental disagreements.

From Liz Holtzman's perspective, "Everyone respected Margaret. I'm very pro-choice and she was not. There was so much more that we agreed on. We knew that we were our strongest when we were together."[25]

Fortunately for the earliest women joining the caucus, abortion did not become more of a partisan issue until the late 1970s.[26]

Heckler and Holtzman recognized that the Congresswomen's Caucus could become a model for highly effective legislating. There were many issues beyond abortion that the women could tackle, including the Equal Rights Amendment (ERA), domestic violence, credit opportunity, employment opportunities, pension rights, and rape and sexual violence.[27]

As Holtzman said of the caucus, "One of their earliest examples of success was when they extended the deadline to ratify the Equal Rights Amendment, a movement that they not only fought for, but they stood side by side for as they marched on Washington. Their win in both the House and the Senate proved that with bipartisan support even the most controversial pieces of legislation could be carried through the process from start to finish; congressmen took notice and began to observe the new women's group a bit more closely."[28]

The congresswomen still endured blatant discrimination in their day-to-day activities on the Hill. One such issue was insufficient restrooms. When Senator Margaret Chase—the only woman in the Senate at that time—retired in 1973, the men converted the women's restroom in the Senate into a TV room. According to Pat Schroeder, it was "like there wouldn't be any more women coming. 'So, well, we had that one and she's gone, so yay! Let's take over the space.'"[29] Schroeder also shared how, walking onto the Speaker's Balcony one day to enjoy the sunshine, she stumbled across a group of congressmen with their trousers down, sunning themselves on what they had deemed an exclusively male balcony.[30] The old boys' network still remained.

While these outrageous incidents were manifold, the Congresswomen's Caucus made the difficult decision to start their work elsewhere. According to Holtzman, "Even though still being barred from spaces like the gym was ridiculous, we would not take that on as a first issue. Later, the gym was desegregated."[31] Their hearts were set on higher aims. They could endure subtle and not-so-subtle harassment and discrimination if it meant they could make lasting changes for all American women.

Speaker Tip O'Neill pledged his "Boy Scout honor" to support the group, saying, "Anything I can do for you, I'm with you all the way."[32] But O'Neill's and other congressmen's responses were primarily curiosity about the caucus and what the women were doing.[33]

"We were *strangers in paradise*," Margaret said. "We were not among the very exclusive male club. So, we had to break the doors down and it took a little defensive strategy. At first, the men overacted to our presence and when they found out we all agreed on something they'd be very shocked and commented on it quite a lot.[34]

However, the women were bolstered by the executive branch. As President Jimmy Carter stated, "Women were unsung and sometimes their contributions went unnoticed, but the achievements, leadership, courage, strength, and love of the women who built America was as vital as that of the men whose names we know so well."[35]

A sign of the caucus's momentum was their one-year fundraiser for the research division, which uniquely brought in supporters from a broad swath of organizations. The first to provide an unsolicited $1,000 check was Margaret's old ally in the fight for the Equal Credit Opportunity Act, the president of Sears Roebuck and Co., Dean Swift. Over fifty businesses and labor groups then pledged sponsorship for the fundraiser. US Second Lady Joan Mondale said of the representation, "Any organization that includes among its sponsors as diverse a group as Atlantic Richfield, General Foods, Campbell Soups, the steel workers, auto workers, and ILGWU [garment workers] has to have its finger on the pulse of this country. You must be doing something right."[36] Margaret said that the success of the caucus had "exceeded our wildest expectations. . . . Cross-fertilization of ideas among the women has been as valuable as has been the 'substantive' work on concerns of common interest."[37]

On February 6, 1978, the Congresswomen's Caucus extended a formal invitation to the newly elected Senator Muriel Humphrey (D-MN), to join. Previously, the group had existed only in the House, as there were no female senators in 1977 when the caucus was formed. Senator Humphrey gladly accepted their invitation.

In the early 1980s, the Congresswomen's Caucus brought to light the fact that pharmaceutical companies only tested new drugs on men, even though there were differences between male and female biology.[38] Even drugs used to treat breast cancer were tested by the FDA only on men.[39] When caucus member Representative Barbara Mikulski (D-MD) confronted the FDA, the protocols were changed. This one policy demonstrated the magic that occurs when education, teamwork, and effort are applied.

When Margaret received an award on behalf of the caucus, she stated it was one of her proudest achievements during her career in Congress.[40] As former representative and senator Olympia Snowe (R-ME), remembered,

> The caucus that Margaret's vision created laid the groundwork for all the other initiatives that were achieved by organizing this group of women where we could work internally to make a difference. The Congresswomen's Caucus created the Office of Women's Health, which led to the Women's Health Initiative. This created the largest women's study trial, from hormone therapy to cervical cancer, including 150,000 women, a major initiative that is still producing results.[41]

Family Medical Leave, pension reform, and child support enforcement were also major programs produced by the Congresswomen's Caucus.

Olympia Snowe extolled the Congresswomen's Caucus as "a hallmark in congressional leadership that sets an example of bipartisanship, that we could work together in spite of our differences, irrespective of the fact that we were pro-life and pro-choice. It was the ideal of putting principle over politics. It really became our foundation. It was an extraordinary achievement."[42]

Under the new leadership of the Congresswomen's Caucus, the women united as a group for the first time. Margaret succeeded in having the queen bees dance together. They spent the next two years busy with ambitious legislative packages and international trips.

The Congresswomen's Caucus turned its attention to Indochina after seeing reports of genocide and mass starvation in Cambodia. Following a seven-year civil war, the communist Khmer Rouge party overthrew the Cambodian regime in 1975. The Khmer Rouge dictator Pol Pot sought to turn Cambodia into an agrarian, classless society. "Intellectuals," such as lawyers, doctors, teachers, and clergy were indiscriminately executed. Agriculture collectivism evicted city dwellers from their homes, sending them to the countryside.

The US played a peripheral part in the chaos in Cambodia. The US had backed the Cambodian monarchy as a part of the Cold War and the Vietnam War, and backed a coup, which established the Cambodian Republic in 1970. In addition, the American military conducted controversial bombing campaigns in rural Cambodia from 1965 to 1973. But after the American withdrawal from Saigon in 1975, the Vietnamese extended their influence into Cambodia. By the time the Vietnamese military overthrew the Khmer Rouge in 1979, it was estimated that a quarter of Cambodia's population perished (1.5 to 3 million people). Of these casualties, 60 percent died in mass execution sites (aka "Killing Fields") and the rest succumbed to starvation and disease.

When Congresswoman Liz Holtzman, chair of the Immigration Committee, saw televised images of Cambodian children in refugee camps, she was moved to ask Margaret to ask whether they should co-lead a humanitarian mission to Cambodia.[43] Margaret's experience with international delegations to China, and her membership on the Agricultural Committee, drove the invitation. Margaret agreed to the trip. The Congresswomen's Caucus strongly supported the mission. The November 1979 trip consisted of Representatives Lindy Boggs, Barbara Mikulski, Patricia Schroeder, and Olympia Snowe. They also invited female political leaders from other countries to join them. Two Australian female politicians agreed to accompany the American congresswomen.[44] Several other key supporters also joined the group. Their mission was to convince the Vietnamese-backed government to allow more aid to enter Cambodia.

Speaker Tip O'Neill lent his plane to the all-women delegation, and they planned to meet the Australian women in Bankok.[45] For the final length of the trip to the Cambodian capital, Phnom Penh, a US Air Force jet was used—the first American plane to land in Phnom Penh since the Vietnam War ended. From the airplane windows, the women somberly took in the airfield, still riddled with scars from earlier bombings. As they deplaned, air force pilots actively guarded the plane.[46] On the ride in the capital city, the women saw surprising debris: piles of eyeglasses and radios that had been confiscated because the Khmer Rouge believed glasses symbolized intellectualism, and radios provided dangerous access

Visiting Phnom Penh, Cambodia, 1979. *Private collection.*

to the outside world. After the Vietnamese overthrow, these items were discarded.

The capital city was still thick with the sights and smells of war.[47] Streets were in shambles and many buildings featured broken windows.[48] Most Phnom Penh residents, who had been forced to relocate to the countryside during the Khmer Rouge regime, had not yet returned. The women saw scattered groups of people huddled near small cooking fires. As the *New York Times* reported, the sights were "astonishing," and the congresswomen witnessed "people frail with deprivation, pick through the rubble of neglect more than of destruction, in a city teetering between desolation and the hope of once more populating its buildings and streets, its empty parks, its idle markets and its hospitals. They remained in doubt whether the hope of life will be realized, because wherever they looked, they saw hunger."[49]

The first stop was the French embassy, where all the windows were smashed. The congresswomen were seated for a banquet lunch. A Cambodian woman who had helped the revolution depose Pol Pot served each congresswoman a glass of Coca-Cola syrup without the carbonation, thinking it was an American delicacy. Barbara Mikulski said to Olympia Snowe, nodding toward the flies floating in her glass, "It looks like there are Olympic swimmers in your Coca-Cola!"[50] The drinks were offered as a toast, so in diplomatic fashion, the congresswomen partook. As Patricia Schroeder bluntly stated, they "couldn't be sissies."[51] Plates of food continued to appear, each also covered in flies—and embarrassment overtook the congresswomen. They were on a mission to address hunger and mass starvation, and yet the Cambodians kept bringing out plates of food.[52]

While trying to eat, the women's minds were also on their upcoming meeting with the new foreign minister of the Vietnamese-backed People's Republic of Kampuchea/State of Cambodia. They were unsure what would happen or whether their requests would be granted. Prior to their meeting with the foreign minister, the women toured an orphanage, a school, and a hospital. Pol Pot's forced emptying of the city had left an eerie impression on the congresswomen, but seeing the remarkably full room of school children renewed their hope for the revitalization of Cambodia.[53]

The meeting with Foreign Minister Hun Sen took place at the former palace of the last monarch, Prince Norodom Sihanouk. Sen was one of the world's youngest foreign ministers at age twenty-six. After the women sat down, Sen bluntly asked them, "What do you want?"

The congresswomen were ready with their request. The cochairs pressed the foreign minister, saying, "We want you to allow relief agencies to bring food over the border into the country and to deliver the food to the people."

To the congresswomen's great surprise, Hun Sen quickly agreed to their request. Margaret peppered the foreign minister with further questions when she felt a kick under the table coming from Liz Holtzman. Margaret's cochair probably thought she should quit while she was ahead since they already had what they wanted.

The foreign minister kept his word. The food, stockpiled just over the border in Thailand, could now be delivered in Cambodia. Almost immediately, relief agencies began flooding into Cambodia to help displaced citizens. Because of the caucus's trip, the Cambodian people received aid they desperately needed.[54]

The *New York Times* reported, "Hun Sen had agreed to allow relief flights at a rate greater than the present one a day, beginning as early as tomorrow. Most relief efforts are being channeled through the United Nations."[55]

Buoyed by their success, the group then traveled to the Thai border to understand how the United States could best support humanitarian efforts in the refugee camps. According to Liz Holtzman, what they saw were "thousands and tens of thousands of refugees on the border who were not being fed . . . children with matchstick bodies."[56]

When the group returned to the United States, they continued to advocate for more Cambodian aid in Congress, which resulted in a first relief installment of $105 million. Margaret also continued using her platform to bring awareness about the mass devastation to her constituents. In her spring 1980 "Reports from Washington," she described in detail the horrors left behind

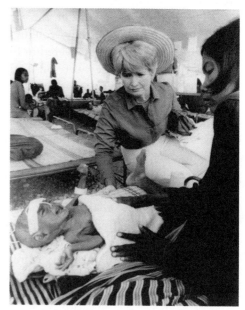

In a Cambodian refugee camp, 1979.
Private collection.

by the Khmer Rouge regime: "We felt that the women of the US Congress could dramatize, as no other delegation could—as women, mothers, and grandmothers—the urgent need for remedial action."[57]

Soon after the congresswomen returned to the States, Heckler and Holtzman were invited to appear on the *Phil Donahue Show*, a popular daytime television program, where they gave a firsthand account of what was happening in Cambodia and what had been accomplished because the women banded together in a united mission.

According to scholar Irwin Gertzog, the Congresswomen's Caucus was the "most effective bipartisan organization in the US House of Representatives."[58] In 1981, it underwent a few changes, including renaming it as the Congressional Caucus for Women's Issues, and then again in 2024 to the Bipartisan Women's Caucus. Additionally, at this time the caucus was also opened to congressmen who were interested in enacting progress for women. But remarkably, it has maintained the same bipartisan structure since it became a mainstay caucus in the House of Representatives.[59]

Almost fifty years after the Congresswomen's Caucus was started, women make up nearly a quarter of the 118th Congress—the highest percentage in US history. Currently, there are 128 women in the US House of Representatives—29 percent of the total, a substantial jump from the 2 percent who were there when Margaret joined Congress in 1967. To date, 376 women have been US representatives.

In her Oral History, Margaret recounted, "It was always my intent and desire to change the playing field for women . . . and the forming of a Congressional Women's Caucus was with the intent to open the doors for more women to enter Congress."[60]

Now that the women had organized, the time had come for them to fight for an amendment that would give them full equal rights under the law.

A Celebrity through the Decades

The Heckler family in Wellesley, Massachusetts, as seen in *People* magazine.
Richard Howard.

*I*n November 1977, Margaret attended the first-ever National Women's Conference in Houston, Texas. She spoke before an audience of twenty thousand attendees, which consisted of mothers, daughters, and grandmothers—women from every walk and stage of life. To thunderous applause Margaret implored, "A country that can put men on the moon

148

can put women in the Constitution! If we really believe in the inscription engraved on the Supreme Court building, equal justice under the law, the ERA is the only way to achieve it. Put your power behind the ERA—now!"

On July 9, 1978, tens of thousands of supporters chanted in unison, "E-R-A now!" and "One-two-three-four, we-need-three-more. Five-six-seven-eight, Congress-must-extend-the-date."[1] Behind the banner for the national Equal Rights Amendment march leaders all held hands and were strikingly dressed in white. This group included Congresswomen Liz Holtzman, Barbara Mikulski, Bella Abzug, and Margaret Heckler. They were joined by feminists Gloria Steinem and Betty Friedan, and actor and activist Dick Gregory.

It took three hours for all the protestors to march down Constitution Avenue to the Capitol steps. When they passed the National Archives, bells were rung to remember the eight thousand suffragists who were spit on, heckled, and battered when they had boldly paraded for women's rights in 1913.[2]

Reporters wrote that the "procession had the look of a huge army advancing into battle."[3] Ultimately, these ERA supporters were successful. A

ERA March on Washington. From left to right: Representative Bella Abzug, feminist Gloria Steinem, activist Dick Gregory, author Betty Friedan, Representatives Elizabeth Holtzman, Barbara Mikulski, Margaret Heckler and another honored guest 1978.
AP photo/Dennis Cook.

month later, Congress approved a new deadline of 1982 for ratification of the ERA, extending it an additional three years: the first time a proposed amendment to the Constitution had a deadline for ratification extended. The women's march in 1978 marked an important changing of the tide, where women of all backgrounds came together to voice their demands for the equal rights of women to be enshrined into the Constitution.

Margaret's brand of feminism was in the minority. She primarily fought for equal justice and economic improvements for women. The one piece of advice Margaret took from her mother, Bridget O'Shaughnessy, was to have her own independent career.

After nearly a decade in Congress, Margaret had achieved celebrity status. Her persona and image made her both a curiosity and a sensation. During her time in Washington she was recognized for her seniority, being a go-getter and a consensus builder, resulting in her being well-liked by her colleagues. Like a movie star, with her Debbie Reynolds–like appearance and spirited personality, she was often recognized in public. At home in the Tenth District, Margaret ran for reelection every two years, campaigning continuously. She met her constituents where they were—and in turn, they loved her and invited her into their homes. Her driver, Danny Converse, shared how in some homes in the predominately Catholic towns of Fall River and Taunton, it was not uncommon for families to display a row of framed pictures running down their hallways of JFK, the pope, and their congresswoman, Margaret Heckler.[4]

Margaret's politics were what was most paradoxical. By the mid-1970s, she'd established herself as a politician with an unconventional, groundbreaking voting record. She did not toe the party line. The *Congressional Quarterly* report for the 93rd Congress reflected that Margaret participated in 90 percent of congressional votes—but only 25 percent of those votes were consistent with the Republican Party's platform. In more than one instance, numerous conservative Republican men peered over her shoulder, waiting to see how she was going to vote; she attributed this to her staunch belief in not voting on a partisan basis.[5]

Hers was not an easy job. What drove her was not partisanship or even power, but rather, as Margaret put it, "a very strong desire to serve the people I represented . . . when people have problems, they love to have someone who will listen and work on the issues. I was ready, willing, and eager to be right there and do everything I could. And I would pursue it very assiduously."[6] It was a difficult balancing act being a Republican representing a Democratic state.

Often, while they were on the road, she would quiz her driver on what her office had done for her constituents. Margaret never forgot Tip O'Neill's slogan: "All politics are local." Her driver Danny Converse recalled, "You had to be on your toes because she believed constituent service, not politics, got her re-elected."[7]

Margaret learned to make it seem like she was everywhere, whether she was addressing a group of sanitation engineers in Fall River or sitting in a meeting with the president in Washington, DC. It was said that "she had one foot on Main Street and one foot in Washington."[8] If the pace she set left her fatigued, she didn't show it. It was said of her that she was more than two people.

An election strategy that Margaret developed was to have her staff secure more nomination signatures than the 74,574 required to enter the election, reaching 500,000 names in some years. For the people who signed the list, it made them feel like they had already made an unofficial endorsement, leading to votes at the polls.[9] She was rewarded with

Speaker Tip O'Neill administers the oath of office for Margaret Heckler's eighth term in Congress, 1980. *Family collection.*

the adoration and commitment of voters in the Tenth District, getting reelected as a Republican in a Democratic state, time after time and twice unopposed.

Margaret was adored and recognized by constituents in her district, sometimes catching her off guard. A former staffer, Ted Fitzgerald, shared, "One gentleman, who stood about six foot four and, noticing Margaret on the street, made his way over to her and proceeded to lift her off her feet, embracing her in a bear hug. When she was safely back on the ground, I quietly whispered in her ear, 'This is Baron Gonkighter. You got his mother her Social Security benefits.'" Another time, in a Taunton restaurant, Margaret had just sat down in the booth when the owner, having heard that "Peggy Heckler" was there, excitedly came over, took off his apron, opened his arms to Margaret and said to her, 'Get out of that booth.' There was a charisma there."[10] It was this empathy with ordinary people, Fitzgerald continued, that "got her elected again and again. Her strength came from the heart—not from organizational skills, nor from political skills, per se." More simply put, it was her "superpower."[11]

Jack McCarthy, another former Heckler staffer, remembered purchasing an amplifier from Radio Shack that worked with the old telephones and made the audio louder. "We had a plan that if she was run-

The Heckler family as seen in *People* magazine, opening Mom's mail in their living room. *Richard Howard.*

ning late, she would pull over, make the call and start talking into this device. We would have all these people waiting to see her and they would get antsy. The effect was magical. . . . I would say to her, 'I'm at Hank and Ruth's house. They can't wait to see you!' She would speak into the phone and her voice would project into the room saying, 'I'm so sorry that I'm not there yet. I had a vote in Congress and I'm trying to do the People's Business. I understand that Bettie Pizarro is there!' It was powerful," Jack said. "This was in the time of radio. People would be staring at the device like she was in there, taking the sting out of her late arrival."[12]

Back in Washington, Margaret expanded her profile in an entirely different way. On the days when the president was to give the State of the Union address, Margaret would arrive early to the Capitol and leave her pocketbook on an aisle seat with a clear vantage point, strategically positioned so that she could *see and be seen*. In those days, no man would *dare* touch a woman's pocketbook. She was able to meet and greet with the other congressman and not have to worry that her seat would be taken.[13]

As a moderate Republican, Margaret felt at home on both sides of the aisle. That being so, her invitation list included both Democrats and Republicans, making her home residence the ideal location for congressional wheeling and dealing.

In the early 1970s, on a hot summer evening, the Hecklers had a pool party at their four-acre, country-style residence in McLean, Virginia. Margaret fluttered about in a pink and orange floral maxi dress, directing caterers and bartenders and asked the children to help with final preparations for members of Congress and friends who would be attending. While John Jr. was outside setting up the tiki lights, Belinda and Alison greeted the VIPs at the front door. The bipartisan group of guests arrived along with players from the Washington Redskins. The partygoers gathered inside and on the sprawling brick patio. The entire Massachusetts delegation showed up, along with others from Congress, including Margaret's longtime friend, George H. W. Bush. Drinks flowed and there was plenty of beef stroganoff and grasshopper pie to go around.

As the full moon lit up the summer sky, the sounds of laughter and splashing water called the guests down to the glowing pool, where the Heckler children took turns riding on the shoulders of Tip O'Neill and Redskins guard Vince Promuto. Some congressmen jumped in the water, others drank cocktails, smoked cigars, and made deals under the canopy of trees. When Tip O'Neill cannonballed off the diving board, he sprayed anyone within a ten-foot radius. The bipartisanship enjoyed during this evening was much more socially acceptable in Washington, DC, in the 1970s, in a gentler time.

From the outside, it looked like a life filled with fame, admiration, and parties, but there was growing strain in Margaret's personal life. John was spending more and more time in Boston with his company, Boston Institutional. Because of this, in 1975 Margaret left the House Banking Committee. To explain the seemingly odd switch to the Agriculture Committee when representing a state that had hardly any farms, Margaret said, "We make the mistake of thinking agriculture is of concern to the producers only. . . . My constituents are consumers. . . . Consumers need to have some insight into the formulation of food policy in the country and until this year they were unrepresented."[14]

Critics decried Margaret for having a restless tenure in Congress, but the reality was that she was being politically shrewd by leaving the House Banking Committee to avoid accusations of conflict of interest and the appearance of impropriety due to her husband's business activities. This was a new phenomenon in American politics. Whereas previously congresswomen replaced their deceased husbands, Margaret had a concern about her husband's job. A similar thing happened in 1984 when Geraldine Ferraro's (D-NY) husband's finances created controversy in her vice presidential campaign.

At home, there were no simple remedies for the growing conflict and stress. The marriage that Margaret had entered into with hopes and dreams of a shared partnership had grown stale. She was grateful that her kids, while lacking attention from their father, were surrounded by a close community and loving caretakers. She had a live-in housekeeper, Fannie Mae Bates, whom the family adored; when she laughed out loud, you could see the wide gap between her teeth. Fannie was the glue that kept the family together. When John Sr. joined the household on weekends, Fannie became the family protector. At six feet tall, with a 220-pound frame, Fannie was the only person who wouldn't tolerate his "antics and could stand up to him." If John Sr., who was hard on little John, began to yell, Fannie would stand in between them saying fiercely, "Now, don't you touch that boy! Where's my nerve medicine?!"[15]

By 1978, all the Heckler children were in college. John Jr. was a freshman at Wake Forest University, Alison was a sophomore at Duke University, and Belinda was a senior at Dartmouth College. The absence of the children exacerbated the loneliness and strain in Margaret and John's marriage. Adding to her woes, the political sands were about to shift, and the timing could not have been more difficult to attempt to salvage a marriage.

· 15 ·

Mission Accomplished

At a White House picnic with President Jimmy Carter (far right)
and his wife Rosalynn (far left). *Public domain.*

*I*n the spring of 1980, the unpopular Jimmy Carter was running against a strong Republican field of moderates and conservatives. Heckler's legislative assistant, Jack Horner, drove Margaret out to a large estate near Marshall, Virginia, where former governor Ronald Reagan was jockeying for support in the Republican presidential primaries against George H. W. Bush. Reagan had used the estate as an East Coast headquarters for his 1980 Republican presidential primary campaign. Although Margaret hoped for Bush's nomination, she was being courted by Ronald Reagan at Wexford, the estate in the heart of horse country that was briefly owned by former president John F. Kennedy and his wife Jackie.

Having served together as freshmen in the House, Margaret and George Bush, both moderates, were longtime friends with similar views on many issues. Margaret was one of the first members of Congress from a state other than Texas to support George H. W. Bush in the presidential primaries. Now in the arena, Bush was vying against Reagan, the conservative Hollywood-star-turned-politician. As the senior Republican congresswoman, Margaret would be a strategic ally for either candidate.

During the hour-long drive, Margaret was already agitated and stressed, enduring a flare-up of her chronic knee problems from her car accident in 1967. Her plan was to grill Reagan about his economic strategy, especially with the country experiencing a 7.5 percent unemployment rate and 14.5 percent interest rate during this recession. As they entered through the gates, Margaret said to her legislative assistant, "Just give me a minute more," as she finished formulating her questions. Then she told him, "They think I'm going to ask about women's issues. They'll be surprised by my actual questions."[1] Her plan to drill them on Reagan's economic strategy would demonstrate her hard-earned mettle from her time on the Joint Economic Committee.

By the time she left, Margaret's stoic front had crumpled. Jack recalled, "After meeting Ronald Reagan, Margaret was in love with the man. He had a charisma that made people instantly like him. When she came out, she said, 'He's so Californian, very relaxed, easy mannered.' Reagan's strong presence and quick wit were captivating from the start. Their shared Irish roots did her in."[2]

Nonetheless, charm was not enough to override Margaret's political calculations. In addition to their aligned views, political considerations also caused Margaret to support Bush. As Massachusetts drifted farther to the Left, Margaret knew Bush would be popular, and her constituents would clash with Reagan and his policies. Her seniority and party affiliation were not assets for Margaret—it was an exploitable vulnerability. As this reality took shape, Margaret eagerly backed Bush, who voted similarly to the people in the Tenth District. It also helped that Bush supported the ERA.

The Tenth District, accustomed to supporting Margaret as a moderate Republican, was easily sold on Bush. He won the Massachusetts primary with 41 percent of the vote, compared to Reagan's 19 percent. But Margaret was worried. If Reagan won the nomination, her days in office could become a ticking time bomb.

As one of the few Republican congresswomen, Margaret was privy to backstage moments that defined the outcome of the 1980 presidential race. One of those moments occurred on the final weekend before the New Hampshire presidential primary in February. Prior to a scheduled debate at Nashua High School, Reagan proposed that he and Bush should split the cost. Bush declined, and Reagan footed the $3,500 bill.

Reagan's campaign manager believed Reagan would do better if he debated all the candidates. Bush was opposed to the idea. On debate night, Senators Bob Dole (R-KS) and Howard Baker (R-TN) and Congressmen Phil Crane (R-IL) and John Anderson (R-IL) all showed up alongside Bush and Reagan. Consequently, Bush's campaign staff refused to allow any of them on the stage. No one seemed to know what was going on.

Margaret felt it was unwise to exclude the other candidates. Advising Bush in a back room, she stressed, "You can't do that. You need to let everybody come up." Meanwhile, Bush's people were saying, "Don't let them on 'cause they're going to interfere here."[3] Margaret's instinct about excluding the others was that it would reflect badly on Bush. Just before the event was about to start, all the opponents except Bush, who was already onstage, stormed the stage.

Chaos erupted. Reagan asked if he could make an announcement before the questions started, but the debate moderator told the soundman to turn off Reagan's microphone. An angered Reagan shot back, "I am paying for this microphone!" The audience roared their approval, showing Reagan to be a charismatic leader. Three days later, Reagan took the New Hampshire primary by a landslide.[4]

Later, reflecting on this incident, Reagan said, "I may have won the debate, the primary—and the nomination—right there [at the Nashua debate]"[5]

By June 1980, Reagan won the Republican nomination. The convention was to be held in Detroit, Michigan. Margaret was tapped for the Republican National Convention Platform Committee because she was a ranking Republican congresswoman. Before heading out to Detroit, Margaret realized she needed a press secretary. Linda Bilmes, a recent Harvard graduate, traveled from Boston to Washington to interview for the job.

When Linda was escorted into Margaret's private office, the scene before her was comical. In a brightly colored suit, Margaret sat with her feet in a bucket of ice and a beagle sitting squarely on her lap. Linda noticed on the floor next to the ice bucket was a pair of well-worn high heels.

The brief interview was a prelude to Linda experiencing Margaret as she was—someone who was "entirely herself, spunky and funny, a real character."[6]

Margaret was one of five women and ninety-five men on the Platform Committee led by David Stockman (R-MI). Her role was to help outline and vote on the party's stated values, goals, and domestic and foreign policy positions. The group stayed at the Detroit Plaza Hotel in the Renaissance Center, along with thousands of reporters who were desperate for news.

Linda described the two weeks in July as "baptism by fire." Margaret wanted Linda with her for meetings, meals, receptions, laps around the hotel, and hairdresser appointments. She spent the remainder of her time on pay phones, reshuffling Margaret's constantly fluctuating schedule.

Linda recalled, "Margaret was dazzling in those days . . . she had a great laugh and a wicked sense of humor." Reporters buzzed around her, intercepting any and all floor discussions, trying to stay abreast of the issues. They were also quick to notice if Margaret had a hair out of place or a run in her stockings.

Margaret phoned Linda around the clock, including in the middle of the night. Eventually, Linda gave Margaret a notepad, asking her to write down whatever she thought of between midnight and 7:00 a.m. It worked for a couple of nights, until Margaret appeared at Linda's door in her bathrobe at 2:00 a.m., saying she'd lost the notepad. They ended up talking all night.

By the time the convention started, there was little doubt that Reagan was about to be crowned the nominee. When Margaret was asked by the Republican Party organizers to join the rest of the Massachusetts delegation in the suburbs, miles away from downtown Detroit, Margaret refused to leave the Plaza Hotel. Her Republican colleagues had supported George Bush and so their accommodations were second rate. She realized if she left the Plaza, she would not have the influence she would need to have access to the presidential nominee Ronald Reagan.

The Secret Service, who had arrived with Reagan, ran around trying to secure the building and block hotel escalator routes. Linda recounted, "It was insane, and Margaret matched the intensity of the mayhem." By that point, Margaret knew every security guard and hotel clerk. "She was the kind of person who naturally spoke to every waiter, every porter, and every hotel bell desk person," said Linda, "leading with her Irish gift of making people feel special. Her popularity was only intensified by her signature strawberry blond hairstyle and bright eighties purple power suits with bulky shoulder pads."[7]

Margaret's primary concern for her work in Detroit was to advance women's rights, particularly to ensure ERA ratification. By 1980, Margaret was one of the few Republican women who supported the ERA. As a lawyer, she differentiated between cultural sexism and legal sexism, focusing on what could be accomplished through the law to improve women's legal protections. The women's rights movement desperately wanted to recruit Reagan to extend the ratification deadline.

At the Republican National Convention (RNC), a small group of Republican political leaders joined forces with Eleanor Smeal, president of the National Organization for Women (NOW), and the cochairs of ERA America: Helen Milliken, First Lady of Michigan, and Sharon Percy Rockefeller. Bush campaign chairman Andy Card recalled that six Republican delegates were advocates for both Bush and the ERA, which Bush openly supported.

Women's advocates at the RNC knew the odds were stacked against them, so they went with a press strategy designed "to keep the ERA in the newspapers, television, radio, whatever . . . we managed for all that time to just keep hammering away at the importance of the ERA."[8]

On July 14, 1980, as part of their media strategy, 4,500 ERA supporters rallied outside the Renaissance Center on the first day of the convention.[9] Margaret stood in front with other feminist supporters Andy Card, Jill Ruckelshaus, and John Leopold, all wearing sashes in solidarity, but not without receiving "a lot of flak for doing it."[10]

After hearing speeches, they enthusiastically marched through downtown Detroit. Former representative Pete McCloskey (R-CA) remembered that "thousands of people [were] marching for women's rights. When we marched by the hotel where the Reagan delegation was, we were booed."[11]

Phyllis Schlafly, a conservative Republican activist, had strongly opposed the ERA for years. At the RNC it seemed that she had Reagan's attention. According to Reagan's campaign manager, Stuart Spencer, "Reagan had a whole clique of guys who were afraid of Phyllis Schlafly. . . . She was tough, vicious, an extremely right-wing person."[12] She had Reagan's ear and a strong coalition of anti-ERA recruits who had found a home in the budding "Moral Majority." Schlafly's influence on the party and the coalition she built was clearly the chosen agenda for the Reagan brand of conservatism.[13]

Aside from winning Reagan's support of the ERA, her broader aim was to use any route that might lead to equal legal protection for women under the leadership of the prospective new president in the next administration. Margaret was described as a strategic pragmatist: "Getting the Equal Rights Amendment enacted was one of the things that Margaret most devoted her life to. And the fact that she came up with a kind of 'Plan B' was very typical of Margaret. She wasn't the sort of person who would hide under a desk in disappointment. She'd be like, 'Okay. If that didn't work, we'll go on to the second-best thing, and here's what it is.'"[14]

Heckler demanded a meeting with Reagan, which was scheduled just before his acceptance speech. Margaret planned to ask him about the ERA, then, knowing his support was unlikely, she'd follow up with a counteroffer: his commitment to appoint a woman to the Supreme Court. As Linda explained, it was a "very, very deliberate discussion . . . she had spent a lot of time researching the fact that there were many women who were judges, and it would not be difficult for him to find someone qualified." Margaret believed that having a woman on the Supreme Court would be highly symbolic of a commitment to women's equality under the law. It would also add a woman's viewpoint into high court jurisprudence. Her purpose for meeting with Reagan was to test this idea.[15]

As a senior congresswoman, Margaret had some sway in getting a private meeting with Reagan. He saw that she was politically savvy enough to maintain a Republican seat in a state trending Democratic, and that she was keenly aware of women's voting inclinations.

For Margaret's forty-five-minute meeting with Reagan, her press secretary sat right outside the door. The ERA was the first issue to come up. Reagan had withdrawn his support for the ERA in the Republican platform and openly expressed his concerns to Margaret:

Reagan: I'm worried that this conservative approach may lose the women's vote.

Margaret: Many women won't take you seriously as an advocate for them.

Reagan: Now what would you suggest I do?

Margaret: Now—you appoint a woman to the Supreme Court.[16]

As the meeting continued, Margaret implored the Republican nominee, "Mr. Reagan, you must appoint a woman to the Supreme Court. Will you commit to it?"

Regan replied, "I'll think about it, but it's a very good idea."[17] The advice was bold, but well received. By the end of Margaret's meeting with Reagan, she had won a concession that he *would* name a woman to the Supreme Court.[18] When they were finished, Margaret left the room and confidently told Linda Bilmes, "Mission accomplished!"

Margaret knew that to be more effective in advancing women's issues, working in consensus with other feminists was fruitful. While Reagan had been clear that he did not want the ERA on the Republican Party platform, female activists at the convention thought they had succeeded when they were summoned for a meeting with Reagan.[19] About two dozen feminist women, including Margaret, attended the meeting. It was likely that none of them knew about Margaret's private conversation with Reagan.

Reagan told the group that he supported equal rights for women, but not in the form of an amendment. He then echoed Phyllis Schlafly's argument that the Equal Rights Amendment would negatively affect labor laws.

With Alice Tetelman standing to the left of presidential contender Ronald Reagan. Seated next to him, with back to camera, is Mary Louise Smith, onetime national GOP chairman. Senator Nancy Kassenbaum (R-KS) is at right and at the opposite end of the table are Representatives Margaret Heckler (left) and Helen Milliken. *Private collection.*

This led to a showdown between Heckler and Reagan. As Margaret described the situation, "The other women in the meeting were also pro-ERA, as was [his daughter] Maureen Reagan, whom he came with. But they remained silent about it. I sat at one end of the table, and he sat at the other. 'I'll support changes in state laws to support more opportunity for women,' Reagan said, 'but not an amendment.' I said, 'This is a negative signal to women.'"[20]

Alice Tetelman, who was in the room, expressed shock at Margaret's boldness, saying, "Representative Margaret Heckler of Massachusetts asked Reagan whether or not he would appoint a woman to the Supreme Court. He said yes. This was the first time that anybody had ever asked him, as far as we knew, and it was astounding."[21]

Reaction outside the meeting was mixed.

> Reporters . . . weren't impressed. They said the GOP feminists were pussycats, easily bought off with a no-cost promise that stopped them from carrying the ERA fight to the full convention—where they could make their argument for equality not to the delegates alone but to the national audience watching on "gavel-to-gavel" television. And anti-ERA strategist, Phyllis Schlafly, angered that Reagan even granted the meeting, remained confident she had shown up the feminists as impotent, wrong-headed idealists whose party had passed them by. [But] when Sandra Day O'Connor took her seat on the US Supreme Court on the first Monday in October of 1981, O'Connor owed her breakthrough in part to Heckler's persuasive argument.[22]

During the time that Reagan announced he would appoint a woman to the Supreme Court, Pam Ou, Margaret's assistant, said, "Congresswoman Heckler identified and recommended to President Reagan Sandra Day O'Connor as a strong candidate."[23]

The RNC's concluding event was Reagan's selection of a running mate. Many believed Reagan would pick Gerald Ford and Representative Jack Kemp's (R-NY) supporters pressed Kemp as a candidate, but it came down to who would help Reagan win the election.[24] The Reagan team needed someone who would draw the moderate vote. The clear choice was George [H. W.] Bush.[25]

Margaret's influence in Republican politics waned after Ronald Reagan's victory in the 1980 presidential election. The political ideology of the Republican Party markedly shifted toward cultural conservatism after Reagan became president. The Moral Majority—born in response to the sexual revolution with greater access to birth control and the legalization of abortion—had redefined the conservative movement. Reaganism now dominated the Republican Party. The Grand Old Party's prior political big tent had shrunk considerably, which threatened to squeeze out moderates like Heckler.

As this cultural conservatism dominated the political conversation during the 1980s, it made it nearly impossible for moderate Republicans to be elected in the Democrat-domineered Massachusetts. While Bay State moderate Republicans were well represented in Congress in the mid-1960s, this shift in voter priorities caused moderate Republicans to start to fade away. This was due to the prominence of the abortion issue. Rather than vote based on who they believed would do the better job representing their interests, in the 1980s, voters became more concerned about the candidates' perceived ideological beliefs.

The first few years after the Supreme Court decided *Roe v. Wade* in 1973, abortion was not a litmus test for party affiliation. Some Republicans were pro-choice; some Democrats were pro-life. During this era, Massachusetts elected Representative Father Robert Drinan, SJ (D-MA), a Jesuit Catholic priest who was pro-choice for five terms. In contrast, Speaker of the House Representative Tip O'Neill (D-MA) was solidly pro-life. But when abortion became a wedge issue for cultural conservatism under Reagan, liberal Massachusetts voters exercised their right to choose pro-choice candidates, and rejected what they viewed as Reagan Republicans. Moderate and pro-life politicians either needed to change their pro-life views or face being thrown out of office.

This was particularly poignant for Margaret, as her entire congressional career was being a moderate Republican in a Democrat-domineered state.

As a leader of the Congresswomen's Caucus, Margaret tried to steer clear of the abortion issue in the group. Margaret's personal views on abortion were profoundly influenced by her early childhood:

> For all of those years when I was the only woman on the committee and fought for women['s rights] and won many, many times, if the prevailing view on abortion had been accepted at the time of my birth, I might not have had the opportunity to be on this planet. I had a very unusual life. . . . I was an unexpected child, and when I arrived, my father was not very pleased to have a child, and especially a daughter.
>
> While we have freedom of religion, we should not have freedom from God and his role in this world. I am acutely aware of it because of my own life, and that role has to be respected. I leave the issue there. To me, [every life] is God's signature, and this has to be honored in our

society and the civil rights have to be honored, at some point, sooner rather than later.[26]

When Margaret even remotely wrestled with the idea of changing her stance to pro-choice to meet the changing tides, one of her Catholic constituents from Fall River brought her back to reality reminding her that "there was a bishop on every corner."[27]

Standing at the crossroads of history, Margaret realized her district's demographics and priorities had changed. The Reagan-inspired "cultural conservatism" dominated Republican ideology. After the Reagan Revolution, not being friendly to the pro-choice position could cost Heckler her seat in Congress.

In a slight move toward a pro-choice position, Heckler opposed a pro-life constitutional amendment that required federally funded clinics to notify parents when teenagers requested and received access to birth control. But this stance was not enough to keep her in step with the women's movement, which believed the right to choose or the right to abort is a woman's issue. After years of feminist action and securing major wins for the women's movement, Margaret soon found herself on the fringe with many women's groups.

For Margaret, a combination of her deep faith, life experience, and the Catholic demographics of her constituents led her to support the Right of Conscience in Abortion Procedures Act, a bill protecting the right of conscience for hospital and medical workers, a topic that was not yet controversial. The bill easily passed.

The Hyde Amendment in 1976 made it illegal to use government-supported Medicaid funds for abortions, except to save the life of the woman. The Hyde Amendment was the pro-life coalition's first legislative success and one of the first bills that forced congressmembers to take a stand on abortion. When it went into effect, Medicaid-funded abortions dropped from three hundred thousand a year to just a few thousand. Victims of rape and incest were later added to the amendment as exceptions. Margaret concluded, "The better part of wisdom is to leave the total issue of abortion to the states."

Up for reelection in 1982, Margaret knew the odds were stacked against her. Massachusetts had lost a congressional seat due to population decline reflected in the 1980 census. The state legislature had to redraw the Tenth District. Their task was made easier when Representative Father Robert Drinan, SJ (D-MA) was required to resign his seat because the Vatican prohibited Catholic religious from holding elective political office. So the Tenth District was redrawn to Margaret's disadvantage and as a result, she was pitted against Barney Frank, a Democratic incumbent. The Massachusetts legislature divided the district to have the appearance that it included equal pieces of Heckler's and Frank's prior districts and while the new district did include much of Heckler's geographic region, the voter ratio became 2.6 Democrats for each Republican.[28] According to Andy Card, gerrymandering made the voting conditions more solidly blue because the Democratic Massachusetts legislature wanted to oust the Republican from the seat.[29] Silvio Conte, the only other Massachusetts Republican representative, was spared—perhaps because his voting record was more liberal than Margaret's.[30]

Even more impactful, the National Organization for Women (NOW) and the National Women's Political Caucus (NWPC), of which Margaret had been a member since its founding in 1971, endorsed Barney Frank in the primary. Margaret was devastated because she was a founding member of the NWPC. That year, the women's groups supported male candidates over a female candidate a total of seven times. NOW president Eleanor Smeal stated that NOW supported these men, especially in the instances of Millicent Fenwick of New Jersey and Margaret Heckler of Massachusetts, because "when it comes to choosing between two candidates, we'll lean toward their position on women's rights rather than the sex of the individual." Now it seemed that feminist groups equated women's rights with abortion rights.

Margaret felt that Smeal's comment was an insult, one that completely disregarded her work on behalf of women's rights over her entire career, effectively erasing her early advocacy for the ERA, her success in getting the Equal Credit Opportunity Act passed, and her work as a cosponsor of Title IX. It was also a far cry from two years earlier, when Congresswomen Schroeder and Heckler were featured together in *Redbook* magazine, as two female candidates to pay close attention to because of their commitment to pro-women policies like the ERA. The *Redbook* article concluded with a call to elect women like "Schroeder and Heckler who are willing to deal with tough problems and to examine them from the point of view of the women in their constituencies."[31]

In 1982, NOW gave $5,000 to Barney Frank's campaign, saying they endorsed Frank because he "is a strong supporter of women's rights issues. His clear stand against Reagan budget cuts—cuts in Social Security, in the women's rights equity program—is of major importance. We need fighters like Barney Frank for American women—women who are heads of households, women who seek equity in educational and employment opportunities, and in pay."[32]

Linda Bilmes, Margaret's former press secretary, described the emotion behind what went down:

> Here she was, one of the original co-authors of the Equal Rights Amendment. She spent twenty years of her life being a trailblazer for women. She spent most of her time in Congress authoring equal credit laws, and the National Organization for Women gave support not to her, but to her male opponent, because of her views on abortion. She was absolutely devastated about this. It was really unfair. It was not close. It was a slap in the face to somebody who embodied everything that the women's movement was about.[33]

Margaret later shared how this betrayal hurt her psychologically. She deeply believed that Republican and Democratic women should work together to advance women's rights and not focus solely on abortion.[34]

Entering the race against Frank, Margaret was still favored to win. Knowing Margaret was vulnerable because of losing support from women's groups and her alignment with several of President Reagan's economic policies, Frank leaned on her allegiance to President Reagan

Campaigning in the 1982 congressional race against Barney Frank (D-MA).
The Providence Journal—*USA Today network.*

even harder. She voted for Reagan's federal tax cuts, which provided fewer government programs for Massachusetts residents. Frank pressed into that, running a TV ad showing an elderly couple walking down a tree-lined street—when suddenly, the screen cuts to a large fist smashing a Social Security check, with the word "cancel" stamped across the front in red lettering.

Margaret's political strategists encouraged her to bring it out in the open that Barney Frank was gay. He had remained closeted publicly. Against their advice, she took the high road and refused to negatively campaign. In the early 1980s, being gay could have been a political risk for a public official.

Despite the odds, Margaret kept her campaign energy high. There was a campaign event in Fall River, which Margaret and Barney Frank attended. An *NBC Nightly News* reporter who saw Margaret shake every hand in the room, exclaimed, "Honest to God . . . I've been in five different races across the country, and I've never seen a Republican campaign like her."[35]

As the campaign dragged on, it began to take a toll on her. As cultural expectations dictated, Margaret wore high heels to appear feminine and to make up for her short five-foot, two-inch stature. At the end of each day, Margaret's feet were killing her. She was advised by doctors to use a microphone because she kept losing her voice, and her hands cramped from the teeming number of handshakes. Now as a fifty-one year old, she needed to take B12 vitamin shots for energy and health. She powered through, attending several campaign events each night—but for the first time, Margaret's morale wavered. At one of her final parades, as she was perched on the back of a convertible, she leaned over and said to her driver, Danny Converse, "I can see it in their eyes. They are not for me."[36]

In the final stretch of the race, Margaret felt frustrated that her staff had scheduled her to spend a few hours at the convent in Foxboro, Massachusetts, instead of being at a bigger, more consequential event. The driver recounted, "She was screaming and hollering the whole drive. 'Why did we agree to do this? I can't believe this! What am I missing because I am here?' But it was too late to change the schedule."

As they pulled up to the beautifully preserved mansion, Margaret was met at the door by one of her former Albertus Magnus classmates, now a nun. Immediately, Margaret was disarmed, feeling a peace she so desperately needed. She had a brief chance to reflect. She was feeling her age and had had a difficult reelection campaign. Everything seemed to be going wrong. The sisters had given vows of silence, so Margaret's friend served as a go-between. All the while, Converse was seated in a back room by an old rotary phone, covered in cobwebs. He made a call to Margaret's executive assistant Mary Anne Thadeu, tying up campaign loose ends.

As the nuns gathered together, Margaret gave a campaign speech, which touched on women's issues, before responding to questions from the sisters. Converse was amazed by how well-read these cloistered nuns were.

Despite Margaret's initial misgivings, the convent visit was perfectly timed. It gave her a sense of serenity. Afterward, Converse said to Margaret, "We were losing it that day. This moment stopped you and reminded you of who you were and why you were here. You were totally different afterwards." The trip made Margaret aware that she might lose the election, but God had a plan for her, regardless of the election outcome.[37]

Margaret lost her seat in the 1982 general election, and she took it personally. Thanks to Reagan's unpopularity that fall, Republicans lost twenty-seven House seats.[38]

After her defeat, condolence letters arrived from everywhere. One of her constituents, Sumner Whittier wrote, "I am very, very sorry for your loss . . . the weirdest idiosyncrasy was the women's movement not being with you." At a Mass she attended in Fall River, the priest gave her a shoutout: "We are losing a great friend [in Congress]." These heartwarming words of encouragement convinced Margaret that losing her seat did not have to be the end of her political career.

After Margaret was defeated, she attended a ribbon-cutting ceremony in Fall River. As Charlton Memorial Hospital president Frederic Dryer remembered,

> We had a big tent with hundreds of people in attendance. I was sitting next to Barney Frank, who was newly representing Fall River, on the stage with me when a car came rolling in. As soon as Margaret stepped out of her car, one of her constituents recognized her, announcing loudly in a thick New England accent, "Look, there's Peggy Heckla!" and hurried over to greet her. Soon, a large portion of the gathering left the tent, surrounding Margaret like she was a celebrity, leaving the speakers on stage baffled. Barney Frank turned to me, frustrated and said, "*Hey, I thought I won the election.*"[39]

III

APPOINTMENTS 1982–1989

Madame Secretary and Minority Health

Walking with President Ronald Reagan (center) and HHS Secretary Richard Schweiker (left) in the White House. *White House Photographer.*

𝒯he phones did not ring and the Capitol halls outside of Margaret's door were empty as she surveyed her office one last time. The heavy silence was a mournful symbol of change. As Margaret described it, "Overnight we went from being a crisis center of Washington to being the local morgue."[1] The boxes containing her mementos from the past sixteen years, including letters from Presidents Johnson, Nixon, Carter, Ford, and Reagan, reflected "the finality of it . . . like a funeral."[2]

After her time in Congress came to a screeching halt in 1982, Margaret needed to step back from Washington to think about what came next. She flew to Massachusetts to reassess her options. She'd received job offers at law offices in Boston and Washington, but those positions wouldn't satiate her drive and political skills. At fifty-one, Margaret knew she had been called into a life of service and her time in politics was not over yet.

Back in Wellesley, Margaret called Gerry Abrams, a well-connected friend and former constituent from Natick who Margaret had helped to protect American fisheries from Soviet aggression. When they spoke on the phone Abrams recalled, "I could hear in her voice that she was choking back tears. She asked, 'Can you get away now?'"[3]

The two met at Ken's Steak House in Framingham. Taking a booth in the back, Margaret's eyes welled up as she told Abrams, "So many of my so-called friends have disappeared and I have $250,000 in campaign debt from the election."

Abrams, like many who knew Margaret on a personal level, believed she was "not the average politician." He assured her they would raise the money through a finance committee, but just as significantly, he helped Margaret reignite her own fire. "Do you know what chutzpah is?" he asked her. Margaret nodded as he continued, "It's the most colossal gall. When you go back to Washington next week for the White House Christmas party and you are in the receiving line . . . when Reagan bends over to kiss you, pull yourself up from your stockings and whisper in his ear, 'Mr. President, I supported you and now I need a job!'"[4]

At the 1982 White House Christmas party, Margaret arrived prepared, accompanied by her son John. She was nervous, thinking that this might be the last time she would see the president. She had one shot, and this was it. She made pleasantries with her friends Secretary of State George Shultz and Vice President George Bush as she walked through the line, but when she approached President Reagan, he leaned down and she immediately put her arm on his shoulder, holding it there as she whispered in his ear, "*I supported you, and now I need a job.*" He smiled genuinely and said, "Okay."

Not long after her brief exchange with the president, Margaret started hearing rumors that Reagan's White House was trying to find a cabinet placement for her. John Heckler, thought his friend George Siguler, who served as associate treasurer at Harvard University, would be a good resource for her. He encouraged her to speak with Siguler. Within a week, Reagan's White House chief of staff Jim Baker called Margaret to say, "There's nothing right now, but before you commit to a law firm, know that you're in our sights."[5]

Shortly thereafter, Lyn Nofziger, assistant to the president, called Margaret, who pitched the position of secretary of the treasury. During this telephone call, Margaret's son John overheard his mother say, "I'm not going to sit in some office, signing dollar bills." John was thunderstruck that it was the White House calling his mother and that she so quickly turned down such a high-profile job.[6] Nofziger then offered her to be the head of NASA. She immediately retorted, "What do I know about spaceships?" Margaret felt emboldened, knowing that she had the president on her side.

Secretary of health and human services (HHS), the largest American government agency, was next on the list from the White House. When Margaret spoke with Elliot Richardson, who previously held the position, he warned Margaret, "HHS is a killer. It's an impossible agency. It's a mammoth job and it goes in so many directions."[7] She knew HHS *was* a mammoth job but due to her work on veterans' affairs, Margaret was more open to HHS than to the Treasury position.

However, there was a catch with the HHS role. The president had promised the role to Jack Svahn, a longtime Reagan supporter from California. This would be a major promotion from Svahn's current position, commissioner of Social Security at HHS. Jim Baker arranged a meeting to see if the contenders could work together at HHS.

They met at the Mayflower Hotel in downtown Washington, DC, sitting in the empty, dimly lit bar. Margaret had invited George Siguler, who was acting as her de facto chief of staff, to the meeting at the Mayflower. According to Siguler, "The meeting did not go well. Jack Svahn was a hard ass." Svahn wanted the top HHS position and was offended that the administration was passing him up in favor of a woman. He did not care that she had over a decade of experience in Washington. As Siguler recounted, Svahn made it clear that he intended to run the department, with Margaret as "second fiddle." With the situation at an impasse, Margaret and Siguler ended the meeting.

Afterward, Siguler said to Margaret, "This guy basically wants your job."

Margaret responded, "Clearly, this meeting wasn't meant to see if we would be compatible. He has it in for me already."[8]

Margaret knew her strengths. She knew she had earned credibility with the president as a Washington insider and had helped Reagan win the women's vote in his 1980 presidential election. According to RNC heavyweight Ron Kaufman, "the GOP needed Margaret Heckler." In 1980, Reagan had received 54 percent of the men's vote and 46 percent of the women's vote. As a result of this gender gap, the Reagan administration was frantically strategizing how to pull in more women.[9]

Republicans had proactively placed women in governmental positions of power in the 1970s and early 1980s.[10] Reagan had heeded Margaret's prompting to put a woman on the Supreme Court. He then nominated Sandra Day O'Connor. Elizabeth Dole became secretary of transportation and Jeane Kirkpatrick was named US ambassador to the United Nations. Margaret knew that top Reagan officials wanted to place at least three women into high-level positions ahead of the 1984 election.

In January 1983, Reagan's chief of staff Jim Baker invited Margaret and George Siguler to attend a White House meeting. Jim Baker, who was a moderate like Margaret, tried to look out for her and "didn't want her to mess up" this meeting. He met her at the White House security entrance and said, "I understand that you met with Jack Svahn and it didn't go well." He then warned her, "Don't use any liberal bullshit in here or this HHS appointment is not going to happen. Your number one task is to avoid stepping on a landmine."[11]

During the White House meeting, Reagan's top advisor, Ed Meese, formally offered her the job of secretary of health and human services. When Svahn, who was also in the room, began expressing his views about how HHS should be run, Margaret stood up and asserted, "I've been in this town for sixteen years. Don't tell me how this thing works. You've been here for sixteen days. I'll tell *you* when you are wrong."

Baker was livid because Margaret's feistiness threatened the appointment. George Siguler thought he was going to fly across the room and strangle her. But Margaret felt she had made her point and left with her aid to discuss the offer privately. Her hesitation elicited a call from Vice President Bush, who told her, "You better take this job, otherwise some hawkish Californian will take it."[12]

In the end, the outright antipathy between Margaret and Svahn was overshadowed by three things. First, Reagan's conservative administration was earnest in their search for an HHS secretary who was pro-life.

The second reason she was chosen was because, as a charismatic, moderate woman, Margaret would be highly successful attracting a broad range of female voters. Thirdly, according to Ed Meese, she had been a long-term congresswoman who knew how to get things done.

As President Reagan stood beside Margaret when she was named as the new HHS secretary, she said, "I feel, frankly, that you have offered me the greatest challenge of my life. I would never have undertaken to accept this great challenge, but for the honor of serving the finest President that I have known. And, indeed, it is with a sense of faith in your vision and

In the Oval Office. Foreground from left to right: Deputy Chief of Staff Michael Deaver, Counselor to the President Ed Meese, Margaret Heckler, Chief of Staff Jim Baker, HHS Secretary Richard Schweiker, and President Ronald Reagan.
White House Photographer.

your goals for America . . . that I accept what I think is the hardest assignment in Washington."[13]

Ahead of Margaret's confirmation hearing, grumbling was heard from both the Right and the Left. Conservatives doubted her "ideological purity" due to her criticism of Reagan's economic programs and her early support of the Equal Rights Amendment. Those on the Left were opposed because she was pro-life, and they used every opportunity to paint her beliefs as extreme. Her photographer, Mel Lukens remembered, "A female cabinet member got more than one raised eyebrow."[14]

On March 3, 1983, Margaret was confirmed as secretary of health and human services with an 83–3 Senate confirmation vote, only the second woman to hold that post. During her acceptance speech, she stated as the nation's health secretary, "I want to be a catalyst for caring." Margaret would become one of the first women cabinet secretaries under President Reagan (with an annual budget of $274 billion). The other was Elizabeth Dole as secretary of labor (with an annual budget of $43 billion).[15]

Six days later, Marine guards directed Margaret and her family past the black iron gates of the White House for her swearing-in ceremony.

The Oval Office was illuminated as the sunlight streamed into the elegant room. Family, close friends, and supporters took their places.

Wearing a red suit, Margaret stood alongside her husband John and her three children. Her cousins from Ireland, Mary Buckley and Theresa Sheehy, had flown in for the monumental day.

In the Oval Office, Margaret was sworn in on March 9, 1983, as HHS secretary by Supreme Court Associate Justice Sandra Day O'Connor. This was a historic moment for both O'Connor and Heckler, as it was a rare display of female empowerment at the highest levels in American government.

At the ceremony, Margaret said, "The glory and honor of this moment belongs to the Lord. I will call on His strength as I strive to carry out my duties . . . there are still people in need, and they will be my special concerns as Secretary of the people's department of the government." She pledged her "desire to indeed symbolize the compassion and caring that I know you [President Reagan] feel for the American people."[16]

President Ronald Reagan rejoined with light-hearted humor: "Now, some have charged that Margaret Heckler was offered this position because this administration is partial to a certain ethnic group in our society

Being sworn in as secretary of HHS by Supreme Court Justice Sandra Day O'Connor while Margaret's daughter Belinda holds the Bible and President Ronald Reagan and Vice President George Bush look on, 1983. *White House Photographer.*

that I want to keep their favor. Now let me be tellin' you," he said, mimicking an Irish brogue, "that Margaret Heckler, being an Irish colleen, it has nothing 'at all a do' with this appointment."

He went on to say:

> Seriously, Margaret is the daughter of Irish immigrants, and her first ambition was to play the concert piano. Lucky for us, she chose a political career instead, where she might add harmony in a much more difficult place to create it. And during these sixteen years in Congress, Margaret has been known for her boundless energy and enthusiasm and she will need it in the job that she takes on as of today. And Margaret, as Secretary of Health and Human Services, I know that you will oversee the federal department with 142,000 employees and an annual budget of $274 billion dollars. Only two budgets in the world are greater than that: the entire budget of the United States' government and the budget of the Soviet Union. . . . Welcome to the team and good luck and I say that with all my heart.[17]

The following day, Margaret entered the HHS headquarters in the brutalist-style Hubert H. Humphrey Building, which was pockmarked with windows. However, the exterior and imposing main hall were in direct contrast with the work done within its walls. HHS serves every person and household in the United States, in particular caring for society's most vulnerable: the impoverished, sick, elderly, and dying. As the second woman to occupy the secretary's office, Margaret understood she would helm an agency that profoundly determined life and death outcomes for many Americans.

Her first day began with a welcome reception in the Great Hall. The Great Hall was a massive two-story space where former department secretaries seemed to watchfully gaze from their full-height portraits lining the walls. The stretch of featured men, interrupted by only one other woman, Patricia Roberts Harris, continued down both sides of the Great Hall.

Seizing the opportunity to set the tone, Margaret turned to Jack Svahn, her undersecretary, and said, "Don't be mistaken as to who is running the agency."

When it was time for speeches, Margaret noticed Svahn rise to give a speech. Margaret quickly took the microphone saying, "Look at the time! We only have time for one speech and that would be mine."[18] She knew that if she gave Svahn an inch of control, he'd try to bulldoze her authority.

Margaret spoke to eight hundred employees at the HHS headquarters and thirty thousand more employees in regional offices via video. Margaret closed the speech by asking for their ideas and she promised to fight for the ones she supported. She added with a grin, "They don't call me a 'heckler' for nothing."[19]

As Margaret started her tenure as HHS secretary, she knew she needed to play multiple roles: 1) to be head of a large government agency; 2) to be a negotiator within the Reagan administration, which was hungry to slash budgets; and 3) to advocate for life-saving programs, to name a few.

Additionally, the day she stepped into her new office she inherited hundreds of lawsuits from her predecessor that now had her name on them. It was a shock to learn she was being sued by so many people on her first day on the job. Equally shocking was the bulletproof vest hanging in her closet.

One of her first tasks was to hire her own staff. The administration wanted to plant their own insiders, but Margaret pushed through George Siguler as her chief of staff and chief policy advisor and Patti Tyson, her executive assistant, who had been working with her since the early 1970s. She would prove to be indispensable, reviewing all the regulations before they went up for the secretary's signature. Another longtime confidant, Roger Woodworth, came on as her special assistant, managing press and public relations, having known Margaret since her days as a private attorney in Massachusetts. With these appointments Margaret was able to create a protective fortress around herself.

Beyond those key roles, the rollover staff from the previous secretary remained and a few others were added. Jackie White, who worked as a policy expert on Medicare and Medicaid, immediately saw Margaret's needs. White had worked at HHS for years and knew the programs inside out. An energetic, godsent angel amid a lair of political hacks, she had no ulterior agenda, she became one of Margaret's fiercest supporters and closest allies.

In her first few weeks, Margaret was bombarded with information and acronyms related to over four hundred HHS programs and eleven operating divisions. The sheer scope of HHS was daunting. Margaret met with the regional office directors in cities across the country—each of them like a mini-HHS agency.[20] When she was in Washington, DC, she attended countless meetings at the White House where HHS budget talks focused more on slashing than creating. Margaret received calls from congressmembers asking her to not cut specific programs. Lowell Weiker (R-CT), for example, asked her to spare the funding for "the most defenseless members of our society," handicapped children.[21]

In the beginning of his term, President Reagan had handed out a guide, "The Blueprint for Leadership," to his leadership team. The president had taken a fairly lax approach in communicating his intent for governance to his new cabinet members. As a result, Jackie White became Margaret's sourcebook, informing her exactly how bureaucratic agencies functioned, explaining the framework of "The Blueprint" and helping her understand each of the four corners of the room. As a result, Margaret felt safe with Jackie.

To the public, a confident woman was at the helm of HHS. But in private, Margaret was cautious. She had a lot to learn, and she did not want to react carelessly. Perhaps the biggest source of her uncertainty was the lack of support from the predominantly male staff she had inherited from former HHS secretary Richard Schweiker. These department heads had a way of talking down to Margaret: "Don't worry your pretty little head!" they would say. "We've got this." In addition to her staff's demeaning comments, Svahn routinely nipped at her heels, hoping she would trip up. Because of the hostility within her office, Margaret didn't feel that she could put her trust in many people except her own appointees.

Her nemesis, Jack Svahn, didn't last long. In the end, Margaret held the keys to the kingdom. Once Margaret established her line of authority, Svahn's role as undersecretary became defunct. No longer under the illusion that he could muscle his way to the top, he left after six months, moving to the White House as an assistant to the president for policy development.

The various HHS department heads and Margaret were like ships passing in the night. Each department had its own foreign language, its own slang, and it was almost impossible to understand. At meetings, Margaret's officers would present ideas to her in large, whole-picture chunks without describing the impact of the program, requiring her to step back and decipher the information, especially on items related to the budget. Jackie White developed a habit of walking back to the office with Margaret after each meeting, translating the information into plain, simple English. She did the same with the lengthy documents, some of them five hundred pages or more. White later recounted how she would look through a document, then explain it to Margaret. For example, "This is actually a cost-of-living adjustment on hospitals. You are determining how much more you want to pay doctors."[22]

❧

Within a few weeks of assuming her new role, a group of five prominent Black medical doctors requested a meeting with Secretary Heckler to present a new study regarding Black health care providers. The meeting took place in late March 1983. The leader of the charge was Dr. Louis Sullivan, president of the Morehouse School of Medicine in Atlanta. Alongside him were a few other prominent Black physicians, including Dr. Rueben Warren, Dr. David Satcher, Dr. Alfred Haynes, and Dr. Walter Bowie. They all took seats around a large conference table in a sixth-floor meeting room at HHS.

Before the meeting started, Margaret and Dr. Warren began discussing Boston. Margaret mentioned she had a dentist in Boston who was Black. Dr. Warren said, "You must be referring to Dr. Walker, because he is the only Black dentist in Boston." Margaret replied, "Yes, I know him very well."

Dr. Warren thought this was the perfect "ice breaker," which "pointed to the fact that there were so few Black health professionals."[23] The exchange between Margaret and Dr. Warren was a "vivid real-life demonstration" and a turning point in the discussion.[24] This was part of Margaret's leadership style, which allowed her to be bold when change was called for. Her small talk established the Boston connection, but it also showed she knew the community.

Dr. Sullivan presented the report, *Blacks and the Health Professions in the 1980s: A National Crisis and a Time for Action.*[25] The study revealed a five-to-seven-year life expectancy gap between Black Americans and White Americans. It also highlighted a severe lack of representation of Black Americans in nursing and medical schools. Black Americans made up 12 percent of the population, but only 3 to 4 percent of health professionals were Black. The doctors wanted to recruit Secretary Heckler to help them address the lack of minority representation in medical professions.

The doctors then described how the historically underfunded Black medical schools were kind of a surrogate for how Black Americans had been treated for centuries. According to Dr. Warren, "When you have this lack of progress, it shouldn't have come as a surprise that Blacks couldn't have had access to proper health care, discriminated against at every turn."[26] The group believed "if they turned to their medical schools as part of the solution, maybe they could change health care discrimination."[27]

Margaret seemed receptive saying, "This is interesting, very important." But Dr. Sullivan was unconvinced that anything would come from their time with her.[28] He felt there was not much support at HHS for this initiative. But Margaret was a mobilizer. A few months later, the doctors learned that she had formed a committee at the National Institutes of Health (NIH) to investigate the issue.

For Margaret, the "burden of death" for Black Americans due to health care disparities brought to mind Christina, the kind Black woman who took on her grandmother's chores and saved her job at a laundry facility when Belinda West fell ill all those decades ago during the Great Depression. Margaret said,

> Reading about the disparity in longevity for minority citizens brought back this memory very vividly. As Secretary of Health and Human Services, I was not satisfied to accept a shorter lifespan for minority Americans of Christina's background and other ethnic groups.[29]

Looking further into the topic, Margaret discovered that these disparities in life expectancy were already documented in HHS's annual *Health, United States, 1983* report.[30]

"It was an affront to our ideals and to the genius of American medicine," she said.[31] But again, Margaret had to cut through the red tape of reform at HHS. Even though the federal government had known about this disparity for centuries, no one had taken up the torch to do anything about it. Margaret stated, "My assistant secretaries unanimously opposed this initiative, because the health disparities had existed since the beginning of record-keeping at the department." Margaret was not willing to accept shorter lifespans for minority Americans without an investigation of what could be done. She believed the question deserved a scientific answer.[32] Margaret believed in the inherent dignity of life. She was an out-of-the-box thinker and refused to settle for bureaucratic lethargy toward minority health issues. Margaret embodied the sentiments of Robert F. Kennedy when he quoted George Bernard Shaw: "Some men see things as they are and ask, 'Why?' I dream things that never were and ask, 'Why not?'"

One year later, in 1984, the Task Force on Black and Minority Health was created. Secretary Heckler appointed highly respected Black biologist Dr. Thomas E. Malone as chairman. His new office was situated close to Secretary Heckler's, showing the importance of this initiative. Senior leaders across the NIH, CDC, and other HHS health departments joined the new task force to research and compose a report on the health status of racial and ethnic minorities. The mission of the task force was to unearth the causes and potential remedies for health inequalities between these groups and White Americans.

In 1985, two years after Louis Sullivan's initial meeting, the Task Force on Black and Minority Health completed the *Report of the Secretary's Task Force on Black and Minority Health*. The report was over six hundred pages and comprised nine volumes on the health of Black Americans, Hispanic Americans, Native Americans, Alaskan natives, and Asian Americans. This study became known as the *Heckler Report*.

The data in the *Heckler Report* was stunning. It documented persistent health disparities that accounted for sixty thousand excess deaths each year.[33] The report confirmed that Black Americans died sooner than White Americans. Six causes of deaths were responsible for 80 percent of total deaths among Black and other minority populations, including cancer, cardiovascular disease and stroke, chemical dependency (measured by deaths due to cirrhosis), diabetes, homicide and accidents (unintentional injuries), and infant mortality.[34]

The *Heckler Report* was the first study conducted by the US government related to minority health. It made sure that the federal government could no longer pretend they were not aware of the numbers. In a preface to the report, Secretary Heckler noted, "[This] should mark the beginning of the end of the health disparity that has, for so long, cast a shadow on the otherwise splendid American track record of ever improving health."

The deaths of Black Americans (and other minorities) were already being counted, and following this report the government admitted they had the ability to chronicle morbidity and mortality based on race.

The practice of hiding these figures changed after the *Heckler Report*. Margaret then set in motion the creation of the Office of Minority Health at HHS, which was established in 1986, with a $3 million fund for monitoring minority public health. In the decades that followed, the *Heckler Report* and the Office of Minority Health facilitated new legislation, more funding, in-depth policy research, development of institutions, local community programs, and the creation of new initiatives.

The *Heckler Report* also generated offices related to minority health in six different HHS agencies.

Reflecting on the achievements of the *Heckler Report*, Dr. Warren said it was "an embarrassment to discover that for over two hundred years, minority health disparities had been chronicled. You could see the figures, but the federal government had never acknowledged it. They ignored it, denied it."[35] Warren continued, "We had been beating that horse, year after year, trying to get the attention of government officials, but the conversation with Secretary Heckler changed the discussion at HHS. She realized from her own life experience that you can be disadvantaged through no fault of your own and have to suffer. . . . Her fight was mission driven. Because she lived it, she had empathy. I'm clear now that she *had* to do it."[36]

According to Dr. Warren, the *Heckler Report* was a miracle because it was released at a bad time to ask for funds from the Reagan administration. "It took courage and ultimately it had the cascading effect of minority health offices opening in every major health division—the CDC, NIH, FDA, and HRSA. Today there are thirty-nine states with offices of minority health and that would not have happened if not for the *Heckler Report*."[37] Margaret's work on behalf of minority health inequality created

At the Annual Leadership and Health Disparities Conference. From left to right: Dr. Luke, Dr. Rene Rodriguez, Dr. Robert Gallo, Margaret Heckler, Dr. Winston Churchill, Dr. Waine Cong, Dr. George H. Pulkries.
Family collection.

something that had never existed before and has benefited millions of Americans since 1985.

In 1989, Dr. Louis Sullivan became HHS secretary and credited the *Heckler Report* as forming the basis for his HHS work. Looking back to his meeting with Margaret in 1983, he said he viewed the work that Secretary Heckler helped initiate "as a continuum; the *Heckler Report* had such a major impact and is still in use today."[38] The *Heckler Report* became one of Margaret's greatest legacies.

In a letter thanking the hosts for the award she received for the *Heckler Report*, twenty years later, Margaret again pointed to Christina. She wrote,

> I thank you for the Lifetime Achievement Award . . . accepted on be-half of all the *Heckler Report* participants. . . . Actually, Christina is the person who deserves my award. . . . Please make the story of Christina part of the history of the cause for the elimination of disparities. One woman's heroic kindness affected the lives and health of millions of her fellow citizens. Christina, *this is for you.*

Working for the largest federal agency in the government, Margaret was continually tasked with placing capable people in roles that women had never served in before. Given the opportunity to place a woman in a high-level leadership position, Margaret named Martha McSteen as the first female Social Security commissioner, in charge of a $170 billion program with more than eighty thousand employees. The *Baltimore Sun* reported that Margaret "felt it fitting to name a woman to head the agency, as 73 percent of its workforce and 54 percent of its recipients are women." Margaret also hired Jo Anne B. Ross to manage Aid to Families with Dependent Children, a $13 billion welfare program serving more than ten million Americans.[39]

In addition to her own women-conscious hiring practices, Margaret created a pipeline to help women to be better positioned for promotions. She said, "When I got to HHS, I saw a department with great power, but the women were concentrated at the bottom rung. So, I started a new executive training program that some said women wouldn't be interested in. . . . I knew they [would be]. We oversubscribed. We had to hold the course three times in one year."[40] The women's management training initiative was a fast track for mid-level women with management potential. It was a triumph for women seeking long-term careers in government.

Leaving Boston on Air Force One after a sucessful campaign trip with President Ronald Reagan. *White House Photographer.*

Meanwhile, Reagan was cashing in on Margaret's ability to campaign for him, especially when it came to addressing the voter gender gap. Her success on the campaign trail was evidenced in the following memo, received by the White House:

Memo for: James Baker III, Michael Deaver, David Gergen, Craig Fuller
From: Karna Small

Just a note to let you know that Secretary Heckler spoke to our group of regional editors and broadcasters in 450 EOB this morning and was positively eloquent in her defense of the president on the subject of the "gender gap" (among other things).

The first question was posed by a woman, and it was regarding the gender gap. Secretary Heckler began by saying she wished that every woman could know Ronald Reagan the way she does; she had the crowd in stitches when she told the story of how she said to the president:

"Do you know, sir, that this is National Secretaries' Week?"

And he replied, "Yes and I'm upset that George Shultz won't wear my corsage!"

She really did a fabulous job, and I believe we should showcase her on this issue as much as possible.[41]

The media also picked up on Margaret's ability to wow a crowd. Reporting on a campaign stop in Maine, Bruce Hertz from the *Somerset Sawdust* wrote:

Heckler was so positive and dynamic that you could almost overlook that she was a Republican. You didn't even mind her laugh. It is hard to report it in print, because the sound intonations aren't reproducible. It was a 'Ha ha' laugh that said that I know and you know that what you said isn't that funny, but I will give this goofy laugh to help us both along.

I've got a small suggestion for Ronald Reagan that would get him about 70 percent of the vote in November. While the Democrats are nambying and pambying about getting a woman on the national ticket, I would drop George Bush and seize Margaret Heckler as the Republican Vice President.[42]

Although Reagan didn't take this advice, it was clear that Margaret had settled into her new role, proving herself as a capable woman in the halls of men. At HHS, Margaret was her best self—advocating for the dignity of human life in profound and moving ways. But her greatest challenge was yet to come, when a deadly disease began to sweep the nation and bring forth controversial questions about the social implications of government-funded care.

AIDS: The Deadly Virus of the Eighties

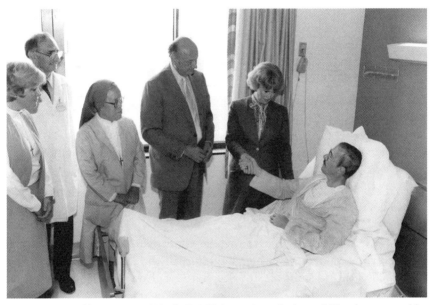

Secretary Heckler, Mayor Ed Koch (D-NY) (center), and others visiting forty-year-old Peter Justice, an AIDS patient, to help calm the hysteria about how the disease was spread, August 18, 1983, at the Cabrini Meical Center in New York City.
Image Bh20240112_090905, Bobbie Hanvie Photographic Archives (MS 2001-039), John J. Burns Library, Boston College.

Three years before Margaret became HHS secretary a mysterious illness began to cause panic in the United States. The illness mainly seemed to attack men, who developed a range of symptoms that resembled pneumonia, Parkinson's disease, or even rare cancers. Puzzled doctors followed the trail and started to piece together that the illness was primarily affecting homosexual men and heterosexual drug users, causing weakened immune systems. Doctors began calling the illness acquired immunodeficiency syndrome, or AIDS. The public responded with hysterical fear, not knowing if the disease was spread through the air, via germs on the hands, through saliva, or something else entirely.

Margaret was warned before she assumed the helm as secretary of HHS that there was a probability of a major health epidemic taking place in the United States on her watch. It did not take long to realize that AIDS could be that epidemic.

In March 1983, during a PBS *Frontline* interview, Margaret recounted how she had sought the advice of Senate Health Committee staffer David Winston. The conversation which defined much of her tenure at HHS followed.

> *Heckler:* David, what are your recommendations for my top priorities as secretary of HHS?
>
> *Winston:* Oh, well, you must begin with AIDS.
>
> *Heckler:* AIDS? What is AIDS?
>
> *Winston:* This is a disease that is killing young people, and the hospital wards in San Francisco are crowded—in fact, bulging.
>
> *Heckler:* Well, I have never been briefed on this. I have never heard of it.

Margaret had gone through the whole confirmation process and AIDS was never mentioned. So, when she returned to HHS headquarters, she dialogued with Assistant Health Secretary Dr. Edward Brant.

> *Heckler:* I just heard of a disease that has never been mentioned to me before: AIDS.
>
> *Brant:* Madame Secretary, you don't want to know.
>
> *Heckler:* I may not want to know, but I must know. I am responsible for this department, for everything that happens here, and this is frightening. I have just heard the worst stories about it.[1]

After learning more about AIDS, Margaret's first step was to visit the White House and discuss the situation with Ed Meese, counselor to the president. She wanted the administration to understand that to fully address the epidemic, she would most likely make requests for additional funds. She believed AIDS "was the most serious priority [she] had."[2]

The initial answer from the Reagan administration after briefing key White House advisors was largely silence. To implement Reaganomics, the country was experiencing a recession to cure skyrocketing interest rates and unemployment. Republicans lost twenty-six seats in the House in the 1982 midterm elections. That being so, the administration was focused on economics. Moreover, AIDS seemed to mostly affect homosexual men and intravenous drug users, which were things that could sully Reagan's clean-cut political persona.

The strategic avoidance from the White House did not stop Secretary Heckler from publicly recognizing the killer disease as the "number one health priority in America" long before other top government officials even knew what its initials stood for.[3] Margaret said, "I made that declaration for two simple reasons: First, the number of reported AIDS cases was doubling every month. Second, AIDS leaves no survivors in its wake, it has been universally fatal. We have rarely, if ever, witnessed a disease as deadly."[4]

From the public's perspective, Margaret's actions were bold and swift, but privately she was reeling with shock about the information. To add to her stress, her marriage with John was now teetering on a precariously thin ledge that was growing thinner by the month. Leaders in positions of power often speak about feeling lonely and in times of crisis, they say, it can feel even lonelier. Margaret, in her brand-new role and without the backing of a spouse, felt lonelier than ever.

Once again, Margaret turned to her good friend and confidant, Gerry Abrams, who made a timely appearance when Margaret most needed a friend.

Margaret and Abrams went to a quiet restaurant. After catching up, Margaret grew serious, asking Abrams, "Have you heard of AIDS?" He nodded. Margaret went on to explain the nuances of the bind she was in. She was clearly stricken with compassion and a sense of moral obligation to help but had little recourse for action. She had a huge budget but couldn't ask for more funds to adequately address the frightening new disease. She confided that she was still waiting to hear back from the White House. As Abrams recalled, "Margaret felt she was alone dealing with AIDS."

In that era, when female executives were rare, she did not have any women peers to turn to who could act as a sounding board, so she confided in Gerry Abrams. In her moment of despair and vulnerability, he was able to talk her off the ledge once again. He reminded her of the superhero-level of good she could accomplish as secretary of HHS. It was the exact push she needed for the ensuing uphill battle. Abrams recalled, "She was a courageous woman and . . . she stood up against the desire of the administration, having to bear this epidemic alone, even with the full weight of AIDS on her shoulders."[5]

Margaret's press secretary at HHS, Roger Woodworth, gave a firsthand insight, which helped her navigate her early response to the AIDS epidemic. Margaret had a planned trip to San Francisco, but it was cancelled. Shortly thereafter Woodworth sent a memo to Margaret lamenting the postponed trip to visit the "frightened, desperate gay community" in San Francisco. Woodworth told Margaret that his "own very strong feelings are that public policy *now* demands that you 'Enter Stage Center.'" Woodworth thought it was time for Margaret "to think seriously about escalating her role as the active, concerned committed-to-cure, out-front spokesperson for the department *and* the administration." He affirmed that the HHS secretary needed to call the signals for the charge to repel the killer.[6]

At a time when being homosexual was not accepted in many circles, Margaret knew Woodworth was gay. Her former press secretary, Linda Bilmes, said, "Margaret was one of the least bigoted people I have ever known. She absolutely couldn't care less about gay or straight or what religion they were. Margaret cared about people suffering and being loyal to her friends. She would fight to the end for her aid of over thirty years."[7]

In contrast to these allies, Margaret received little support from the White House. Once the early medical research began to reveal that the illness was concentrated among homosexual men who averaged sixty different sexual partners a year, President Reagan and other key conservative figures were notably silent. The Moral Majority soon added homosexuality and AIDS as part of their litmus test for conservatives and Republicans. Knowing the Moral Majority considered homosexual behavior a sin, and not wanting to lose their support, Reagan skirted the topic of AIDS.

While social and cultural taboos surrounding AIDS grew, deaths multiplied rapidly and horrifically. In 1982, the number of AIDS cases doubled every five months and on average, patients died fifteen months after diagnosis.[8] By the end of Margaret's first six months at HHS, the AIDS count was 2,259 victims and 917 deaths, with an 80 percent death rate for victims who survived up to two years after first contracting the illness.[9] The average was 165 new cases per month.

The United States was not alone. This was a worldwide problem, as AIDS was identified in seventeen other countries. In 1983, in a status report by one of the leading researchers at the National Institute of Allergy and Infectious Diseases, Dr. Anthony Fauci, said, "Thus far, there is no cure for AIDS and its source remains unknown."[10]

As Americans learned about AIDS, their fear was often reported as a collective hysteria. Although health professionals and scientists knew by 1983 that AIDS was spread through sex, unclean needles, or blood donated by victims, the public treated those with AIDS like lepers. One paper reported that a new social caste system had developed as a result of avoiding leprosy. Dr. Matil Krim referred to children with AIDS as the new lepers. Even among scholars, "AIDS was described as the leprosy of our times."[11]

Bus drivers would not touch transfer tickets—fearful they would catch the disease. People stopped "eating in restaurants, using public facilities and beauty salons."[12] In some hospitals, even nurses were known to leave food on trays outside their patients' doors. AIDS victims died in isolation because friends and family members shunned them. This illustrates how crazy people can get when there's an epidemic they don't understand.

One young man, Steve Forrest, got sick in Dallas and sought refuge in his native West Virginia. "But a small town, he soon learned, is no haven for an AIDS victim. Vandals shot out his car windows. Friends and kin shunned him . . . he could still see the faces of people at the pool that day, their mouths drawn taut and eyes granite-hard and flecked with fear. A woman screamed, 'Why don't they lock him up?'"[13]

Rock Hudson, a Hollywood movie star who Ronald and Nancy Reagan knew personally, was the first A-list celebrity to publicly admit he had contracted AIDS. Hudson was denied boarding for a Los Angeles–bound flight. He needed to charter an Air France flight for $250,000 to return home, where he would die two months later.[14] The social ostracization and indifference was appalling, and it chafed at Margaret's deeply held Catholic compassion for those who were sentenced to suffer and die.

In June 1983, Margaret announced that HHS would provide Social Security disability payments to AIDS victims.[15] *Time* magazine reported: "In order to allay fears that AIDS is widely contagious, Secretary of Health and Human Services Margaret Heckler last week visited the Warren Magnuson Clinical Center in Bethesda, Maryland, where she shook hands with AIDS patient Peter Justice and sat at his bedside, as the media and cameramen leaned in to record it for the evening news. [Secretary Heckler said]: 'What's just as bad as the disease is the fear of the disease. The fear has become irrational.'"[16]

Blood donations nationwide plummeted. The hysteria that dangerously reduced the number of blood donors became another concern for health officials. At the end of June 1983, in one week alone, the Red Cross reported a 16.4 percent reduction in blood donations. Some urban areas reported being 30 percent below their previous year's supply. To lead by example, in early July Margaret donated blood at a local American Red Cross blood donation center. As the television cameras filmed Margaret being stuck by a needle, she said, "I want to assure the American people that donating blood is 100 percent safe."[17]

Margaret directed various HHS departments to begin publishing a biweekly report with the latest research findings. She also established a toll-free hotline that allowed those with questions about AIDS to speak with a public health service worker.

The hotline served the purpose of monitoring the public's reactions to the disease. Assistant secretary for health, Dr. Edward N. Brandt Jr., observed that "many, many callers perceive AIDS as an insidious, invisible and uncontrollable threat to them, personally. They imagine themselves to be potential victims of a fatal disease that is spreading the way measles once did when they were in grade school." He went on to say those fears were not justified.[18]

Margaret concluded that bathhouses were a key component in the spread of AIDS. Bathhouses were among the most popular spaces for homosexual populations to congregate, often operating in the basements of hotels and in more run-down sectors of cities. They offered pools, steam rooms, saunas, gyms, and salon-like settings for men to socialize—but more significantly, bathhouses were one of the places where anonymous sex was most accessible in the gay community. Secretary Heckler and other health professionals believed if they could decrease the number of locations for casual, unsafe sex gatherings, it could prevent, or at least slow, the spread of AIDS.

The problem was acute in New York and San Francisco where there was a large gay population. So Margaret contacted her former congressional colleague Ed Koch (now the mayor of New York City) and Diane Feinstein (mayor of San Francisco) and urged them to close the bathhouses in their cities. Mayor Ed Koch obliged, while Mayor Diane Feinstein initially refused. As a result, New York cases came under control but cases in San Francisco soared. Feinstein's indecision may have been driven by the power of the homosexual vote in the City by the Bay.

Closure of the bathhouses became a social, cultural, and political lightning rod in the early 1980s. For the gay community, it was symbolic of anti-gay prejudice, an infringement on their liberties, and a severely isolating experience at the same moment an unknown terror had taken hold of their lives. Margaret's reaction was to counter this with an aggressive campaign saying, "We've beaten other diseases, and we're determined to beat this one too."[19]

"During the summer of AIDS, Margaret was very unfairly criticized for her role in the Reagan administration's recognition of AIDS, but really it was her finest hour," Linda Bilmes recalled. "I watched her go to hospitals, meet patients, hug and kiss them, and hold their hands, beg the White House for more resources, spend hours with the NIH researchers, praying for the patients and their families and mourning for those dying."[20] Even though her actions were unpopular in the Reagan administration, Margaret was motivated to end the terror that accompanied the disease.

The stumbling block to effectively fight the AIDS epidemic was convincing the White House and congressional Republicans to provide more funding. Between the CDC and NIH, $14 million had been spent on AIDS research in the previous year, and Margaret's department initially requested $12 million more.[21] The more conservative members in Congress reacted unfavorably to this budget increase request. Senator Jesse Helms (R-NC), a staunch conservative, sent her a letter, saying, "You are not helping gays! We don't care what they do in the halls of HHS, Madam Secretary, but we're not funding it."[22]

Ignoring these threats, Margaret continued to encourage the NIH and CDC to speedily search for a cause and cure for the mysterious, deadly illness. Educating the opponents about the need to discover a way to detect the virus in the blood was a key goal for making the national blood bank secure. Without this safeguard in place, any person needing a blood transfusion could be a victim of the deadly disease. Once conservatives understood the full scope of the virus and the harm it could cause to their wives or children, funding followed.

From 1980 to 1984, $200 million was spent on AIDS research and treatment. For fiscal year 1984–1985 Margaret sought another $126 million for AIDS research and treatment. For those who balked at the amount, Margaret asked, "How much is enough? If the $331 million we have already allocated were doubled or even tripled, would the time it takes to solve the AIDS devastation be reduced proportionally?"[23] This was not a request to fund new roads—this was an urgent request for funding to save human lives, American lives.

On April 23, 1984, Margaret called a press conference to announce a breakthrough on AIDS. National Cancer Institute scientist Dr. Robert Gallo claimed he had found the virus that causes AIDS. But this news created an international imbroglio, as Gallo had previously agreed to jointly present the breakthrough with Dr. Luc Montagnier from the Pasteur Institute, as French scientists had found the virus a year earlier.[24]

Sorting out this scientific snub took two years and the involvement of French president Jacque Chiraq and President Reagan to agree that both Montagnier and Gallo should share credit for discovering the human immunodeficiency virus (HIV). Despite this Franco-American finesse for scientific credit, when the Nobel Prize for Medicine was awarded in 2008 for the discovery of HIV, Dr. Gallo was not mentioned.[25]

Nevertheless, the discovery of the virus led to the creation of a blood test to discover AIDS, which was approved by the US Food and Drug Administration. This blood test paved the way for the development of treatments. Abbott provided over six hundred thousand test kits initially, producing two million tests per month. Although Secretary Heckler's ambitious target of two years fell short, progress was made in AIDS treatment via antiretroviral therapy (ART). The life expectancy of those diagnosed with HIV went from fifteen months upon diagnosis in the early 1980s to almost the same lifespan as the general population today.

Having an HIV blood test ensured the country's blood supply was once again safe for donations and transfusions. To date, no HIV vaccine has been developed. However, since the earliest days of the AIDS epidemic, Margaret's support for development of extensive procedures and infrastructure for HIV vaccine research have helped to make major gains for the scientific community and those suffering from the disease.

In a bit of eerie foreshadowing, a *Time* magazine article about the quest to find the source of AIDS, CDC director Dr. William Foege shared that what he worried about most was the return of a familiar flu virus: "I fully anticipate that possibly in our lifetime we will see another flu strain that is as deadly as 1918. We have not figured out good ways to counter that."[26] Dr. Foege was not wrong. Because of the work done through NIH, the National Cancer Center, and the CDC, and thanks to the determination of research, the way was paved for vaccine research and development for COVID-19.

In early 2020, the *Washington Post* lauded Margaret Heckler's visionary leadership at HHS. Her very public, all hands-on approach to HIV established a framework for combating COVID-19. In the thirty-six years between HIV and COVID, AIDS research helped scientists accumulate experience and information about the immune system and vaccine technologies. Laboratories and test sites could easily and rapidly be repurposed for a pandemic such as COVID-19.[27]

Ed Meese would later say that perhaps Margaret's "best-known work was making AIDS the number one public health priority."[28] Ron Kaufman, former national political director of the Republican National Committee, said, "Margaret Heckler was way out in front of everyone . . . as a warrior pushing for a solution for the AIDS problem. It was her legacy. She was courageous."[29]

Many of those surrounding Heckler wanted to pretend the deadly illness didn't exist. It was not until 1985 that Reagan first used the word "AIDS" in public. Eventually, he gave a nod to Margaret, acknowledging that AIDS was a "top priority" for the administration, and he ensured that necessary funding was provided to the NIH and CDC despite budget cuts.[30]

As Margaret would later say, "It was the encounter with David Winston which sent the message to me to work on this problem [AIDS]. I have always considered that a divine encounter. And this divine intervention, in my view, is what made the difference in terms of accelerating the AIDS answer, although we're still seeking the real cure."[31]

In later years, Margaret was honored by the American Medical Association as their person of the year for her early and prominent response to this deadly disease against all odds.

· 18 ·

Hospice: Dying with Dignity

At a cabinet meeting. From left to right: Secretary of Education William Bennett, Secretary of HHS Margaret Heckler, Secretary of Energy Donald Hodel, President Ronald Reagan, Secretary of State George Schultz, Secretary of Defense Caspar Weinberger, Attorney General William French Smith, Secretary of Transportation Elizabeth Dole and in the foreground Director of the Office of Management and Budget David Stockman. *White House Photographer.*

$\mathcal{I}$n the mid-1970s, Margaret was back in her congressional district in Massachusetts, meeting with her assistant, Eddie Cabrall, at a restaurant. During their meal, Eddie shared shocking news: He had cancer. Before Margaret could open her mouth to ask about his prognosis, they noticed a woman at a nearby table break into tears. It turned out the woman's husband had been diagnosed with terminal cancer and she had just overheard Eddie telling Margaret about his diagnosis.

As Eddie stepped over to comfort the woman, a waitress chimed in, "Dogs are treated better than our government treats the dying."

This sardonic comment personalized the pain for Margaret. At the time, hospice—end-of-life care for the terminally ill—was a relatively new concept in the United States. In fact, the first hospice in the country, Connecticut Hospice, had opened in Branford, Connecticut, in 1974.[1] And then, in the same year, Senators Frank Church (D-ID) and Frank E. Moss (D-UT) introduced the first hospice legislation in Congress, but it wasn't enacted.[2]

Congresswoman Heckler was keenly interested in the possibility of a federalized hospice program. Unfortunately, the legislation didn't pass. When she became HHS secretary, Margaret quickly realized she now had the authority and a direct path to guarantee federalized care for those who lay dying.

In Western civilization, end-of-life care can be traced back to biblical times. In the Middle Ages, Roman Catholics provided hospitality for the sick, wounded, and dying. These missions also provided housing and care to pilgrims making arduous long journeys to holy sites. Sadly, clinics began disappearing when religious institutions dispersed.

The 1800s had a resurgence of institutionalized care for the dying. Jeanne Garnier coined the term *hospice* as a resting place for travelers or pilgrims, conveying that the facility functioned somewhere in between a hospital and a home. Garnier opened her hospice in 1842 as a place of comfort for those living out their last days.

In 1879, the Irish Sisters of Charity established a hospice in Ireland, then expanded their work to England.[2] In 1967, British physician Dame Cicely Saunders opened St. Christopher's Hospice (London), which was the first modern end-of-life care center. Word of St. Christopher's Center spread and Dr. Florence Wald, dean of the Yale School of Nursing, traveled to London to observe Dr. Saunders's work. Afterward, Dr. Wald enlisted the help of two pediatricians and a chaplain to open the Connecticut Hospice in Branford.

A year before Margaret joined HHS, Congress passed the Tax Equity and Fiscal Responsibility Act of 1982. Senator Bob Dole (R-KS) was instrumental in establishing the Medicare hospice benefit that took effect in December 1983. However, the costs for the benefit were high. Concerned about containing the costs associated with the program, Congress slated the benefit to end in 1986. To put a cap on annual per-patient expenses, they also instituted a daily reimbursement system for the Medicare hospice benefit.[3] It was a Band-Aid program with a scheduled expiration date, and Margaret felt the government could do much more. The hospice program passed by Congress had not been put into effect by the Reagan administration.

Unfortunately, Margaret quickly learned that she was limited by two things: the Reagan administration's lack of support for extending the hospice benefit and the HHS budget. HHS had an annual budget of $315 billion, or 34 percent of the entire federal budget. Medicare was a government program paid for by HHS. Since Reagan was firm in his "hellbent-for-leather determination to hold down domestic spending,"[4] the administration outright rejected Margaret's initial proposal to extend a hospice benefit as a Medicare entitlement program. As reported in 1984, "Medicare was the most expensive government health program [in 1983]. It cost $57.4 billion, with $40.4 billion going for hospital care."[5]

The Reagan administration's fear that hospice would significantly drive up the cost to Medicare was misguided. As Margaret and her team determined, hospice care would actually be "less expensive than the hospital care which Medicare would cover in many of the same circumstances."[6]

After an HHS hearing. From left to right: Senator Bob Dole (R-KS), Margaret's daughter Alison Heckler, Senator Daniel Patrick Moynihan (D-NY), Secretary Margaret Heckler, Senator Ted Kennedy (D-MA), and Margaret's daughter Belinda Heckler.
Public domain.

While Margaret scrambled for ways to make hospice more palatable to the administration, her favored HHS policy expert, Jackie White, worked on a new payment system for Medicare. Under the prior Medicare system, the federal government reimbursed hospitals for extended-stay Medicare patients, so it was in a hospital's interest to retain a terminally ill patient for weeks or months until they died, then charge the government for the expense. This pay structure was a major drain on HHS's Medicare funds.

Jackie White was responsible for creating a new system called the Diagnostic Related Group (DRG). Under this system, hospitals would charge a flat rate for each medical procedure, so HHS knew exactly how much they would be billed, saving an exorbitant amount of money. Once the procedure was done with an agreed-upon amount of time to recover, it was time for the patient to leave—or any additional hospital time was on the patient's dime.

Hospitals were suddenly incentivized to provide hyperefficient services—often not a virtue in health care. If a patient didn't have the necessary funds to remain in the hospital to receive the full medical treatment they required, they were discharged—quicker and sicker. Jackie White later recounted her own personal experience: "When I had my first child, they kept me in the hospital for a whole week. By the time I had my last child, you delivered the baby in the morning, and they were discharging you by the end of the day."[7]

Introduced in 1984, the Reagan administration's health-care reform using the DRG model was reported as a major success in controlling Medicare spending. The new DRG model saved the federal government $7 billion after only two years.[8]

When Margaret learned how the new DRG payment structure would affect those who were terminally ill, she got angry. The new system would incentivize hospitals to send patients home to die with no medical support or oversight. With all of this in mind, Margaret felt a new urgency to establish the federal hospice program that had become law but had not been put into effect by the Reagan administration.

There were so many unaddressed questions. If the patient was sent home, how would they access pain medication and nursing assistance for basic medical care? How could they afford at-home care? Some might have a family member who could take on the role, but caretaking of the dying is often a full-time job and around-the-clock care from a family member was certainly not guaranteed. While few people wanted to spend their final days in a hospital, the thought of people spending their last weeks or months in immense pain at home with little to no care filled Margaret with sickening horror.

One morning when Jackie White arrived at work—eight months pregnant, having dropped her children off at day care, arms filled with papers and reports—a security guard stopped her as she was walking to her office. "Secretary Heckler is in the basement [parking garage]," the guard said. "She's looking for you."[9]

White found Margaret, upset, in the driver's seat of her car. She was on her way to the National Institutes of Health (NIH) and would be there all day. Margaret rolled down the window and asked her to get in the car, saying, "I need to talk to you."

They had a forty-five-minute drive to NIH headquarters. Margaret explained, "We cannot have terminally ill patients sent home from the hospital early, leaving them to die at home. We have to display some kind of compassion."[10]

Margaret realized that the Reagan administration implemented the new system to cut costs and send the terminally ill home to die. The federal government would save millions of dollars in the hospital costs of Medicare patients.

Before she went to her meeting, she turned around and implored Jackie, "I want you to fix this. Remember, death with dignity!"[11]

White was flummoxed, her head spinning just thinking about how she was going to move forward. She needed time to sort through the complex knot of issues: current Medicare programs, the budget-slashing administration, a new, but broken, medical payment structure—and how to create an industry for the dying that had never before existed in the United States.

White needed to notify the Office of Management and Budget (OMB) staff about Secretary Heckler's request for additional funding for an entirely new program. Margaret needed approval from OMB to provide funding for programs outside the scope of what was allocated to her department.

OMB director David Stockman and other officials were not receptive. Every time White visited the OMB offices, she would report back to Margaret about the frustrating conversations that went nowhere. Margaret would respond, "Go back over there. This is a complicated endeavor. You are creating something from scratch. Imagine that there was no nursing home industry. We're in the same situation here." Officials at OMB scoffed at this request, which only seemed clear to Secretary Heckler and

Jackie White. There were only a few hospice services available in the United States, and none received any form of federal funding.

The administration and Margaret were in a gridlock. White later described Margaret as a Joe Palooka punching bag, "She'd get hit and she'd bounce back."[12]

Slowly, Margaret began to wear her opponents down. OBM became weary of the two women from HSS and finally told them that they could write a proposal. As White said, "It was the guys trying to shut her up." But it was soon clear that OBM didn't intend to grow a new industry or consider their proposal seriously, especially since there were no other government leaders who wanted the new program. Margaret's chief of staff George Siguler was told, "This idea of offering hospice as a government program is ridiculous," as it was a "budget buster."[13]

Adding to the complexity, Margaret did not just want White to craft a new industry, she wanted her to draft a proposal that would completely alter the new medical industry's payment system. A patch job to the faulty DRG system would only set hospice up for failure a few years down the line. With this in mind, the two women devised six different payment streams for hospice. The benefit would be restricted to only those who had been determined by a doctor to have six months or less to live and the treatment would have to cost less than in-hospital care, seeking only to increase comfort and manage pain.

"What I was describing to OMB was a new benefit, but it would add to the cost of Medicare," said White. It's taking up half the federal budget, they responded. As White continued drafting the full proposal for OMB, Margaret advised her to research different Catholic models, to see if they employed any unique cost-saving measures. According to White, the experience felt like "building the airplane as she was flying it."[14]

With a proposal drafted and given preliminary approval, White called the Executive Office of the President and met with the chief actuary. White echoed Margaret's long held sentiment that the terminally ill at home were treated unjustly, "Even a dog wouldn't be treated this way." She continued that "hospice is the answer, but it is going to *ring that cash register.*"[15]

The staff at the Executive Office of the President were confident the proposal would never be approved. David Stockman, David Kleinberg, deputy associate director and head of Health and Income Maintenance, as well other top OMB staff members, said they "basically hated the whole thing."[16]

White wrote numerous drafts until finally, OMB agreed to put the proposal out for public comment as a tactic to temporarily quiet the ladies' persistence. The two women waited for input while the same questions circled between them: "Is this going to work? Is it good enough? Does it need to be changed?"

The proposed hospice coverage wound up receiving overwhelming praise from the public, but President Reagan still withheld support. OBM, strategizing how they might be able to stop Heckler and White's endless barrage, decided to move forward with the proposal but with a key revision: cutting the payments for caregivers in half. Secretary Heckler was hysterical. The budget team had butchered her proposal. Rather than give her a flat-out "no," they set the payments so low that no industry could develop. Margaret called White, who by that time was on maternity leave and had two more weeks left at home. With metaphors of child-rearing on her mind, White later recalled that OBM's final rule "was like killing something in the crib."[17]

George Siguler told Margaret that OBM's final rule was the best she was going to get. George encouraged her, saying "it was enough money" and "it was going to work."[18] Reluctantly, Margaret accepted the change.

As a former congresswoman, Margaret's mind started to turn with new tactics. Since HHS and the president wouldn't budge on giving more money, she devised another way to get the funding she needed for a federally backed hospice program.

The secretary had a plan: It was time to "bring in the nuns." Margaret went to Saint Agnes and Saint Thomas Moore, two parishes in Arlington, Virginia, where she met with the local nuns. Given the long history of Catholic-sponsored end-of-life care, the nuns were thrilled about Margaret's mission to add hospice as a Medicare benefit. Margaret needed help lobbying Congress for the terminally ill, and the nuns gladly took on the responsibility. Armed with plenty of experience from maneuvering and strategizing in Congress, Margaret's aim was to whip up a House and Senate majority to pass a law that would allow hospice to operate as a *fully funded* Medicare program. At the same time, the nuns were prepared to go to the Capitol and do whatever it took to secure full funding for end-of-life care.

Dressed in habits, the nun's first stop was to see Speaker of the House Tip O'Neill. After O'Neill's assistant greeted the nuns, she walked into his office, announcing, "I have half a dozen nuns who want to see you."

"What do they want?" O'Neill asked.

"They want to speak with you."

Taking seats in the Speaker's office, the nuns told him they were there on behalf of Secretary Heckler, who was very upset. "So you're ambassadors for Margaret Heckler?" O'Neill said with a laugh. "That's my girl!"[19]

Tip O'Neill was an easy sell as a fellow Irish Catholic and close friend of Margaret's. With the Speaker's support, there was a good chance the rest of Congress would fall into line. But just to be sure, the nuns didn't leave the Capitol until they had met with all significant members of Congress to make their plea. The nuns created a stir as they walked through the halls of Congress, lobbying members who were essential to the bill's passage.

Americans would soon not have to choose between being sent home to die in pain or to die buried in debt. The bill passed. The legislation included Secretary Heckler's initial proposed rate and made those payment rates law.[20] Congress came up with six payment schemes to ensure Medicare recipients would receive hospice benefits, and those benefits remain the same today. According to Jackie White, "The legislation built an entire industry; now, hospice is everywhere."[21]

The press gave glowing reports for Secretary Heckler's commitment to care for the most vulnerable in society. According to one report, "An estimated 31,000 people with a life expectancy of six months or less are expected to take advantage of the [hospice] program during the first year. Thanks to Mrs. Heckler and the more sensible regulations she personally pushed through the White House, those patients will be entitled to up to $6,400 in benefits, a sum which should assure them of quality hospice care, and which is more in line with Congress' original recommendation. Mrs. Heckler, keep on rising."[22]

Although it was costly to the government, the program made a huge difference in the lives of average Americans. Six months into the program, when Jackie White visited the former associate director of OMB, David Kleinberg, who was suffering from cancer, she said, "David, you were right—it *was* a budget buster. But I don't care, and I know you don't care either, because here you are using the hospice benefit for yourself right now!"

Today, hospice is available everywhere in the country. Anyone who is a Medicare-eligible beneficiary can enroll in the program. Improvements have been made, including better funding and reimbursement rates, but for over four decades, hospice has worked[23] miracles for the dying and their families. Currently, more than four thousand hospice providers are available in the United States, and over 1.5 million Americans receive hospice services annually.

Margaret was driven by her faith. Her compassionate heart refused to settle for anything less than the most humane and dignified government policies. As her daughter, Alison Heckler, commented, "It was God using her in a mighty way! She was the first to suggest the use of chaplains in hospice care. She said that policymaking was her favorite political work, and she loved putting a chaplain to serve in the hospice program."[24]

Margaret's tireless work on behalf of AIDS, minority health, and hospice demonstrated her compassion and took her to the apex of her political career. Nevertheless, she would soon find herself in the midst of circumstances that threatened her tenure at HHS.

• 19 •

Parties, Scandal, and Nancy

With President Ronald Reagan and Jack Pierce, treasurer of Boeing, at a White House dinner. *White House Photographer.*

After a year at the helm of HHS, Margaret Heckler had become one of the most powerful women in America.[1] She was now the nation's health secretary. People were recognizing her in this challenging role, and she was gaining notoriety. In November 1983, to publicize National Diabetes Month, Olympic gold medalist Bruce Jenner (now known as Caitlyn Jenner) was invited to the White House. Margaret was by President Reagan's side in the Oval Office for the proclamation signing ceremony. When the "King of Pop" Michael Jackson was honored on the White House lawn in April 1984 for allowing his song "Beat It" to be used in a Mothers Against Drunk Driving campaign, Margaret was there.

Danny Thomas wrote a note to Margaret thanking her for her continued support of St. Jude Children's Research Hospital. The editor in chief of *Cosmopolitan*, Helen Gurley Brown, was enchanted with Margaret and wrote her to say, "I'm sure very few people actually realize the budget that you oversee—mind-boggling doesn't begin to describe it! I loved my luncheon—one of the nicest I have ever had. I am now a total nutcase fan!"

According to former White House chief of staff Andy Card, "When Margaret Heckler walked into the room for cabinet meetings President Reagan would announce to everyone, 'Here she is!' No one else received that kind of shout out."[2]

The Reagan administration had her front and center, giving speeches around the country. In August 1984, she was a keynote speaker in Dallas at the Republican National Convention, promoting President Reagan for his reelection campaign. In November 1984, Reagan won in a landslide, 49 states en route to amassing 525 electoral votes, compared to Mondale's 13—one of the biggest landslides in US election history.

A month after President Reagan won his reelection, he wrote a tongue-in-cheek tribute to Margaret:

> I am happy to send greetings to the Circus Saints & Sinners Club to pay tribute to Health and Human Services Secretary Margaret M. Heckler as this year's 'Fall Gal.' As head of our largest federal department, Margaret Heckler plays an invaluable role at cabinet meetings—she makes the coffee. Without her, I'd sleep through more of those meetings. And yet, some people don't appreciate Secretary Heckler. A few complain that she's not conservative enough. This really puzzles her. For years, she was the most conservative Representative from the People's Republic of Massachusetts.

Reagan ended the tribute on a sincere note: "If I may be serious for a moment, I must say that there is no more able, no more dedicated, no more public-spirited person in government than Margaret M. Heckler. Margaret, I'm proud to have you on my team."[3]

When President Reagan was out of town, Margaret was often gifted the use of the presidential box at the Kennedy Center for the Performing Arts.

Despite the mutual appreciation and respect between the president and the HHS secretary, it did not come without some tension. The First Lady was reluctant to share the spotlight with any other woman in the administration. Nancy could not tolerate the jocular exchanges between

Margaret and her husband. Margaret recalled, at social events, "When President Reagan came over to me, Nancy would say, 'Come on Ronnie,' and would start pulling on his coat, trying to keep him on schedule, all while he was trying to tell me another Irish joke."[4] If Margaret showed up to events wearing red—Nancy's signature color—it irritated the First Lady to no end.[5] From the moment Margaret was sworn into office, she encouraged President Reagan to visit Ireland. When President Reagan invited Margaret to join him on the trip to Ireland in the summer of 1984, "Nancy had a total fit."[6] Margaret declined his offer.

As the second term began, Nancy Reagan accumulated an unusual amount of authority as a First Lady. Secretary of labor Raymond Donovan was forced to resign because of an indictment case brought against him. It was an open secret in the White House that the First Lady wanted Donovan out. It was also common knowledge that she held similar sentiments toward CIA director William Casey and HHS secretary Margaret Heckler.

The First Lady's biggest concern was the public perception of the president and his administration. The *New York Times* described her

President Ronald Reagan's 1985 cabinet. *White House Photographer.*

sphere of influence as "a role that combines what her friends call a powerful protective streak for her husband and her own input in the day-to-day workings of the administration."[7] At times, Reagan pushed back against his wife—as was the case with her desire to swap out the CIA director and the HHS secretary. Still, the First Lady exercised a surprisingly high degree of power. In the same *New York Times* story, one Washington insider said, "She's the president's best friend, his closest confidante and his most trusted adviser." Michael Deaver added, "If Ronald Reagan owned a shoe store, Nancy would be pushing shoes. Nobody was under the illusion that she was merely an accessory to Ronald Reagan's presidency—she carved out a job for herself in the White House."[8]

Nancy Reagan's antipathy toward Margaret put her in a precarious position. As Margaret's life began to unravel personally and professionally this added fuel to the First Lady's fire.

For decades, while Margaret's star rose, John Heckler was rising too, but not without significant strains on the marriage. John chose to reside at the Wellesley house in Massachusetts for most of their married life. Margaret and the children lived in Virginia, and he visited on weekends. Hiding his infidelities strained family relationships and created a lack of trust. "I dedicated my life to her" he said bitterly. "She has the highest position of any woman in the land." While he had supported her early political aspirations, those in the Heckler social network believed a large part of John's reason for seeking a divorce was his pride. In a devastating *Washington Post* news item, the Hecklers' impending divorce was made public."[9]

Mark B. Sandground, who referred to himself as the "prince of darkness," was John Heckler's lawyer. Sandground was known for his underhanded tactics. John, Margaret's estranged husband, did not hold back. "I'm no nice guy," he said in an interview.[10] Sandground framed the case to demonstrate that Margaret had deserted her husband.

Over thirty years of marriage, Margaret had never wavered from her Catholic faith and her marriage vows of "for better or worse." She had tried to balance her career and her children alongside John.[11] Margaret told the *Washington Post*, "This is a very difficult time and a time of great sadness for me and my family. I hope that everyone will understand that it is also a personal time. Because of these factors and especially in consideration of my children, I intend no further public comment, but I will carry on my public obligations."[12] Margaret sought to schedule a hearing to keep the divorce proceedings closed to the public, while her attorney made sure the court forbade those familiar with the case from discussing it publicly.[13]

Sadly, the damage was already done. Divorce was still not common and was often considered taboo. Margaret's staff observed how she handled her embarrassment about her divorce while still managing to run HHS. One staff member said, "A lesser person would have just collapsed. She was very strong."[14] Margaret would later say that their divorce was her greatest failure.

Heartbreak was only one part of Margaret's concern. She also worried about how the Reagans would react to the bad press. The tabloids printed the story for months. Ronald Reagan was divorced from actress Jane Wyman in 1949. Ronald Reagan was the first divorced US president. Still, Margaret felt uneasy about discussing her personal situation with the president. When they finally spoke of it, she apologized to him, expressing her concern that her divorce might reflect badly on him or his administration. "Margaret," Reagan responded. "Don't be silly. I'm divorced. You've done a great job. You've raised three wonderful children. Your position is not threatened because of this."[15] The First Lady was another story. She viewed Margaret's divorce as another opportunity to discuss her removal from office.

When the divorce went to trial in early 1985, there was no public testimony. The case was finalized on February 14, 1985. The date was ironic, because the marriage to her first love ended on Valentine's Day. Margaret shared with the press that the president had remained "very supportive."[16]

Yet the storm was not over. Margaret was locked in a battle with Don Regan, who had served as secretary of the treasury from 1981 to early 1985. Regan began feuding with Margaret when he stepped into his new role as President Reagan's chief of staff. Most of the tension came down to differences in personality and governing style. Regan, a former Merrill Lynch CEO, was a number cruncher, while Margaret was perceived as a budget buster. During a cabinet meeting, director of the Office of Management and Budget (OMB) David Stockman, and Chief of Staff Regan wanted to cut a series of programs across the board, Margaret objected, saying, "Well I don't think cutting a program that benefits unwed mothers would look very good for the president."

When Don Regan joined the White House staff in February 1985, Margaret realized that he was starting to clean house, and she now had to watch her back. Former chief of staff Jim Baker, who swapped roles with

Regan, as the secretary of the treasury, confided, "When I left, I couldn't protect Margaret anymore."[17]

Don Regan was trying to cut spending and at the same time increase compassion. As reported in the *Washington Post*, "In practice, this meant the White House almost constantly said no to Heckler's expansion ideas and [they] were constantly in disagreement over which populations to show compassion, such as the HIV/AIDS victims."[18] As Chief of Staff Regan placed stumbling blocks in her path, Margaret was continually challenged.

∾⊱⊰∾

Despite these power plays, Heckler still played a prominent role in the Reagan administration. Prior to Don Regan stepping in as chief of staff, Margaret Heckler was chosen as the first woman ever selected to be the "designated survivor" on January 20, 1985. The function of the designated survivor, who is chosen by the president, is to maintain continuity in the presidency if the president dies and others in the line of succession also die. An article in the *Washington Times* noted, "Health Secretary Margaret Heckler had to pass up attendance at President Reagan's private oath-taking at the White House yesterday under the tradition of keeping one cabinet official away for security reasons."

In spite of the rumors that were circulating about her performance, Margaret Heckler still had initiatives to complete that were near to her heart. As a woman, Margaret had a particular interest in women's health, especially breast cancer. Until the 1980s, little research had been done on breast cancer—and ironically, what research had been done was conducted only on men. Even when rats were used to study the effects of drugs, female rats were never used. In 1985, one of every eleven American women developed breast cancer, and the death toll was thirty-eight thousand women a year.

At a conference of women's groups at the National Institutes of Health, Margaret boldly called out that women were dying "unnecessarily because a cancer which could have been recognized and treated early went undetected out of fear or ignorance."[19] She said that the responsibility of the women's groups was to "conquer that fear, to abolish that ignorance."

Of the over one hundred programs under the HHS umbrella, Margaret was able to make several significant contributions to topics ranging from child support to Alzheimer's disease to homelessness. The issue of child support, which fell under the Administration for Children and Families, became a particular focus for Margaret, a continuation of the work she sought to do when she was in Congress. She brokered a rare display of bipartisan camaraderie between the Reagan administration and Congresswomen Barbara Kennelly (D-CT), a chief sponsor of the legislation, to ensure that noncustodial parents, mostly fathers, paid their agreed-upon child support. At a time when 8.4 million American women were single mothers, only half received the child support due for their children—totaling $4 billion a year of unpaid support owed to children.[20] Convincing President Reagan to support the legislation would secure financial support for "two million mothers and many more children."[21]

In a televised meeting, President Reagan signed the Child Support Bill, saying, "It is an unfortunate fact of our times that one in four American children lives in single-parent homes, and [experiences] needless deprivation and hardship due to lack of support by their absent parent. The failure of some parents to support their children is a blemish on America."[22] Under the new law, the federal government now garnishes the ex-husband's pay, making it much more difficult for any employed father to avoid paying owed support.

Alzheimer's was another area of concern and a seldom-discussed disease in the United States at the time Margaret was HHS secretary. The illness had been discovered in 1906 but was then largely ignored by the scientific community. Despite two million Americans being afflicted with Alzheimer's disease in 1984, little was known about its origins.[23] Until 1980, fear of the unknown stifled conversation and isolated patients and their caretakers—even within hospitals. Valerie Megerian, who was the caretaker for her husband, an Alzheimer's patient, shared with the media that "judgmental" doctors, who knew little about the disease and had even less compassion, treated her (the wife) as if something was also wrong with *her*.[24] It was inexcusable to Margaret that the medical community neglected the disease, its victims, and caretakers. Mary Anne Thadeu, former HHS assistant, said Margaret had become invested in Alzheimer's research when a woman she knew died from the disease. In order to increase public awareness, when *Good Housekeeping* and *Glamour* asked Margaret for an interview, she agreed under the condition that they run an article about Alzheimer's.[25] In hopes of developing better policies and programs for aging Americans, Margaret set up a task force of nine medical professionals to conduct research on the disease.[26] By 1984, the federal government was projected to spend $37.1 million on Alzheimer's research, with plans to increase the figure to $38.5 million in 1985.[27]

Homelessness was yet another area covered in the department of HHS. In September 1984, Margaret met with Mitch Snyder, the most recognizable activist in DC for homelessness, who went on a hunger strike to advocate for renovations of an eight-hundred-bed shelter to house the homeless population in DC. Fifty-one days later, sixty-two pounds lighter, and thanks in part to Margaret's negotiations with President Reagan, Snyder broke his hunger strike after the administration finally agreed to fund the shelter.[28] Margaret addressed a group of homeless people saying, "You have as much right to dignity and respect as anyone in this society."[29] At many points during her HSS tenure, it seemed as if the Reagan administration was doing everything in its power to reduce government spending, while Margaret was doing everything in *her* power to meet the basic health needs of Americans and expand research that would lead to better care. Margaret's HHS actions often began with stories of individual lives that scaled up to the big picture: hundreds of thousands of Americans experiencing similar difficult conditions.

In the words of Mel Lukens, Margaret's head of advance, "Margaret was a top-down visionary. She was operating at thirty thousand feet, and she needed us to bring it in for a landing. 'Here are my ideas,' she would say to her staff, now you assemble the ingredients and bake the cake. She knew what the problem was, she knew what the solution was, but she wanted us to work on the stuff in the middle."[30] This skill set resulted in some of Margaret's greatest achievements as secretary of HHS: greater focus on minority health, increased HIV/AIDS research, creation of a federally funded hospice program, and more attention given to women's health, child services, Alzheimer's disease, breast cancer research, and much more.

Her visionary approach was also the source of one of her greatest weaknesses: It fed the perception of many, including Don Regan and Nancy Reagan, that Margaret was too progressive. These powerful individuals were fully prepared to exploit this weakness.

By mid-1985, Margaret's third year at HHS, a storm was brewing. In his book, *For the Record*, Don Regan wrote, "[Margaret] was in the midst of a divorce action, which increased Mrs. Reagan's uneasiness. 'We've got to get rid of her,' the First Lady told me. 'You know Ronnie will never fire her.'"[31] Soon after, George Siguler, Margaret's chief of staff, recalled White House secretary to the cabinet, Craig Fuller saying to him, "George, the fat lady's singing. It's time for Margaret Heckler to move on."[32]

Margaret held on until September 1985. By then, the media was in a full-out frenzy over whether she was going to be asked to step down. Rumors leaked that Margaret would be asked to leave HHS but would receive an ambassadorial position. Some reports said the administration was "dissatisfied" with her performance, while others claimed President Reagan was openly supportive of her work.[33] On September 27, an article published through the *Associated Press* featured the headline "Heckler Won't Be 'Hustled Out,' Hatch Promised." Senator Orrin Hatch (R-UT), one of Margaret's "strongest defenders on Capitol Hill" was "outraged at the unattributed attacks on her."[34] His vocal support of Margaret had led Don Regan to publicly promise Hatch that she wouldn't be pushed out of her position.

On September 30 in the White House Press Room, a reporter recorded the following exchange with President Reagan:

Q: Mr. President, will you fire Margaret Heckler today or soon?

Reagan: There's never been any thought in my mind of firing Margaret Heckler. I don't know where these stories have come from. They are not true.

Q: You're perfectly satisfied with her performance, then?

Reagan: Yes.[35]

Then, after Reagan vehemently denied all suggestions that the White House planned to fire her, the administration released the news that Margaret was being removed from HHS. News of her departure dominated the headlines for several days. The *Washington Post* placed the blame on Don Regan.[36] Other White House officials shared with the press that it was common knowledge Margaret had been on Regan's "axe list."

The press was under no delusions about the dynamics at play. Laying it out for the public, the *Los Angeles Times* described how "conservatives have never liked Heckler" and saying that she was appointed in 1983 to help with Reagan's reelection under the impression she would serve as a "figurehead." To the administration's disappointment, however, Margaret turned out to be a "scrapper," wanting to be a "cabinet officer, not a token," so she "battled with the White House over an effective safety net for the poor and other disadvantaged people." Ultimately, it was her "independence" that led to her downfall.[37]

Margaret was vocal that she wanted to remain at HHS and that the accusations that she was too progressive and an incompetent leader were misplaced. "I have faithfully carried out the president's portfolio," she said. "If we had great difference of opinion over major issues or enormous prior confrontations it would be understandable, but none of these [things] occurred."[38] Even Reagan tried to set the tone that the gossip was unjust and that "she executed the policies that I wanted for the agency."[39]

The media reported that the power struggle took on an adversarial flavor with Don Regan's and Margaret's personality differences and their misalignment over which policies to prioritize. In the end, Margaret wouldn't be hustled out. She told Don Regan, "I'll resign when President Reagan tells me to resign."[40]

After it was announced she was leaving HSS, the president attempted to quiet the negative reports—in a press conference, he said he was "promoting" Heckler to another role in his administration, US ambassador to Ireland. However, the press felt that calling it a promotion was an "embarrassing performance."[41] No one was convinced the motives were benign, least of all Margaret, who responded with the words, "That's a lovely position—for someone else."[42]

After meeting with President Reagan for nearly an hour, Margaret finally caved. The headlines read, "Heckler Resists Shift to Dublin" and "Reagan's Reluctant Ambassador." But in Ireland, especially among Irish women, it was predicted that the appointment would be received "quite well."[43]

With Margaret's departure, Transportation Secretary Elizabeth Dole suddenly became the only woman left in Reagan's cabinet. Pithily, the *Los Angeles Times* noted, "The Administration deserves some credit for its record of appointing women to high government posts. It has not done so well in keeping them, particularly those who exercise any sort of independence."[44] The *Chicago Tribune* was even more searing. On October 10, 1985, Ellen Goodman published a piece titled "Margaret Heckler's Out and Chauvinism Is In."[45] Particularly spicy lines included, "The way things are going, she might easily have been sent for coffee" and "Donald Regan has gone back to the white male talent agency for his central casting." The article quoted Margaret saying, "There's far more tolerance of incompetent males." Goodman agreed and concluded by writing, "It's fair to observe that Heckler was judged by that old double standard: Any woman less than twice as good wasn't good enough."[46]

While she ascended to heights of political prominence as a woman and did as much as she could to ensure the laws and health priorities of

With Senator Ted Kennedy at her Senate confirmation hearing for her ambassador to Ireland post. *Private collection.*

the federal government protected women, minorities, and other vulnerable Americans, the reality was that Margaret's dismissal at HHS revealed how much harder it was for women to stay in the political game without facing consequences if they acted too much outside the norms or expectations of the men around them.

The Senate unanimously approved Margaret's appointment as ambassador to Ireland and on December 19, 1985, Supreme Court Justice Sandra Day O'Connor swore her into her new position. Among others, Margaret's longtime friend Vice President George Bush attended the ceremony. President Reagan stood alongside Margaret, demonstrating his support.[47] An article titled "Peggy and Ronnie . . . Heckler and the Reagan Connection," noted, "During all of this time, Heckler was very much part of the Reagan inner sanctum and a special favorite of the president, who always called her 'Peggy.'"[48]

Margaret was not able to remain upset about leaving HHS for long. "I will go to Ireland in good cheer—hoping that I will be able to unravel some of the ancient threads of bitterness and hate," she said. "I'm anxious to represent my country in the country of my ancestors."[49] The time for change had arrived. Margaret was ready for the land laced in green.

An Irish Homecoming

In the back of her car reading Irish newspapers.
Kathy Borchers Photojournalism Collection, Robert S. Cox, Special Collections &
University Archives Research Center, Umass Amherst Libraries.

*O*n January 27, 1986, the newly sworn-in US ambassador to Ireland boarded an Aer Lingus flight to Dublin with her oldest daughter Belinda. Being ambassador was unlike any other position Margaret had held. It was imbued with deep meaning and pride in her heritage as the daughter of Irish immigrants, a bookend to the personal history that had been the basis of her lifelong drive and determination.

As she crossed the Atlantic, putting miles between her and America, the political circus of Margaret's appointment—and her recent divorce—fell into the past. She'd put her heart and soul into shaping HHS to effectively serve a wide variety of Americans. In a season of professional and personal challenges, her passion and conviction propelled her forward. In the words of Senator Ted Kennedy, "The cabinet's loss is Ireland's gain. Margaret O'Shaughnessy Heckler will bring the same warmth and dedication to the causes and concerns of the Irish people as she has brought to the elderly, the poor, the sick, and the millions of others in our society whom she has ably represented in an administration that too often neglects their needs."[1]

The ambassadorship to Ireland was viewed as one of the most coveted assignments for the US State Department. Shaking off the heavy dust of Washington, Margaret was finally able to look ahead, grateful that President Reagan had appointed her as an ambassador to a country of shared significance to both of them. She always trusted Ronald Reagan to have her back even when others did not. For the rest of her life, she referred to him as "My President."

At Dublin Airport, the midwinter sun struggled to break through the cloudy, early morning skies. In the Aer Lingus lounge, which was used to welcome diplomats and VIPs, the Irish press and Margaret's Irish relatives waited. Margaret's first cousins, Mary Buckley, Kay Moynihan, Theresa Sheehy, and Anthony Sheehy were there to greet her.

Bulbs flashed and cameras rolled as television and print journalists clambered to capture the moment when Margaret Heckler made history, arriving in Dublin as the first woman American ambassador to Ireland.

In her speech, Margaret lauded her mother:

> During my years of service in the Congress, my mother—Bridget O'Shaughnessy—was a counselor, a critic, a confidant. She did not come to Washington often, but she read—voraciously—and she watched the morning, noon, and night TV news with an almost professional dedication.

We talked on the telephone several times a week. And she invariably opened those conversations with what was to become a familiar refrain: "You and Congress are helping Israel—you're helping Italy, you're helping countries whose names I can't even spell or pronounce—*but what are you doing for Ireland today, Peggy?*"

Today in Dublin, for the first time, I have the right answer. "Mother, I've come home to Ireland, and I've brought America with me.[2]

After she made her speech, she took questions from the press.

Reporter: Do you have any misgivings being in Ireland, Ambassador Heckler?

Heckler: I'm very pleased and honored to be here, the place of my parents' birth.[3]

Another reporter: What are your plans for Ireland?

Heckler: I'd like to get the lay of the land first and then hopefully, make a difference for the economy, the culture, and the people.[4]

Many photographs later, Margaret and her daughter Belinda were picked up in a black limousine and brought to the residence. Driving through Dublin, Margaret was abuzz with the novelty of a new country. One of the small luxuries Margaret relished was having her own car phone, a technology she hadn't had access to in Washington and something that was not yet widely available to the general public.

They arrived at Phoenix Park, a seventeen thousand–acre park, the largest enclosed park in Europe and home to three official residences: Áras an Uachtaráin, the home of Ireland's president; the Papal Nuncio (head of the Catholic Church in Ireland); and Deerfield, the American ambassador's residence. When turning into the residence, they were met by two US Marines manning the guard house, then passed through the massive iron gates and continued another quarter mile along a perfectly landscaped winding drive to the Deerfield mansion. She was immediately met by an official motorcade to take her to the residence of Patrick Hillery, the president of Ireland, to present her credentials to him as the new American ambassador to Ireland.

The year before Margaret arrived, President Reagan had visited their shared ancestral land and in preparation for his visit, the State Department had Deerfield fully redecorated. The interiors were redone to resemble the splendor of the White House, with rooms named by their colors—gold, green, red, and blue. Margaret was as impressed as Reagan

Deerfield, the US ambassador's residence in Phoenix Park, Dublin, Ireland. *Family collection.*

was with the lavish mansion's interior and setting, which rivaled that of other great manors in Ireland.

Deerfield was truly breathtaking. Ireland's natural beauty was enough to make any diplomatic assignment there unforgettable, but the 28,395-square-foot, white Georgian home, built in 1776, elevated the posting to near-royal proportions. To live at Deerfield was to share this house with the ghosts of its previous inhabitants: General Cornwallis, sent to serve in Ireland after his defeat at Yorktown; the Duke of Wellington, who lived in the house before his great victory at Waterloo; and Sir Winston Churchill, who lived there as a child.[5] Adding to the air of historical importance, Margaret's neighbor across the street would be the president of Ireland.

The residence had six bedroom suites, a ballroom, a library, a kitchen, an office, and a dining room with seating for twenty-four. The sixty-two-acre property featured three additional cottages, formal gardens, and a tennis court. Deerfield's staff consisted of a driver, a butler, cooks, a social secretary, an upstairs maid, a downstairs maid, and a gardener.

As Margaret said, "The palatial residence helped minimize the difficulty of this transition. . . . Along with access to Phoenix Park, it comes with my own herd of deer that run wild here. I can take long walks, snatching breaths of the gorgeous Irish air."[6] Heckler, then one

With her dog, Jackson O'Toole, at the front door of Deerfield. *Kathy Borchers Photojournalism Collection, Robert S. Cox, Special Collections & University Archives Research Center, Umass Amherst Libraries.*

of the most powerful women in American government, was now the most powerful American in Ireland.[7]

Margaret would not be the only new resident at Deerfield. Her new best friend walked on four legs, not two. After the painful divorce from John, Margaret's beau, Jack Pierce, arranged for her to have a companion who would remind her of him. There was a special surprise waiting for her at the residence. Margaret was met by an Irish wolfhound puppy, which Jack had playfully named Jackson O'Toole. With his shaggy gray coat, big brown eyes, and spirited personality, Jackson O'Toole quickly captured the hearts of the media, celebrities, world leaders, and business tycoons alike. The staff adored the puppy, and overnight, he helped transform the atmosphere of the cavernous house, making it feel like a home. The dynamic duo was ready for their diplomatic responsibilities.

Margaret's story had come full circle. Shortly after her arrival to the Emerald Isle, she was asked to be a guest on *The Hal Roach Show*. The Irish comedian opened the show saying, "We would like to welcome our friends from the American Embassy in Dublin, but the *icing on the cake* is to welcome our new Ambassador to Ireland, her Excellency, Mrs. Margaret Heckler." As the room filled with applause, Roach continued, "*Now, there is a woman who loves our land with its forty shades of green as much as we do.*"[8]

Margaret's social secretary kept her schedule humming. She reported, "This morning, the ambassador has two appointments in Dublin: tea with the Lord Mayor, to discuss how the United States can help celebrate Dublin's one thousandth anniversary; and a private policy meeting at the Department of Foreign Affairs, Ireland's State Department. This afternoon, she has her weekly meeting with the career diplomats on her staff. Heckler has to get it all done by 6 p.m., when the president-elect of the American Medical Association is due at Deerfield for cocktails."[9]

Margaret, at age fifty-seven, suddenly found herself juggling two love interests. One evening, at the Ballyseede Castle Hotel in Tralee, County Kerry, Ireland, the Irish playwright John B. Keane tried to act as a matchmaker between Margaret and Morris Sullivan. Sullivan, a distinguished, successful American businessman, was the owner of Sullivan Bluth Studios, which produced the hit movies *All Dogs Go to Heaven* and *The Land Before Time*. He had lost the love of his life years earlier but was smitten with Margaret from the moment they met. As their relationship shifted from professional to romantic, Sullivan proposed marriage. He took her to the finest restaurants in Dublin and showered her with expensive gifts. But as Margaret would later share, "Morris Sullivan was still very much in love with his deceased wife who had passed more than a decade ago. He spoke about her constantly, as if she was still alive. Why would I wish to compete with that?"[10]

Another admirer, Ireland's first billionaire, Tony O'Reilly—the owner of the *Irish Times* and famous international rugby player—courted Margaret, but the attraction was not there for her. The interaction with these suitors made Margaret realize that Jack Pierce, the man who was by her side after her divorce, truly did love her, and their romance survived, although they were oceans apart.

Margaret's diplomatic mission to Ireland was set against the backdrop of the Troubles, a conflict in Northern Ireland, which was still part of the United Kingdom, that lasted from the late 1960s until 1998. The fight was between the Unionists (Protestants) who wanted to remain loyal to the British Crown and the Irish Republicans (Catholics) who wanted to secede from the UK and join with the Republic of Ireland.

The Irish Republican Army (IRA)—an Irish republican paramilitary group—conducted bombings and attacks primarily in Northern Ireland and England, but they sometimes hit targets in the Republic of Ireland, as well. In total, over the course of the Troubles, the IRA directed more than forty-three thousand violent acts. When Margaret became ambassador, she explained to the American media that the 2,500 lives lost to the Troubles from 1969 until then, were the equivalent, based on population, to losing 350,000 US lives.[11]

Because Margaret was the American ambassador to the Republic of Ireland, she was a prime potential target. Underscoring safety concerns for her were drastic security measures taken both at Margaret's residence and the American embassy at Ballsbridge, which was a fortress that had bulletproof glass and reinforced steel doors that could withstand gunshots or a sledgehammer.

The ambassador's limousine, built to protect presidents, was known as a "fortress on wheels." The limo "could not be pierced by a shrapnel grenade, a 9 mm machine gun, or a .357 or .44 Magnum."[12] Margaret's driver was equipped with a special set of goggles that used infrared technology so he could see through smokescreens or drive without headlights in the dark.

The great caution taken to protect Margaret's life was not overblown. The IRA often conducted car bombings and planted landmines, as occurred in the 1976 killing of the British ambassador to Ireland, Christopher Ewart-Biggs.[13]

Upon her first visit to Northern Ireland near Derry, Margaret encountered a security officer at the airport.

Ambassador Heckler: Has the Ambassador's car arrived?

Security officer: The Ambassador is not here.

Ambassador Heckler: I was inquiring about the Ambassador's car.

Security officer: I told you, the Ambassador has not yet arrived.

Ambassador Heckler: Sir, the Ambassador *is* here. The question is, where is my car? You have a Prime Minister [Margaret Thatcher] who is a woman. How is it possible that you do not think a woman can be an ambassador?

The security officer's eyes widened in amazement. He "was quite chagrined" from the interaction.[14]

Margaret's priorities for her time in Ireland were to (1) quell the Troubles and (2) expand economic opportunity between Ireland and the United States. Speaking of the peace effort, she said, "President Reagan and a magnificent bipartisan coalition in the Congress have pledged their support for peace and reconciliation . . . to be in a position to play a role in such a historic development is not just a significant challenge but a very heartwarming honor." She added, "This is the only country in the world for which my government has a policy: 'Invest in Ireland.'"[15]

In 1985, the country was experiencing very high inflation with high unemployment; younger workers had little opportunity for jobs and were leaving the country. Margaret seized the opportunity to be an advocate and liaison between world leaders. Seeking peace and reconciliation, Margaret worked with Queen Elizabeth II of England, UK prime minister Margaret Thatcher, and Irish prime minister Garret FitzGerald, the Taoiseach. One newspaper reported that Margaret "arrived in Dublin at what could be a pivotal time in relations between Ireland and Britain over troubled Northern Ireland."[16]

When Margaret first stepped into her post as ambassador, there were reasons for apprehension in the region, but there was also hope. Two months before her arrival, the Anglo-Irish Agreement had been signed. This peace treaty, made between British prime minister Margaret Thatcher and Irish prime minister Taoiseach Garrett FitzGerald, granted the Irish government an advisory role over Northern Ireland's government, with a goal of ending the Troubles. In return, the Republic of Ireland made a commitment to uphold whatever the majority of the Northern Irish citizens decided: remaining part of the United Kingdom or joining the Republic of Ireland. It was hoped that this agreement would help end the Troubles.

Unfortunately, this enthusiasm was dampened a few months later, on April 15, 1986, when the United States carried out an airstrike in Libya. Ireland had, for years, been exporting cattle and other dairy products to Libya, and Libya had been exporting firearms and explosives to the Irish Republican Army (IRA). This complicated the US response to the Troubles.[17] In retaliation for British support of the US airstrike, Libya's president, Muammar Gaddafi, saw to it that several large shipments of weapons and bombs were sent to the IRA.

Two years later, on December 21, 1988, Pan Am Flight 103—flying between London and New York City—was blown up by a Libyan terrorist over Lockerbie, Scotland, killing all 270 passengers, including 190 Americans. This was the deadliest terrorist attack in the history of the United Kingdom. Muammar Gaddafi took the blame. The United States responded by bombing Gaddafi's palace in Libya, killing the Libyan leader's family, but he escaped by chance, having stepped outside to take a walk. However, his final fate would take place not long after.

Despite these tense international developments, Margaret promoted a vision for peace and prosperity in Ireland. To celebrate the Anglo-Irish Agreement, she gave a speech on St. Patrick's Day, saying, "Prime Ministers FitzGerald and Thatcher have joined hands—across both the Irish Sea and centuries of enmity and travail, in an act of vision and statesmanship which creates a framework for dialogue, understanding, reconciliation and peace."[18] She pledged the financial support of the United States.

The *Irish Times* shared that "she's won the praise of the government for being such a good cheerleader for the new accord."[19] In Ambassador Heckler, the Irish government saw a fighter, someone who had a "characteristic zest for action."[20]

Margaret believed that peace and the economy were inextricably linked. "The success of the peace process is really critical not only to the economic future of Ireland and the United States, but to world peace and the terrorism that affects all of us," she said.[21] Margaret pushed the United States to contribute to the International Fund for Ireland, an independent fund created as a part of the Anglo-Irish Agreement to promote economic mobility in both the Republic of Ireland and Northern Ireland. In her St. Patrick's Day speech, Margaret shared a message to the US Congress and the rest of the world: "I look forward to the speedy adoption by the Congress of the legislation I have proposed which provides immediate, tangible support. And I urge other nations to contribute and cooperate in bringing about an economic and political renaissance in Northern Ireland and the parts of the Republic which have, for so long, been affected by instability and insecurity."[22]

True to her word, Margaret traveled back to the United States to testify before the House International Relations Committee. She made a case for supporting the "Overseas Private Investment Corporation (OPIC) to establish a $60 million Ireland Equity Fund for US businesses to set up operations in North and South Ireland, which will leverage $240 million in investment from private sector sources." As she continued to explain, the fund "would be targeted to small- and medium-sized companies. They are the sleeping giants of American industry. They offer the greatest jobs and are the most innovative."[23] Toward the end of her testimony, she reiterated that economic development was an essential way for the United States to "see the bomb and the bullet put out of the lives of Irish people and out of the news broadcasts in Northern Ireland on a daily basis" and that the United States needed to "stand behind its commitment with more than statements and expressions of support. . . . Speaking out is not enough. It's important that we bolster this new framework agreement in Northern Ireland through concrete economic assistance."[24]

By June, Congress was debating the two legislative proposals, which totaled $250 million in aid. Through Margaret's advocacy, the United States became one of the largest contributors to the International Fund for Ireland. By 1998, 95 percent of the funds available originated from the United States.[25] Of the millions of dollars secured, a $120 million grant for economic development in Ireland was specifically attributed to Margaret Heckler.[26]

But securing funds was just one aspect of Margaret's work. The next step was enticing American businesses to set up shop in Ireland.

In the 1980s, Ireland was still inching toward the modern global economy. From the potato blight of the early 1800s to the massive emigration of its citizens to the United States, nearly two centuries of hardship had taken its toll.[27] It was no accident that Ireland had earned the moniker, "Europe's only Third-World nation."[28]

As ambassador, Margaret knew that strategic introductions of American and Irish stakeholders, with a goal of millions of dollars of economic expansion in Ireland, was essential. The key to these introductions was creating an engaging social scene. As a congresswoman and cabinet secretary, Margaret had kept an active social calendar, but it only indirectly influenced political outcomes. In Ireland, the social component was a core feature of her political and diplomatic responsibilities. At her Deerfield residence, philanthropic soirées, elite dinner parties, musical performances on the patio, and lawn games were all part of the job description; however, coordination between the cook, butler, and social secretary was no simple task. She would need the creative energy to bring it all together.

Carlton Varney, a friend and the American interior designer best-known for his work on The Greenbrier said, "I first met Margaret when she came down to Dromoland Castle. We got along like a *house on fire*, dancing the night away." Varney went on to say, "Margaret was not monetarily driven," instead "she was very generous in her parties and in her spirit. She had lots of sparkle."[29]

In her role as ambassador, Margaret gave toasts and speeches and regaled visitors who included Supreme Court Justice Sandra Day O'Connor and her husband John; four-star general and Marine Corps commandant Paul X. Kelley; comedian Joan Rivers; Irish American actresses Maureen O'Hara and Roma Downey; and the Irish poet and Nobel laureate, Seamus Heaney. Margaret transformed the residence into a salon where poets, politicians, and movie stars intermingled. The magical ambience of Deerfield transported her guests into a world filled with rich culture, tradition, and merriment.

From the start of her ambassadorship, economic opportunity for Irish youth became one of Margaret's passions. The country suffered from a steady stream of young people who received higher degrees, then left the country. A "brain drain" was taking place, with talented graduates having no choice but to seek opportunities in other European countries and the United States because none were available in Ireland. James R. Carroll, a US reporter who visited Margaret in 1987, said he heard constantly that "there is no future in Ireland" from the younger generation of Irish emigrants.[30] In Margaret's words, "Many Americans have a vision of Ireland romanticized by tradition and fixed in time, but . . . the young Irish, graduating from an Irish university today, in a demanding academic environment, face scarce job opportunities."[31]

Margaret traveled across Ireland, organizing meetings with business leaders. She had ambitious ideas to grow Ireland's economy and hire from within. One such idea was to take Irish tourism to a new level by attracting more American visitors.

In a speech titled, "A Very Special Place," given on October 26, 1986, Margaret said, "From the thatched-roof cottages beside county lanes to the dramatic coastlines and cliffs . . . from outstanding theater to traditional Irish music . . . tourists will surely come away as mesmerized as I am." She continued, "It seems to me that Ireland is one of the best-kept secrets in Europe, and I plan to do all I can to change that."[32]

Women's advancement was always at the forefront of Margaret's mind. She recognized the need to lift up Irish women in business, and she was well positioned to create the Women in Enterprise Conference by using her contacts from Congress and HHS. Her goal was to bring together American women business owners with aspiring Irish women in a conference to create a dynamic exchange of ideas and contributions for the benefit of launching women in Ireland. In a thank you note to Margaret on May 12, 1988, Pamela Kearney wrote, "Dear Excellency, I would like to congratulate you on conceiving and bringing to fulfillment such a superb conference last Friday. . . . Thank you for the work you have done in the cause of women in business and for helping me launch Network as a national organization."[33]

During Margaret's ambassadorship, three prominent American companies invested in Ireland: Intel, Boeing, and Anheuser-Busch. In 1949, Ireland had created the Industrial Development Authority (IDA) to attract foreign businesses to the country. According to Padraic White, IDA managing director from 1981–1990, "Margaret's success with the International Fund for Ireland had a significant ripple effect in enticing American businesses to Ireland at the right time. Trust in the Irish economy had been low for years, but when Charles Haughey was elected prime minister in 1987, he was able to cut programs and reduce inflation, increasing the confidence of foreign companies to invest in Ireland. A series of business incentives were also implemented, such as tax abatement, loans, research, construction, and training grants. . . . Margaret was passionate about bringing new American businesses to Ireland. She was 'ceaseless.' The decision of Intel to invest in Ireland happened during Margaret's tenure as ambassador. It was the largest business investment in Ireland to date and afterwards. It was the most advanced technology as well."[34]

As Margaret shared in her testimony to the House International Relations Committee, "Ireland is a gateway to Europe, a huge tax-free market of 380 million customers, with young, well-educated English-speaking people."[35] The case was strong for the American government and American businesses to invest in Ireland, and Margaret was the energetic advocate the Irish government needed. White said, "She focused on the economic aspect and promoting business in Ireland more than most Ambassadors" and her ability to "attract US investment and promote Irish exports across the Atlantic . . . was a godsend."[36] Years later, on behalf of the IDA, at a special dinner, White presented Margaret with a silver plaque, "honoring her vigorous and dynamic support" in promoting industry in Ireland.

One of Margaret's outstanding accomplishments as ambassador was bringing Boeing, the world's largest aerospace company, to Ireland in the 1980s. It was Boeing's first operation outside of North America. According to White, "Margaret put huge pressure to get Boeing to come here and, in my opinion, we would not have got them without her. She had *good guts*."[37] She also had a strong connection with the owner of Sullivan Bluth Studios, an animation studio started by former Disney animators who moved their business from Los Angeles to Dublin in 1986. Margaret attended the premiere of their creation, *The Land Before Time*, with the studio owner, Morris Sullivan, who became the father of the animated film industry in Ireland, leaving a legacy of animation programs at Irish colleges and universities.

Anheuser-Busch, the "King of Beers," made a significant investment in Ireland during Margaret's tenure as ambassador. In 1985, Dennis Long, president of the Anheuser-Busch Company, traveled to Ireland with the St. Louis Busch Soccer Club. During the visit, the team visited the Curragh Racecourse, where Long was approached by the board and asked if Anheuser-Busch was interested in sponsoring the Irish Derby. Dennis Long, who was a fourth-generation Irish American, showed serious interest in this unexpected offer.

The Irish Derby was already an extremely popular 118-year-old horse race, but the racecourse facilities were in need of repair. Long agreed that "Anheuser-Busch would sponsor the race and rehabilitate the

With the Aga Khan (left) and Dennis Long (right), COO of Anheuser-Busch,
at the Irish Derby, 1989. *Family collection.*

facilities for $1 million, as long as some of the money would go into the
stands, where the 'real beer drinkers' (who would also ideally drink Budweiser) would be."[38] They agreed to the terms, and in 1987, the first-ever
Anheuser-Busch–sponsored Irish Derby took place.

Margaret gladly hosted the Anheuser-Busch senior executives, as
well as their top distributors and a host of celebrities at Deerfield. She also
served as the unofficial hostess at the horse race itself. She was handed a
press kit with notes about the history of the "venerable race," as well as
two prewritten statements, dependent on the winner: the favorite horse
or the longshot. The memo also included the reminder, "Most important
of all: *Remember this is Budweiser's debut as sponsor of the Irish Derby so you
must give them a resounding plug.*"[39]

On July 6, 1987, all over Ireland and around the world, people
watched the Irish Derby on television. The battle between eight three-
year-old horses proved to be one of Ireland's greatest days on the turf. Off
the track, the scene was extremely stylish.

Margaret presented the Waterford crystal trophy to the owner of
the winning horse, Sir Harry Lewis. Budweiser's participation flawlessly
represented the merger of an iconic American business and a longstanding
Irish tradition.

Two years later, at a breakfast speech, Margaret described the first "Budweiser Derby" as an "explosive success" and "*the* social event of the racing season in Ireland." For Anheuser-Busch, the return on investment was almost immediate. In addition to the exchange of beer, the horse industry between Ireland and the United States also flourished. The year prior, the United States exported bloodstock totaling $37 million and Ireland sent several million dollars' worth of their own horses to the United States.[40]

Margaret had become an expert hostess for the Irish Derby by her second year of entertaining eclectic groups of celebrities. A news clip, "People, Places, Parties," featured Margaret's itinerary and guest list for the weekend: To kick off the fun, Margaret and her son John, who was visiting for Derby week, attended a dinner on Saturday night at Luttrelstown Castle hosted by Mike Roarty, vice president and director of marketing for Anheuser-Busch.

The next morning, Margaret hosted a breakfast with the entire crowd that was brought over for the derby: American actor Gene Autry; American actor John Forsythe; American actress Stephanie Powers; Ed McMahon, from *The Tonight Show Starring Johnny Carson*; Steve Garvey, Hall of Fame baseball player; and Mick Jagger of the Rolling Stones.

In a dinner toast to a group of OPIC executives, Margaret stood at the head of the large dining room table and said, "The Irish Derby is the Kentucky Derby, the Preakness, and the Belmont Stakes, all rolled into one magnificent race."[41]

Budweiser continued to sponsor the Irish Derby until 2007. It helped to place the event on the world stage as one of the richest horse races in Europe, while also converting the Irish into Budweiser drinkers.[42] Margaret's hosting power during those first critical years left a lasting legacy when Ireland most needed the economic support. Padraic White described Margaret as a strong female leader, one who paved the way for the number of American businesses in Ireland to grow from 350 in the 1980s to over 800 in the thirty years that followed.[43] It was a "restoration of international confidence" in Ireland and Margaret's strong political background in the United States gave her the best possible experience and contacts to promote businesses in Ireland. "I thought she was a dynamo, a ball of energy, and no nonsense. We worked very well together," remembered White.[44] Margaret naturally stepped into the ambassadorial role with the same spirit and work ethic that she used to help drive change in America.

The Final Hurrah

Ambassador Margaret Heckler looking up.
Thomas Laylor Photographer, The Irish Times.

*F*or decades, Margaret had held a number of grand roles, but the Irish people and the Irish pace of life helped to reveal a very different side of her personality. Ireland was changing her. Margaret loved the way her Irish colleagues always found time to tell a droll tale. "I have definitely learned to enjoy life more. . . . I don't think I could ever be as serious as I was before. I can laugh at anything now."[1] Between the green hills and jest-filled spirit of the Irish, she was entering a new season of life.

As much as Margaret appreciated connecting with her extended family, proximity to her Irish relatives was bundled with its own set of challenges. This was the case with Mary Buckley, Margaret's first cousin, and the matriarch of the Sheehy and O'Shaughnessy clan. Mary called the American embassy and spoke in her thick Irish brogue to Margaret's assistant, Jack Horner, in hopes of arranging a tribute for the O'Shaughnessy family. Mary wanted to have Margaret's father's cottage in County Limerick memorialized.

Mary's intent was not just to glorify the O'Shaughnessy name, it was to celebrate how the daughter of an Irish immigrant from a small village in western Ireland returned as the US ambassador to Ireland. Margaret hesitated to accept Mary's request. She felt that it was not within the scope of her ambassadorial role and the "honor" seemed self serving. But because of Mary's persistence, Margaret finally consented, so long as the occasion was private and did not involve the press. Mary gave assurances that the event would be understated and well-managed.

On the day of the event, Margaret was accompanied by her assistant Jack Horner for the two-hour drive to County Limerick. When they turned the corner of the small country town of Askeaton, they were immediately confronted by a large banner that stretched high above the road saying, "Welcome Ambassador Heckler!" As Margaret stepped out of the limousine, it was total pandemonium. Children were chasing after the limo, townspeople were waving and cheering and American flags were flying, reporters from two Irish radio and television stations were present. At the entrance of the cottage, they caught a glimpse of Mary Buckley, standing tall and proud. It was at that moment that Horner got "the look" from Margaret as if to say, "Thanks Jack!"

In front of the stone hearth of the tiny two-room cottage, Margaret gave a speech about returning to the ancestral home of her parents, sharing what the United States had given her and what Ireland had given her. She spoke about having a foot firmly planted in both countries. She finished by expressing her gratitude for America as being a land of op-

With Vice President George H. W. Bush (back row on the right) and Secretary of State George Schultz (back row on the left) while Irish prime minister Garrett FitzGerald (front row on the right) presents a crystal sculpture of the Statue of Liberty to President Ronald Reagan (front row on the left) on the White House steps, 1986. *White House Photographer.*

portunity, a place where with hard work and determination all things are possible.[2]

Margaret Mary O'Shaughnessy Heckler had come full circle. She marveled at the significance of the "how" and "why" of being in this place. At the pinnacle of her career, she was brought back to the home of her father. Margaret realized that "*these were her Irish roots.*" Instead of bitterness over the wound from her childhood, she chose thankfulness for all the ways she was able to channel that hurt into caring.

As ambassador to Ireland, Margaret reminisced, "There has been such an unusual trend line to my career. . . . I feel I was meant to come to Ireland, and it certainly has been a great personal blessing to me."[3]

She reflected on her life's journey by saying:

I am the child of Irish immigrants. . . . My parents came with nothing. America was the place of all possibilities. I grew up in New York City, became a lawyer, served on the Governor's Council for four years, was a member of the US Congress for sixteen years, was appointed to the cabinet under President Ronald Reagan as Secretary of Health and

In the Wicklow hills. *Kathy Borchers Photojournalism Collection, Robert S. Cox, Special Collections & University Archives Research Center, Umass Amherst Libraries.*

Human Services, and served as the first woman US Ambassador to Ireland. I *am* the American dream.

Margaret was a woman of firsts. She became the first woman to serve as Speaker of the House for the Connecticut Intercollegiate Student Legislature. She was one of the first women to graduate from Boston College Law School and to be on the *Boston College Law Review*. She was one of the first women to serve on the Massachusetts Governor's Council. She was the first congresswoman from Massachusetts elected in her own right. She was the first congresswoman to enter a warzone in Vietnam. She was the first congresswoman to enter communist China in the 1970s. As HHS secretary, she was the first woman to be named "designated survivor." Finally, Margaret became the first female American ambassador to Ireland.

Margaret recognized that there was a divine order and purpose to her life. She converted her feelings of fragility from being an unwanted child into a burning drive to help the vulnerable. When she began to realize her gifts, Margaret used her various positions of power to effect long-lasting change. She was able to make a world where women were given a right to credit in their own names. She fought to highlight racial inequalities in health care. She also created the first hospice program under Medicare. Her fierce passion for justice and equality changed the lives of millions of Americans.

In spite of her many challenges, Margaret Heckler was led to have an extraordinary destiny. At the end of her public life, she proclaimed, "I feel like a pawn on the chessboard, and I'm a great believer in the Lord's plan for each of us. When it's your turn to move, *you move*."[4]

THE END

Author's Note

$\mathcal{U}$pon her return to the United States from Ireland, Margaret settled in Arlington, Virginia, retired from politics and dedicated her life to God and her family.

Margaret served on many boards and organizations. She was on the board of the Allied Irish Bank, their American affiliate bank in Maryland, the National Alliance for Hispanic Health, the Women's Research and Education Institute, Catholic Values Investment Trust, and the Mission of Mercy. She became a member of the Dames of Malta, a worldwide Catholic order whose mission is to work with the sick and the poor. Themes of compassion, conviction, justice, equality, and bipartisanship were constant fixtures of her lengthy career and in her personal life.

Margaret O'Shaughnessy Heckler died on August 6, 2018, at the age of eighty-seven. She bequeathed her official papers to the John J. Burns Library at Boston College in Newton, Massachusetts.

In addition to Margaret's three children, she was the grandmother to four grandchildren: John Maguire Heckler III; Amanda Rose Heckler; Elizabeth O'Shaughnessy Heckler; and John Hallett Mulliken IV.

Acknowledgments

$\mathcal{W}$hen I first met Margaret Heckler in 1988, she was serving as the ambassador to Ireland. She had flown back to the States for the official unveiling ceremony of her portrait being hung in the great hall of the Hubert Humphrey Building, the home of the Department of HHS in Washington, DC. I was overwhelmed by my first impressions of this amazing woman. My love for her grew exponentially in the years following.

During the last five years of her life, we began a new Heckler tradition, where the family gathered for Sunday night dinners with Margaret. It was after hearing the countless stories of her extraordinary life that I felt compelled to share her life in this book.

Not being a trained professional writer, I realized that I would need the help of editors and writers to help me develop the stories into a chronological biography. If I succeeded at all, it is due to two people: Belinda Heckler Mulliken, my sister-in-law, and Aryana Petrosky. Belinda agreed to work alongside me, and together, we combined the stories in a chronological order, performed over 130 interviews, and spent countless hours writing and editing our manuscript.

Aryana Petrosky, a talented writer, came from the American Enterprise Institute. For over two years, her gifted language helped bring our stories to life. She saw the vision for the project and stayed with us through the creation of the agent pitch letter and book proposal.

Cynthia Swanson, a content editor, helped cut forty thousand words from the manuscript and added colorful details. Laurie Sprague, a family friend and talented editor, came to my aid as I crossed the finish line.

Brilliant Brian Matt helped edit and fine-tune the final draft. I thank you for your dedication and time spent in the final hours.

I am deeply grateful for the untiring support of my family—my husband John, who gave generously as a reader and offered input, and my three children—John, Amanda, and Elizabeth. I want to thank my mother for loving me, reading through chapters, and being by my side. I so appreciate my nephew John Mulliken IV for his support with Microsoft Word and offering to be our computer and footnote guru, a total lifesaver. Alison Heckler-Haensler helped unearth stories and offered feedback. Susan Heckler Smith was one of our readers and gave invaluable edits and suggestions. My dear friend, Janet Mountz, used her journalism skills to help me cut many unnecessary words from the manuscript.

I very much appreciate Senator Ed Markey (D-MA), who stepped out on a limb for us during very partisan times, painting a picture of Massachusetts politics in the sixties and seventies. Former congressman Jim Gardner (R-NC) talked about his time with LBJ as president. Former congresswoman Liz Holtzman (D-NY) shared about the early formation of the Congresswomen's Caucus. Former congresswoman and senator Olympia Snowe shared stories of traveling to Cambodia with Margaret and their work on the Congresswomen's Caucus.

Former aide extraordinaire Jack Horner was indispensable. His humor and splendid memories kept us on track and entertained. Former driver and assistant Danny Converse added much color by sharing behind-the-scenes stories about Margaret. Mary Anne Thadeu, Margaret's administrative assistant, made herself available to share her unvarnished insights of what it was like fifty years ago. Carol Bauer regaled me with tales from Congress and HHS. Jacquelyn White shared her role with Margaret's in creating the Medicare hospice benefit.

Linda Bilmes, Margaret's former assistant and press secretary, was an eyewitness to Margaret's years at the Republican National Convention and the Reagan years. Beth Hinchliffe, former speechwriter for Margaret lent her advice on numerous occasions with written words at crucial times. Her encouragement kept me going through the tough times.

College classmate from Albertus Magnus, Sister Dolores Liptak, RSM, offered help early on with the history of Albertus Magnus and time spent with Margaret as a member of the Connecticut Intercollegiate Student Legislature. She supported me steadfastly, as did the faculty and staff of Albertus Magnus College. The Library of Congress Women's History and Gender Studies Discussion Group was a source of inspiration, and LeRoy Bell unlocked mysteries for me by locating records. Dan

Coquillette, author, historian, Harvard Law School professor and Boston College Law School professor helped piece together a better picture of the early history of Harvard Law School. Janice Connell introduced me to Joelle Delbourgo, who became my agent.

I want to thank Christian Dupont, Boston College, Burns Library, who came to my aid time and again patiently helping locate boxes in Margaret's collection. Vicki Sanders, at Boston College Law School was always so helpful finding artwork and photos for the book.

I am most grateful to Irish ambassador Geraldine Bryne Nason and her assistant Norma Ces for their networking and hospitality. Mort Taubman went above and beyond offering legal counsel and friendship. His wife, Allyson Taubman, one of my close friends, has been a sounding board and advocate. My longtime soul sister Eunice Mazloom walked beside me through many stages of the book's production, especially promotion.

I am also grateful to my acquisitions editor Brittany Stoner at Lyons Press, who believed in my book project and partnered with me as an editor, and to my production editor Mary Wheelehan for her continuous support and kindness in the final stages of production. And lastly, Joelle Delbourgo, my agent, who took a chance on me as a new writer. Her vast experience in the industry helped land me a book publisher and an audio publisher. Thank you to all my friends who have come alongside me during this journey. I hope I have given credit where credit is due and haven't neglected anyone. Everyone who has helped me is in my heart. I remain deeply grateful.

Notes

INTRODUCTION

1. Beth Hinchliffe, "A Claim on my Heart," *MetroWest Daily News,* August 8, 2018, accessed May 5, 2024. https://www.metrowestdailynews.com/story/news/local/2018/08/08/claim-on-my-heart/6527229007.

2. Ted Fitzgerald (congressional district staff), in discussion with the author, November 12, 2020.

CHAPTER 1

1. Joel Mokyr, "Great Famine Ireland 1945–1949," accessed March 16, 2020, https://www.britannica.com/event/Great-Famine-Irish-history.

2. "The Stock Market Soars," *Centricity,* accessed November 11, 2023, https://www.scuc.txed.net/cms/lib/TX02204767/Centricity/Domain/1979/Chp%209-1.html#:~:text=The%20bull%20market%20of%20the,a%20company%27s%20earnings%20and%20profits.

3. Mark Bulik, "1854 No Irish Need Apply," *New York Times*, September 8, 2015, https://www.nytimes.com/2015/09/08/insider/1854-no-irish-need-apply.html.

4. John Kuroski, "55 Harrowing Photos of the Great Depression in New York City," *All That's Interesting*, December 4, 2016, https://allthatsinteresting.com/great-depression-new-york-city.

5. Joy Blackburn, "Former Health Secretary: Simple Act of Kindness Inspired her Work," *The Virgin Islands Daily News*, October 16, 2009.

CHAPTER 2

1. "Margaret Heckler," *Bornacoola Parish Paper*, 1987.
2. Christopher Reed, "Unveiled: For the First Time, a Recluse's Treasures Go Traveling," *Harvard Magazine*, March–April 2003, https://www.harvardmaga zine.com/2003/03/unveiled.html.
3. Stephen Wolohojian, *A Private Passion* (New York: The Metropolitan Museum of Art, ed., 2003), vii.
4. "The Many Faces of Ingres," harvardartmuseum.org, July 7, 2015, accessed November 12, 2023, https://harvardartmuseums.org/article/the-many-faces-of -ingres.
5. "The Breakfast Table," harvardartmuseum.org, accessed November 12, 2023, https://harvardartmuseums.org/collections/object/299794.
6. Margaret Heckler, interview by author, Arlington, VA, March 25, 2015.
7. Heckler interview, June 21, 2016.
8. Heckler interview, June 21, 2016.
9. Heckler interview, June 21, 2016.
10. J. Gordon Hylton, "Adam's Rib as an Historical Document: The Plight of Women Lawyers in the 1940s," accessed November 12, 2023, https://law .marquette.edu/facultyblog/2013/06/adams-rib-as-historical-document.
11. Heckler interview, June 21, 2016.
12. Heckler interview, June 21, 2016.
13. "Our Legacy," accessed October 4, 2022, https://www.dominicanacademy .org/about-us/legacy.
14. Heckler interview, June 21, 2016.

CHAPTER 3

1. Margaret Heckler, interview by author, Arlington, VA, March 8, 2015.
2. Carter Gilbert, "Women in College During the 1950s," March 30, 2020, accessed January 18, 2024, https://sites.lib.jmu.edu/sc-interviews/2020/03/30/ women-in-college-during-the-1950s/#:~:text=During%20the%201950s%20 it%20was,science%20would%20be%20almost%200%25.
3. Dolores Liptak, interview by author, Arlington, VA, February 4, 2021.
4. Jody McPhillips, "The Ambassador," *Magnum Opus*, February 1988.
5. Anne Crellin Seggerman, interview by author, Arlington, VA, November 3, 2020.
6. Heckler interview, February 16, 2016.
7. George Heckler, interview by author, Arlington, VA, October 8, 2018.
8. George Heckler interview, October 8, 2018.
9. Margaret Heckler, interview by author, Arlington, VA, October 14, 2016.

CHAPTER 4

1. Phyllis Mays, interview by author, Arlington, VA, September 28, 2022.
2. Mays interview, September 28, 2022.
3. Heckler interview, April 10, 2016.
4. Jody McPhillips, "The Ambassador," *Magnum Opus*, February 1988.
5. Family archives.
6. Family archives.
7. Oobie Butler, interview by author, Arlington, VA, November 1, 2018.

CHAPTER 5

1. Daniel Coquillette, interview by author, Arlington, VA, April 22, 2020.
2. Coquillette interview, April 22, 2020.
3. Daniel R. Coquillette and Bruce A. Kimball, *The Intellectual Sword: Harvard Law School, the Second Century* (Cambridge, MA: Harvard University Press, 2020), 457–62.
4. Coquillette and Kimball, *The Intellectual Sword*, 465.
5. Summarized/adaption from Stephanie Mansfield, "The Heckler Breakup," *Washington Post,* October 16, 1984, https://www.washingtonpost.com/archive /lifestyle/1984/10/16/the-heckler-breakup/812213ed-d2c5-4d08-8d6e-e5bf 2d54d917.
6. Margaret Heckler, interview by author, Arlington, VA, March 11, 2015.
7. Heckler interview, February 16, 2016.
8. Edward Markey, interview by author, October 19, 2021.
9. "The Honorable Margaret M. Heckler Oral History Interview," Office of the Historian, US House of Representatives (June 6, 2017 and October 26, 2017), https://history.house.gov/Oral-History/Women/Representative-Heckler.
10. Larry Fagan, interview by author, Arlington, VA, February 12, 2020.
11. Vincent Marzilli, interview by author, Arlington, VA, February 11, 2020.
12. Frank Privitera, interview by author, Arlington, VA, February 19, 2020.
13. John Brebbia, interview by author, Arlington, VA, February 11, 2020.
14. "Margaret Heckler Proves Tougher Than Expected." *Business Week,* November 7, 1983.
15. Heckler interview, February 16, 2016.
16. Heckler interview, February 16, 2016.
17. Heckler interview, February 16, 2016.
18. Margaret Heckler, interview by author, March 8, 2015.

CHAPTER 6

1. Margaret Heckler, interview by author, March 8, 2015.
2. Judith Richards Hope, interview by author, Arlington, VA, October 7, 2020.
3. Martin Tolchin and Susan Tolchin, *Clout: Womanpower and Politics* (New York: Coward, McCann & Geoghegan, 1974).
4. Margaret Heckler, interview by author, Arlington, VA, June 21, 2016.
5. Linda Bilmes, interview by author, Arlington, VA, November 4, 2019.
6. Heckler family archives.
7. Heckler interview, March 8, 2015.
8. Heckler family archives.
9. Heckler family archives.
10. Heckler family archives.
11. Heckler interview, January 25, 2017.
12. Fred Brady, "Mrs. Heckler Has No Plans to Heckle Council," *Boston Herald*, 1961.
13. Heckler family archives.
14. Heckler interview June 21, 2016.
15. Heckler family archives.
16. Heckler family archives.
17. James G. Colbert, *The Newton Graphic*, 1963.
18. Betty Friedan, *The Feminine Mystique* (New York: W.W. Norton, 1963), 305.
19. "Bribe Jury Names Ex-Gov. Furcolo; He and 4 Are Indicted in Boston for Conspiracy," *New York Times*, October 14, 1964.
20. Tolchin, *Clout: Womanpower and Politics*.
21. Folder 9: "13th Annual Republican Women's Conference—Washington, D.C., 2 April 1965," Robert J. Dole Speeches Collection, 1958–1996, Robert and Elizabeth Dole Archive and Special Collections, https://dolearchivecollections.ku.edu/collections/speeches/002/c019_002_009_all.pdf.
22. Heckler family archives.
23. Margaret Heckler, interview by author, March 25, 2015.

CHAPTER 7

1. Heckler family archives.
2. Martin F. Dolan, "Mrs. Heckler Claims Victory," *Boston Globe*, September 14, 1966, 9.
3. "The Honorable Margaret M. Heckler Oral History Interview," Office of the Historian, US House of Representatives (June 6, 2017 and October 26, 2017), https://history.house.gov/Oral-History/Women/Representative-Heckler.

4. Richard Daly, "Mrs. Heckler Eyes Martin" and "Martin's Plans GOP Quandary," *Boston Herald*, April 16, 1966.

5. Daly, "Martin's Plans GOP Quandary."

6. Daly, "Mrs. Heckler Eyes Martin."

7. Heckler family archives.

8. Vera Glaser, "Lady in Congressional Race," *Baltimore Sun*, October 27, 1966, 27.

9. Frank Privatera, interview by author, Arlington, VA, May 20, 2019.

10. Daly, "Martin's Plans GOP Quandary."

11. "The Honorable Margaret M. Heckler," Office of the Historian.

12. "The Honorable Margaret M. Heckler," Office of the Historian.

13. "The Honorable Margaret M. Heckler," Office of the Historian.

14. Robert Turner, "Margaret Heckler: A Rose With Thorns." *Boston Globe*, September 15, 1966, https://www.proquest.com/historical-newspapers/margaret-heckler-rose-with-thorns/docview/366027338/se-2?accountid=12084.

15. Martin Tolchin and Susan J. Tolchin, *Clout: Womanpower and Politics* (New York: Coward, McCann & Geoghegan, 1974).

16. Heckler family archives.

17. Margaret Heckler, interview by author, Arlington, VA, October 14, 2016.

18. Heckler family archives.

19. "Joe Martin Accepts the Taste of Defeat," *Newsday*, September 15, 1966, 7.

20. Glaser, "Lady in Congressional Race."

21. Tolchin, *Clout: Womanpower and Politics.*

22. Heckler family archives.

23. Tolchin, *Clout: Womanpower and Politics*, 131.

24. "Joe Martin Accepts."

25. "Joe Martin Accepts."

26. Dolan, "Mrs. Heckler Claims Victory."

27. Tolchin, *Clout: Womanpower and Politics.*

28. Glaser, "Lady in Congressional Race."

29. Heckler family archives.

30. Vera Glaser, "A Heckler in Washington," *Boston Globe*, January 15, 1967.

31. Glaser, "A Heckler in Washington."

32. "The Year They Stayed In," *Time Magazine*, November 18, 1966, 14, 28, 29.

33. Glaser, "A Heckler in Washington."

34. "The Honorable Margaret M. Heckler," Office of the Historian.

CHAPTER 8

1. "Women Transforming Congress" C-SPAN, November 19, 1998, https://www.c-span.org/video/?156582-1/women-transforming-congress.

2. "Margaret Heckler, A Woman on the Go in Washington," *Boston Herald,* January 13, 1967.

3. "Margaret Heckler, A Woman."

4. Margaret Heckler, interview by author, March 11, 2015.

5. Heckler family archives.

6. Beth Hinchliffe, "A Claim on My Heart: Remembering Margaret Heckler, Massachusetts' Political Trailblazer," August 8, 2018, accessed May 20, 2024. https://www.metrowestdailynews.com/story/news/local/2018/08/08/claim-on-my-heart/6527229007.

7. "A Changing of the Guard: Traditionalists, Feminists, and the New Face of Women in Congress, 1955–1976," *History, Art & Archives: United States House of Representatives,* accessed November 17, 2023, https://history.house.gov/Exhibit ions-and-Publications/WIC/Historical-Essays/Changing-Guard/Introduction.

8. Edward Markey, interview by author, Arlington, VA, October 19, 2021.

9. Heckler family archives.

10. Margaret Heckler, interview by author, Arlington, VA, March 11, 2015.

11. Photo in the Heckler family archives.

12. Carol Bauer, interview by author, Arlington, VA, June 26, 2019.

13. Heckler family archives.

14. Heckler family archives.

15. "The Honorable Margaret M. Heckler Oral History Interview," Office of the Historian, US House of Representatives (June 6, 2017, and October 16, 2017), https://history.house.gov/Oral-History/Women/Representative-Heckler.

16. "The Honorable Margaret M. Heckler Oral History Interview."

17. Margaret Heckler, interview by author, April 10, 2016.

18. Margaret Heckler, interview by author, March 25, 2015.

19. Young, "Mrs. Heckler Cutting."

20. Heckler interview, January 25, 2017.

21. Stephanie Mansfield, "The Heckler Breakup," *Washington Post,* October 16, 1984, https://www.washingtonpost.com/archive/lifestyle/1984/10/16/the-heckler-breakup/812213ed-d2c5-4d08-8d6e-e5bf2d54d917.

22. Jim Gardner, interview by author, Arlington, VA, June 3, 2021.

23. Gardner interview.

24. Heckler interview, February 11, 2018.

25. Heckler family archives.

26. Heckler family archives.

27. Lyndon Johnson, "Remarks Upon Signing Bill Providing Equal Opportunity in Promotions for Women in the Armed Forces," *American Presidency Project,* November 8, 1967. Online by Gerhard Peters and John T. Woolley. https://www.presidency.ucsb.edu/documents/remarks-upon-signing-bill-provid ing-equal-opportunity-promotions-for-women-the-armed.

28. Heckler family archives.

29. Heckler family archives.

CHAPTER 9

1. Kaitlyn Crain Enriquez, "April 1968 Washington, D. C. Riots," April 5, 2023, accessed February 19, 2024. https://unwritten-record.blogs.archives .gov/2023/04/05/april-1968-washington-dc-riots/#:~:text=Rioting%20and%20 protests%20lasted%20in,over%206100%20individuals%20were%20arrested.

2. National Guard Educational Foundation, "The D. C. Riots of 1968," accessed February 19, 2024. https://www.ngef.org/the-d-c-riots-of-1968/#:~: text=All%20of%20these%20emotions%20erupted,a%20second%20round%20 of%20rioting.

3. "Patsy Mink and the 1967 Protest at the US House of Representatives' Gym," New York Historical Society, New York History.org, 1967, accessed July 10, 2024, https://www.nyhistory.org/blogs/members-only-patsy-mink.

4. History, Art, and Archives: United States House of Representatives, "Women in Congress: New Patterns," accessed November 18, 2023. https://his tory.house.gov/Exhibitions-and-Publications/WIC/Historical-Essays/Changing -Guard/New-Patterns/.

5. Susan Hartmann, "When Republicans Were Feminists," accessed November 18, 2023. https://www.ohioacademyofhistory.org/wp-content/uploads/2017/08/ revd-OAH-Distinguished-Historian-Address-2017-by-Susan-Hartmann _when-republicans-were-feminists-PROCEEDINGS.pdf.

6. Kenneth Thompson, *The Nixon Presidency* (Lanham, MD: University Press of America, 1987), 233.

7. Florence Dwyer, July 8, 1969, Box 39, Clapp files.

8. John W. Dean, *The Rehnquist Choice: The Untold Story of the Nixon Appointment that Redefined the Supreme Court* (New York: Free Press, 2001), 61, 63.

9. Margaret Heckler's papers in the John J. Burns Library, Boston College.

10. Hartmann, "When Republicans Were Feminists," 3.

11. "The Women's Caucus and Roaring," 1997.

12. Hartmann, "When Republicans Were Feminists," 11.

13. "The White House Fact Sheet: Women in the Federal Government," April 28, 1972.

14. "The White House Fact Sheet."

15. Hartmann, "When Republicans Were Feminists," 11.

16. Heckler family archives, AP Wire Story, August 21, 1972, Miami Beach, FL.

17. "Child Care and the Working Woman: Report and Recommendations of the Secretary's Advisory Committee on the Rights and Responsibilities of Women 1975," 41, https://files.eric.ed.gov/fulltext/ED138779.pdf.

18. Joe Western, "Fall River Survey on Childcare," Newsletter from Congresswoman Margaret Heckler to the Tenth Congressional District, Massachusetts, December 3, 1971.

19. William Roth, "Institute for Research on Poverty Discussion Papers. The Politics of Daycare: The Comprehensive Child Development Act of 1971," 1976, accessed November 18, 2023, https://www.irp.wisc.edu/publications/dps/pdfs/dp36976.pdf.

20. Matt Schudel, "Margaret M. Heckler, Congresswoman, HHS Secretary and Ambassador Dies at 87," *Washington Post*, August 6, 2018.

21. Matthew Andrew Wasniewski, editor, *Women in Congress* (Washington, DC: Government Printing Office, 2006).

22. Congress, Senate, Committee on the Judiciary, The "Equal Rights Amendment": Hearings before the Subcommittee on Constitutional Amendments of the Committee on the Judiciary, Ninety-first Cong., second session, May 5, 6, and 7, 1970, http://historymatters.gmu.edu/d/7020.

23. History, Art, and Archives.

24. Margaret Heckler, interview by author, Arlington, VA, October 14, 2016.

25. Letter from House Minority Leader Gerald R. Ford to President Richard M. Nixon, accessed August 13, 2021, http://www.archives.gov/education/lessons/ford-nixon-letter.

26. Danny Converse, interview by author, Arlington, VA, February 21, 2023.

27. History.com editors, "Watergate Scandal," accessed April 20, 2024. https://www.history.com/topics/1970s/watergate.

28. David Rosenbaum, "An Explanation: How Money that Financed Watergate was Raised and Distributed," *New York Times,* May 17, 1974, https://www.nytimes.com/1974/05/17/archives/an-explanation-how-money-that-financed-watergate-was-raised-and.html.

29. A letter from Mrs. William G. Campbell to Congresswoman Margaret Heckler on October 5, 1972 regarding a *Boston Globe* article by Robert Healy. From the John J. Burns Library.

30. Heckler family archives.

31. Joe Byrnes interview by author, Arlington, VA, August 12, 2021.

32. Margaret Heckler papers in the John J. Burns Library, Boston College.

33. Danny Converse, interview by author, Arlington, VA, February 21, 2023.

34. John Chancelor, "Saturday Night Massacre| Nixon," *American Experience,* 1972.

35. Heckler family archives.

36. Banking and Currency Committee statement on Watergate, July 1974, John J. Burns Library.

37. Glenda Leggitt Etchison, interview by author, Arlington, VA, August 16, 2021.

CHAPTER 10

1. Heckler family archives.

2. Margaret Heckler, "Women's Right to Credit," *119 Congressional Record (Bound)—House of Representatives,* July 23, 1973, 25, 486, https://www.govinfo .gov/app/details/GPO-CRECB-1973-pt20/GPO-CRECB-1973-pt20-2-2.

3. Enid Nemy, "Congress Passes Bill Banning Bias Against Women on Credit," *New York Times,* October 11, 1974, https://www.nytimes.com/ 1974/10/11/archives/congress-passes-bill-banning-bias-against-women-on -credit-women.html.

4. Leandra Ruth Zarnow, *Battling Bella: The Protest Politics of Bella Abzug* (Cambridge, MA: Harvard University Press, 2019) 121; Edmund Rice (administrative assistant for Margaret), in discussion with the author, May 18, 2020.

5. Edmund Rice, interview by author, Arlington, VA, May 18, 2020.

6. Rice interview.

7. Rice interview.

8. Margaret M. Heckler, subcommittee on Consumer Affairs Hearings on Credit Discrimination, November 13, 1973.

9. Heckler, subcommittee on Consumer Affairs Hearings.

10. Heckler, subcommittee on Consumer Affairs Hearings.

11. Heckler, subcommittee on Consumer Affairs Hearings.

12. Heckler, "Women's Right to Credit."

13. Rice interview.

14. Heckler, subcommittee on Consumer Affairs Hearings.

15. Heckler, subcommittee on Consumer Affairs Hearings.

16. Rice interview.

17. "Women Transforming Congress," C-SPAN, April 14, 2000, accessed November 25, 2023. https://www.c-span.org/video/?156582-1/women-transforming -congress.

18. Donnie Radcliffe, "A Show of Support for Women's Issues," *Washington Post,* April 26, 1978.

19. "BOGGS, Corinne Claiborne (Lindy)," History, Art & Archives US House of Representatives, accessed November 19, 2023, https://history.house.gov/Peo ple/Listing/B/BOGGS,-Corinne-Claiborne-(Lindy)-(B000592)/#assignments.

20. "The Equal Credit Opportunity Act," justice.gov, accessed November 19, 2023. https://www.justice.gov/crt/equal-credit-opportunity-act-3.

21. Margaret Heckler papers in the John J. Burns Library, Boston College.

22. Lynn Olanoff, "Silver Anniversary: Founder of Women's Caucus Marks Group's Milestone." *Roll Call, Life After Congress,* April 18, 2002, 42.

23. "Women Transforming Congress," C-SPAN.

CHAPTER 11

1. Jack Horner, interview by author, Arlington, VA, December 11, 2019.

2. "The Honorable Margaret M. Heckler Oral History Interview."

3. Margaret Heckler, interview by author, Arlington, VA, February 21, 2016.

4. Jack McCarthy, interview by author, Arlington, VA, January 11, 2023.

5. McCarthy interview.

6. McCarthy interview.

7. HR 12965, 18252, 17958, 10130, and 10494, respectively.

8. "The Honorable Margaret M. Heckler Oral History Interview."

9. Margaret Heckler, interview by author, Arlington, VA, January 25, 2017.

10. "The White House Fact Sheet: President Biden's Budget Honors Our Nation's Sacred Commitment to Veterans and Military Families," March 9, 2023, accessed March 5, 2024. https://www.whitehouse.gov/omb/briefing-room/2023/03/09/fact-sheet-president-bidens-budget-honors-our-nations-sacred-commitment-to-veterans-and-military-families/#:~:text=Prioritizes%20VA%20Medical%20Care.,%2417.1%20billion%20in%20the%20TEF.

11. "Heckler Thanks Supporters of Her Health Bill." *Congressional Record,* September 10, 1979, https://www.govinfo.gov/content/pkg/GPO-CRECB-1979-pt18/pdf/GPO-CRECB-1979-pt18-4-3.pdf.

12. Heckler family archives.

13. The 1950s Great Leap Forward economic campaign killed an estimated forty million people and then Mao's Cultural Revolution in the 1960s killed up to a million more people, with a total estimate of forty to eighty million deaths over the reign of Mao's rule.

14. Michael E. Ruane, "China Was a Brutal Communist Menace. In 1972, Richard Nixon Visited, Anyway," *Washington Post*, February 20, 2022, https://www.washingtonpost.com/history/2022/02/20/nixon-china-mao-visit-1972/.

15. Margaret Heckler, "China 1975 A Firsthand View."

16. Pete McCloskey, interview by author, Arlington, VA, February 13, 2020.

17. McCloskey interview.

18. McCloskey interview.

19. Margaret Heckler, "China 1975 A Firsthand View."

20. Heckler, "China."

21. "The Honorable Patricia Scott Schroeder Oral History Interview," Office of the Historian, US House of Representatives, June 3, 2015.

22. Laurie Johnston, "Notes on People," *New York Times*, December 13,1975, https://www.nytimes.com/1975/12/13/archives/notes-on-people-12-women-in-house-to-make-china-trip.html.

23. Heckler family archives.

24. Heckler family archives.

25. Heckler family archives.

CHAPTER 12

1. Marene Nyberg Allison, interview by author, Arlington, VA, May 25, 2021.

2. "New Opportunities Seen for Women in US Army," *Lincoln News Bridgewater Edition—New England Newsclip*, October 25, 1978; "Heckler Praises Army for Women," *Dover-Sherborn Suburban Press*, October 12, 1978.

3. Allison interview, 2021.

4. Marene Nyberg Allison, "At the Gates of West Point." All excerpts in this piece are taken from the Marene Nyberg Allison Collection, October 21, 2006, transcript, Women's Memorial Foundation Oral History Collection, Women's Memorial Foundation, Arlington, VA.

5. Allison, "At the Gates of West Point."

6. Allison, "At the Gates of West Point."

7. Allison interview, 2021.

8. Allison, "At the Gates of West Point."

9. Allison interview, 2021.

10. Allison interview, April 12, 2024.

11. Bee Haydu, interview by author, Arlington, VA, November 8, 2019.

12. Stephen Arionus, "Women Airforce Service Pilots and their Fight for Veteran Status," *Air Force Personnel Center, Air Force,* November 11, 2021, https://www.af.mil/News/Article-Display/Article/2838960/women-airforce-service-pilots-and-their-fight-for-veteran-status/.

13. "Women Airforce Service Pilots (WASP)." *US Army,* accessed October 25, 2021. https://www.army.mil/women/history/pilots.html.

14. Arionus, "Women Airforce Service Pilots."

15. Arionus, "Women Airforce Service Pilots."

16. "The Honorable Patricia Scott Schroeder Oral History," 2015. Office of the Historian, US House of Representatives, June 3, 2015.

17. Arionus, "Women Airforce Service Pilots."

18. Haydu interview.

19. Haydu interview.

20. "Women Members' Lives and Experiences," C-SPAN, April 26, 1996, https://www.c-span.org/video/?71467-1/women-members-lives-experiences.

21. "Women Members' Lives."

22. Arionus, "Women Airforce Service Pilots."

23. HR 3277, September 20, 1977, Washington, DC: US Government, 29, https://babel.hathitrust.org/cgi/pt?id=mdp.39015082545826&view=1up&seq=7.

24. Katherine Sharp Landdeck, *The Women with Silver Wings: The Inspiring True Story of the Women Airforce Service Pilots of World War II* (New York: Crown Publishing, 2020) 313.

25. Arionus, "Women Airforce Service Pilots."

26. Landdeck, *The Women with Silver Wings*, 314.
27. Landdeck, *The Women with Silver Wings*, 314.
28. Landdeck, *The Women with Silver Wings*, 315.
29. HR 3277, 235.
30. HR 3277, 235.
31. HR 3277, 235.
32. Landdeck, *The Women with Silver Wings*, 315.
33. "Women Airforce Service Pilots (WASP)."
34. "Women Members' Lives."
35. Landdeck, *The Women with Silver Wings*, 317.
36. Bee Haydu, interview by author, Arlington, VA, January 15, 2019.

CHAPTER 13

1. Jack Horner, interview by author, Arlington, VA, December 11, 2019.
2. Donnie Radcliffe, "A Show of Support for Women's Issues," *Washington Post*, April 26, 1978.
3. Carol Bauer, interview by author, Arlington, VA, June 26, 2019.
4. "The Honorable Margaret M. Heckler Oral History Interview," Office of the Historian, US House of Representatives (June 6, 2017, and October 26, 2017). https://history.house.gov/Oral-History/Women/Representative-Heckler/.
5. Olanoff, "Silver Anniversary," 42.
6. "The Honorable Margaret M. Heckler Oral History Interview."
7. "The Honorable Margaret M. Heckler Oral History Interview."
8. "The Honorable Margaret M. Heckler Oral History Interview."
9. "The Honorable Margaret M. Heckler Oral History Interview."
10. Horner interview.
11. Horner interview.
12. Olanoff, "Silver Anniversary," 42.
13. "The Honorable Margaret M. Heckler Oral History Interview."
14. Elizabeth Holtzman, interview by author, Arlington, VA, June 13, 2019.
15. Holtzman interview.
16. "The Honorable Margaret M. Heckler Oral History Interview."
17. Patricia Schroeder, interview by author, Arlington, VA, October 30, 2020.
18. Holtzman interview.
19. "The Honorable Elizabeth Holtzman Oral History Interview."
20. Margaret Heckler, interview by author, Arlington, VA, March 8, 2015.
21. Laila Kazmi and Stephen Hegg, "What Former Presidential Candidate Shirley Chisholm Said about Facing Gender Discrimination," September 13, 2016, accessed May 12, 2024. https://www.pbs.org/newshour/politics/what-former-presidential-candidate-shirley-chisholm-said-about-facing-gender-discrimination.

22. "The Honorable Margaret M. Heckler Oral History Interview."

23. Holtzman interview.

24. "The Honorable Margaret M. Heckler Oral History Interview."

25. Holtzman interview.

26. Daniel K. Williams "The Pro-Life Movement, a History," accessed March 8, 2024. https://mcgrath.nd.edu/assets/458944/the_pro_life_movement_a_his tory.pdf.

27. Holtzman interview.

28. Holtzman interview.

29. Schroeder interview.

30. Schroeder interview.

31. Holtzman interview.

32. Radcliffe, "A Show of Support for Women's Issues."

33. "The Honorable Margaret M. Heckler Oral History Interview."

34. Heckler interview.

35. "Statement by the President on National Women's History Week." The American Presidency Project, February 28, 1980, https://www.presidency.ucsb .edu/documents/statement-the-president-national-womens-history-week.

36. Donnie Radcliffe, "A Show of Support for Women's Issues," *Washington Post*, April 26, 1978.

37. Donnie Radcliffe, "The Women's Caucus," *Washington Post*, April 27, 1978.

38. "History of Women's Participation in Clinical Research." National Institutes of Health, accessed April 23, 2024, https://orwh.od.nih.gov/toolkit/ recruitment/history.

39. Patricia Schroeder, interview by author, Arlington, VA, October 30, 2020.

40. Margaret Heckler, interview by author, Arlington, VA, February 11, 2018.

41. Olympia Snowe, interview by author, Arlington, VA, April 18, 2023.

42. Olympia Snowe, interview by author, Arlington, VA, April 18, 2023.

43. Holtzman interview.

44. Holtzman interview.

45. Holtzman interview.

46. Holtzman interview.

47. Holtzman interview.

48. Schroeder interview.

49. Henry Kamm, "Cambodia Tells US Group It Will Allow More Aid; Cambodia Assures US Group It Will Allow More Aid," *New York Times*, November 13, 1979.

50. Snowe interview.

51. Schroeder interview.

52. Holtzman interview.

53. Kamm, "Cambodia Tells US Group."

54. Holtzman interview.

55. Kamm, "Cambodia Tells US Group."

56. Holtzman interview.

57. Margaret Heckler, "Cambodia: Still a Nightmare," *Margaret M. Heckler Reports from Washington,* Spring 1980.

58. Irwin Gertzog, "The Congressional Caucus for Women's Issues was the most effective bipartisan organization in the US House of Representatives," says Irwin Gertzog, "until the Republican revolution of 1994 threatened its survival." (Author of 2004 *Women & Power on Capitol Hill,* Boulder, CO: Lynne Reinner Publishers.)

59. "Congresswomen Admit 46 Men to Their Caucus," *New York Times,* December 14, 1981.

60. "The Honorable Margaret M. Heckler Oral History Interview," Office of the Historian, US House of Representatives (June 6, 2017 and October 26, 2017), https://history.house.gov/Oral-History/Women/Representative-Heckler/.

CHAPTER 14

1. James Lardner and Neil Henry, "Over 40,000 ERA Backers March on Hill," *Washington Post,* July 10, 1978, https://www.washingtonpost.com/archive/politics/1978/07/10/over-40000-era-backers-march-on-hill/880a1a29-c7ba-46f7-afd3-ade684653e63/.

2. Karen de Witt, "100,000 Join March for Extension of Rights Amendment Deadline," *New York Times,* July 10, 1978, https://www.nytimes.com/1978/07/10/archives/100000-join-march-for-extension-of-rights-amendment-deadline-100000.html.

3. Lardner, "Over 40,000 ERA Backers March on Hill."

4. Danny Converse, interview by author, Arlington, VA, February 21, 2023.

5. Carol McCabe, "Margaret Heckler: She's Different," *Providence Sunday Journal,* April 13, 1975.

6. "The Honorable Margaret M. Heckler Oral History Interview," Office of the Historian, US House of Representatives (June 6, 2017, and October 26, 2017), https://history.house.gov/Oral-History/Women/Representative-Heckler/.

7. Converse interview.

8. Ted Fitzgerald, interview by author, Arlington, VA, November 12, 2020.

9. Converse interview.

10. Fitzgerald interview.

11. Fitzgerald interview.

12. Jack McCarthy, interview by author, Arlington, VA, January 11, 2023.

13. Jack Horner, interview by author, Arlington, VA, December 11, 2019.

14. McCabe, "Margaret Heckler: She's Different."

15. John Heckler Jr., interview by author, Arlington, VA, October 11, 2018.

CHAPTER 15

1. Jack Horner, interview by author, Arlington, VA, December 11, 2019.

2. Horner interview.

3. Danny Converse, interview by author, Arlington, VA, February 21, 2023.

4. Karen Tumulty, *The Triumph of Nancy Reagan* (New York: Simon and Schuster, 2021), 519.

5. Tumulty, *The Triumph.*

6. Linda Bilmes, interview by author, Arlington, VA, November 4, 2019.

7. Bilmes interview.

8. Alice Tetelman, "I Hope the Next Generation Will Continue to Hold Up the Banner in Whatever Way They Can," *VFA Pioneer Histories Project: Veteran Feminists of America*, interviewed by Judith Waxman, February 2021, https:// veteranfeministsofamerica.org/vfa-pioneer-histories-project-alice-tetelman/in terview-alice-tetelman.

9. Bill Peterson, "The Republicans in Detroit," *Washington Post,* July 15, 1980, https://www.washingtonpost.com/archive/politics/1980/07/15/the-republicans -in-detroit/10824cab-3a0c-436d-a9b6-34565bab5297.

10. Andy Card, interview by author, Arlington, VA, March 11, 2020.

11. Pete McCloskey, interview by author, Arlington, VA, February 13, 2020.

12. Stuart Spencer, interview by author, Arlington, VA, August 20, 2021.

13. Tetelman, "I Hope the Next Generation."

14. Bilmes interview.

15. Bilmes interview.

16. Stephanie Mansfield, "The Heckler Breakup," *Washington Post,* October 16, 1984, https://www.washingtonpost.com/archive/lifestyle/1984/10/16/the -heckler-breakup/812213ed-d2c5-4d08-8d6e-e5bf2d54d917.

17. Bilmes interview.

18. Alice Tetelman, interview by Elizabeth Griffith, February 5, 2021.

19. Tetelman, "I Hope the Next Generation."

20. Margaret Heckler, "Letter to Carl Sferrazza Anthony, former speech writer to Nancy Reagan," December 11, 1998.

21. Tetelman interview.

22. Margaret Simpson, "The New Secretaries, Margaret Heckler," *Working Woman.*

23. Pam Ou, interview by author, Arlington, VA, May 28, 2021.

24. Card interview.

25. Tetelman, "I Hope the Next Generation."

26. "The Honorable Margaret M. Heckler Oral History Interview," Office of the Historian, US House of Representatives (June 6, 2017, and October 26, 2017), https://history.house.gov/Oral-History/Women/Representative-Heckler/.

27. Margaret Heckler, interview by author, Arlington, VA, March 8, 2015.

28. NBP Staff, "Longtime Republican Survivor Margaret Heckler Dies, 87," *New Boston Post*, August 7, 2018. https://newbostonpost.com/2018/08/07/longtime-republican-survivor-margaret-heckler-dies-87/.

29. Card interview.

30. Card interview.

31. Sey Chassler, "Between the Lines," *Redbook*, November 1980.

32. "NOW Endorses Barney Frank," *Jewish Times*, October 21, 1982.

33. Bilmes interview.

34. Lynn Olanoff, "Silver Anniversary: Founder of Women's Caucus Marks Group's Milestone," *Roll Call*, April 18, 2002.

35. Converse interview.

36. Converse interview.

37. Converse interview.

38. NBP Staff, "Longtime Republican Survivor," *New Boston Post*, November 3, 1982.

39. Heckler interview, March 11, 2015.

CHAPTER 16

1. David Van Biema and Garry Clifford, "Washington's Revolving Door," *People*, February 14, 1983, 34–35.

2. Biema and Clifford, "Washington's Revolving Door," 34–35.

3. Jerry Abrams, interview by author, Arlington, VA, October 17, 2020.

4. Abrams interview.

5. George Siguler, interview by author, Arlington, VA, March 23, 2021.

6. John Heckler Jr., interview by author, Arlington, VA, October 11, 2018.

7. Siguler interview.

8. Siguler interview.

9. Bella Abzug and Mim Kelber, "Despite the Reagan Sweep, a Gender Gap Remains," *New York Times*, November 23, 1984, https://www.nytimes.com/1984/11/23/opinion/despite-the-reagan-sweep-a-gender-gap-remains.html.

10. Susan Hartmann, "When Republicans Were Feminists," accessed November 10, 2023. https://www.ohioacademyofhistory.org/wp-content/uploads/2017/08/revd-OAH-Distinguished-Historian-Address-2017-by-Susan-Hartmann_when-republicans-were-feminists-PROCEEDINGS.pdf.

11. Siguler interview.

12. Siguler interview.

13. "Remarks Announcing the Resignation of Richard S. Schweiker as Secretary of Health and Human Services and the Nomination of Margaret M. Heckler for the Position," January 12, 1983, accessed September 12, 2022. https://www

.reaganlibrary.gov/archives/speech/remarks-announcing-resignation-richard-s
-schweiker-secretary-health-and-human.

14. Mel Lukens, interview by author, Arlington, VA, March 8, 2021.

15. Kathy Sawyer, "Budget Briefing: Safety Enforcement Faces Cut," February 10, 1983, accessed May 18, 2024. https://www.washingtonpost.com/archive/pol itics/1983/02/11/budget-briefing/46c69288-e66b-446a-9014-92ce38bfdc23/.

16. "The Swearing in of Margaret Heckler as the new Secretary of Health and Human Services by Justice Sandra Day O'Connor then Remarks by President Reagan in the Oval Office on March 9, 1983," https://www.youtube.com/watch?v=2mHM1QuIQLE.

17. "The Swearing in of Margaret Heckler."

18. Siguler interview.

19. "Heckler Foresees Six More Years," *Washington Post*, March 15, 1983.

20. Siguler interview.

21. "Secretary Heckler Addresses Employees," *NIH Record*, March 29, 1983.

22. Jacquelyn White, interview by author, Arlington, VA, September 8, 2020.

23. White interview.

24. Dale Dirks, interview by author, Arlington, VA, May 15, 2023.

25. Ruth S. Hanft, *Blacks and the Health Professions in the 1980s: A National Crisis and a Time for Action* (Washington, DC: The Association of Minority Health Professions Schools), 1983.

26. Ruben Warren, interview by author, Arlington, VA, June 7, 2023.

27. Warren interview.

28. Louis Sullivan, interview by author, Arlington, VA, April 18, 2023.

29. C-SPAN 2000, "Women Transforming Congress," accessed November 25, 2023. https://www.c-span.org/video/?156582-1/women-transforming-congress.

30. *Health, United States and Prevention Profile, 1983*, National Center for Health Statistics, 1983, accessed October 18, 2024. https://www.cdc.gov/nchs/data/hus/hus83acc.pdf.

31. Heckler interview, March 25, 2015.

32. Heckler interview.

33. Akilah Johnson, "Black Communities Endured Wave of Excess Deaths in Past Two Decades, Studies Find," *Washington Post*, May 16, 2023, https://www.washingtonpost.com/health/2023/05/16/black-communities-excess-deaths/.

34. "Part 2 Trends in Priorities in the Heckler Report," accessed April 25, 2024, https://www.ncbi.nlm.nih.gov/books/NBK581106/.

35. Reuben interview.

36. Warren interview.

37. Warren interview.

38. Sullivan interview.

39. Heckler family archives.

40. Heckler family archives.

41. Heckler family archives.

42. Bruce Hertz, "My Experience with a Cabinet Officer," *Somerset Sawdust*, in the family archives.

CHAPTER 17

1. PBS *Frontline* interview with Margaret Heckler. This is the edited transcript of an interview conducted on January 11, 2006, https://www.pbs.org/wgbh/pages/frontline/aids/interviews/heckler.html.

2. PBS *Frontline* interview.

3. James Morrison, "Ex-Envoy Fights AIDS," *Embassy Row*, November 9, 1995.

4. Heckler family archives.

5. Gerry Abrams, interview by author, Arlington, VA. October 17, 2020.

6. Heckler family archives.

7. Linda Bilmes, interview by author, Arlington, VA, November 4, 2019.

8. Boyce Rensberger, "AIDS Cases in 1985 Exceed Total of All Previous Years," *Washington Post*, January 17, 1986, https://www.washingtonpost.com/archive/politics/1986/01/17/aids-cases-in-1985-exceed-total-of-all-previous-years/38c933d7-260c-414b-80f7-0dd282415cc6/.

9. Associated Press, "AIDS Threat is Exaggerated, Officials Say," *Atlanta Journal*, September 15, 1983.

10. Walter Isaacson, "Hunting for the Hidden Killers: AIDS Disease Detectives Face a Never Ending Quest," *Time*, July 4, 1983, http://content.time.com/time/subscriber/article/0,33009,950937-1,00.html.

11. Willem A. Saayman, "Diagnostic Medievalism: The Case of Leprosy's Stigma," Summer 2019, accessed May 13, 2024. https://dsq-sds.org/index.php/dsq/article/view/6410/5409#:~:text=At%20the%20height%20of%20the,in%20Africa%20by%20Willem%20A.

12. Associated Press, "AIDS."

13. "AIDS: When Fear Takes Charge," *US News & World Report*, October 12, 1987.

14. Daniel Bates, "Airlines Refused to Fly Rock Hudson After His AIDS Diagnosis Became Public, Claims Hollywood Actor's Former Manager," *Daily Mail*, April 22, 2015, https://www.dailymail.co.uk/tvshowbiz/article-3050932/Airlines-refused-fly-Rock-Hudson-home-AIDS-diagnosis-public-claims-Hollywood-actor-s-former-manager.html.

15. "Heckler Tells Mayors of AIDS Battle Plan: Says US Will Provide Health Advisers, Hot Line, Disability Pay," *Los Angeles Times*, Part I, June 15, 1983.

16. Margaret Heckler papers in the John J. Burns Library, Boston College.

17. "Heckler Donates Blood," *Boston Globe*, July 11, 1983.

18. Associated Press, "AIDS."

19. Isaacson, "Hunting."

20. Linda Bilmes, interview by author, Arlington, VA, November 4, 2019.

21. Isaacson, "Hunting."

22. Heckler family archives.

23. Heckler family archives.

24. Lawrence K. Altman, "US and France End Rift on AIDS," *New York Times,* April 1, 1987, https://www.nytimes.com/1987/04/01/us/us-and-france-end-rift-on-aids.html.

25. Alice Park, "The Man Who Co-Discovered HIV 30 Years Ago on Why There Won't Be a Cure for AIDS," *Time,* April 23, 2014, https://time.com/72938/the-man-who-co-discovered-hiv-30-years-ago-on-why-there-wont-be-a-cure-for-aids.

26. Margaret Heckler papers.

27. Lenny Bernstein and Carolyn Y. Johnson, "Decades of Research on an HIV Vaccine Boost the Bid for One Against Coronavirus," *Washington Post,* July 14, 2020, https://www.washingtonpost.com/health/decades-of-research-on-an-hiv-vaccine-boosts-the-bid-for-one-against-coronavirus/2020/07/13/3eb1a37a-c216-11ea-b4f6-cb39cd8940fb_story.html.

28. Ed Meese, interview by author, Arlington, VA, November 13, 2019.

29. Ron Kaufman, interview by author, Arlington, VA, September 2, 2020.

30. Karen Tumulty, *The Triumph of Nancy Reagan* (New York: Simon and Schuster), 986.

31. PBS *Frontline* interview.

CHAPTER 18

1. Saul Ebema, "What Are the Unique Origins of Hospice?" *Hospice Chaplaincy*, January 3, 2018, https://hospicechaplaincy.com/2018/01/03/hospice-origns.

2. Ebema, "What Are the Unique Origins."

3. "Hospice: Background," Homecare and Hospice: National Association for Home Care & Hospice, October 14, 2017, http://www.nahc.org/wp-content/uploads/2017/10/14-NHCHM-Hospice-Background.pdf.

4. Margaret Heckler papers in the John J. Burns Library, Boston College.

5. "Budget Success," *Argus Leader* (SD), October 11, 1984.

6. National Hospice and Palliative Care Organization, "New Research Shows Hospice Care Reduces Medicare Costs, Hospice Care Contributed $3.5 Billion in Medicare Savings in One Year," 2023, accessed April 27, 2024. https://www.nhpco.org/new-research-shows-hospice-care-reduces-medicare-costs/#:~:text=(Alexandria%2C%20VA%20and%20Washington%2C,patients%2C%20families%2C%20and%20caregivers.

7. Jacquelyn White, interview by author, Arlington, VA, September 8, 2020.

8. Jane Whitlow, "Health Chief Stumps State for Reagan-Bush," *Star Ledger* (NJ), October 16, 1984.

9. White interview.

10. White interview.

11. White interview.

12. White interview.

13. White interview.

14. White interview.

15. White interview.

16. White interview.

17. White interview.

18. George Siguler, interview by author, Arlington, VA, March 23, 2021.

19. Margaret Heckler, interview by author, Arlington, VA, March 25, 2015.

20. The Omnibus Budget Reconciliation Act of 1985 gave a 10 percent increase in reimbursement rates, made the Medicare hospice benefit permanent, and allowed hospices to care for residents of nursing facilities. States were given the option of including hospice in their Medicaid programs. There were 158 Medicare certified agencies. http://www.nahc.org/wp-content/uploads/2017/10/14 -NHCHM-Hospice-Background.pdf.

21. White interview.

22. Margaret Heckler papers in the John J. Burns Library, Boston College.

23. White interview.

24. Alison Heckler, interview by author, Arlington, VA, April 6, 2022.

CHAPTER 19

1. Beth Hinchliffe, "A Claim on my Heart," *MetroWest Daily News*, August 8, 2018, accessed January 12, 2024. https://www.metrowestdailynews.com/story/ news/local/2018/08/08/claim-on-my-heart/6527229007/.

2. Andy Card, interview by author, Arlington, VA, March 11, 2020.

3. Heckler family archives.

4. Margaret Heckler, interview by author, Arlington, VA, February 11, 2018.

5. Jack Pierce, interview by author, Arlington, VA, August 5, 2019; Bernard Weinraub, "The Washingtonization of Nancy Reagan," *New York Times* Archives, March 26, 1985, https://www.nytimes.com/1985/03/26/us/the-washingtoniza tion-of-nancy-reagan.html.

6. Mary Anne Thadeau, interview by author, Arlington, VA, April 30, 2023.

7. Weinraub, "The Washingtonization."

8. Weinraub, "The Washingtonization."

9. Lois Romano, "Heckler Sued for Divorce," *Washington Post*, August 8, 2018.

10. Donnie Radcliffe, "The Heckler Breakup," *Washington Post,* October 16, 1984.

11. Belinda Heckler Mulliken, interview by author, Arlington, VA, November 7, 2018.

12. Romano, "Heckler Sued."

13. Romano, "Heckler Sued."

14. Mary Beth Bloomberg, interview by author, Arlington, VA, March 10, 2021.

15. Heckler interview, February 16, 2016.

16. "Hecklers Reach Divorce Accord," *New York Times Archives*, February 14, 1985, https://www.nytimes.com/1985/02/14/us/hecklers-reach-divorce-accord .html.

17. James A. Baker, interview by author, Arlington, VA, October 23, 2020.

18. David Hoffman, "Heckler's Ouster Shows Regan's Power," *Washington Post*, October 2, 1985, https://www.washingtonpost.com/archive/politics/1985/ 10/02/hecklers-ouster-shows-regans-power/6382a38d-0d34-4392-8397-5f62e 6e028a2.

19. Margaret Heckler, "Breast Cancer Prevention," speech at the National Institutes of Health, 1985.

20. Dale Mezzacappa, "Reagan Urges Child-Support Reforms," *Philadelphia Inquirer*, September 16, 1983.

21. Spencer Rich and Dale Russakoff, "Reagan Signs Bill Increasing Power To Collect Child-Support Payments," *Washington Post*, August 17, 1984.

22. Robert Pear, "Reagan Signs Bill Forcing Payments for Child Support," *New York Times*, August 17, 1984, https://www.nytimes.com/1984/08/17/us/ reagan-signs-bill-forcing-payments-for-child-support.html.

23. Mark W. Bondi, Emily C. Edmonds, and David P. Salmon, "Alzheimer's Disease: Past, Present, and Future," NIH National Library of Medicine, February 28, 2018, https://www.ncbi.nlm.nih.gov/pmc/articles/PMC5830188.

24. Valerie Megerian, interview by author, Arlington, VA, May 24, 2019.

25. Thadeau interview.

26. Heckler family archives.

27. "Grants Given for Study of Alzheimer's Disease," *Taunton Daily Gazette* (MA), October 2, 1984.

28. "Headliners; Fast Serves its Purpose," *New York Times Archives*, November 11, 1984, https://www.nytimes.com/1984/11/11/weekinreview/headliners-fast -serves-its-purpose.html.

29. "Margaret M. Heckler Who Championed Women's Issues in Congress Dies at 87," *Washington Post,* August 8, 2018, https://www.washingtonpost .com/gender-identity/margaret-m-heckler-who-championed-womens-issues -in-congress-dies-at-87.

30. Mel Lukens, interview by author, Arlington, VA, March 8, 2021.

31. Donald T. Reagan, *For the Record from Wall Street to Washington* (Orlando, FL: Harcourt Brace Jovanovich, 1988), 291.

32. George Siguler, interview by author, Arlington, VA, March 23, 2021.

33. William Kronholm, "Heckler Won't Be 'Hustled Out,' Hatch Promised," *AP News,* September 27, 1985, https://apnews.com/article/bb8637a0bcdd3073 ba5c97f2660ae392.

34. Kronholm, "Heckler Won't Be."

35. Informal Exchange With Reporters on Secretary of Health and Human Services Margaret M. Heckler, September 30, 1985, Ronald Reagan Presidential Library and Museum, https://www.reaganlibrary.gov/archives/speech/informal -exchange-reporters-secretary-health-and-human-services-margaret-m-heckler. "*Note: The exchange began at 10:10 a.m. in the Oval Office at the White House, prior to discussions with King Hussein I of Jordan. Donald T. Regan was Assistant to the president and Chief of Staff. A tape was not available for verification of the content of this exchange.*"

36. Hoffman, "Heckler's Ouster."

37. Baker interview.

38. Sean Cronin, "Heckler Resists Shift to Dublin," *Irish Times,* September 30, 1985.

39. Bernard Purcell, "Reagan's Reluctant Ambassador," *Irish Independent,* October 1, 1985.

40. Siguler interview.

41. Hoffman, "Heckler's Ouster."

42. Heckler family archives.

43. Robert Pear, "Woman in the News; A Shrewd and Combative Envoy to Ireland: Margaret Mary O'Shaughnessy," *New York Times,* October 2, 1985, https://www.nytimes.com/1985/10/02/us/woman-shrewd-combative-envoy-ire land-margaret-mary-o-shaughnessy.html.

44. Heckler family archives.

45. Ellen Goodman and *Washington Post* Writers Group, "Margaret Heckler's Out and Chauvinism Is In," *Chicago Tribune,* October 10, 1985, https://www .chicagotribune.com/news/ct-xpm-1985-10-10-8503090223-story.html.

46. Goodman, "Margaret Heckler's Out."

47. Andy Card, interview by author, Arlington, VA, March 11, 2020.

48. Heckler family archives.

49. Heckler family archives.

CHAPTER 20

1. Heckler family archives.

2. Margaret Heckler, interview by author, Arlington, VA, March 25, 2015.

3. Heckler family archives.

4. Heckler family archives.

5. Elizabeth Shannon, *Up in the Park: The Diary of the Wife of the American Ambassador to Ireland 1977–1981* (New York: Antheneum, 1983), 18.

6. Heckler interview.

7. Sarah Booth Conroy, "Margaret Heckler, All Emerald Smiles," *Washington Post*, March 17, 1987.

8. Video footage of *The Hal Roach Show* introducing America's Ambassador to Ireland, January 1986.

9. Heckler family archives.

10. Margaret Heckler, interview by author, Arlington, VA, March 8, 2015.

11. George D. Moffett, "Anglo-Irish Accord: A Route to Peace, Says Heckler," *Christian Science Monitor*, June 12, 1986, https://www.csmonitor.com/1986/0612/aheck.html.

12. Com Keena, "Behind Barbed Wire and Bullet-Proof Glass, the Embassies: The Other Great Risk Area From Terrorism is Our Foreign Embassies Reports," *Irish Independent*, October 9, 1986.

13. Keena, "Behind Barbed Wire."

14. Heckler interview.

15. Heckler family archives.

16. Moffett, "Anglo-Irish Accord."

17. "Ireland and Libya: The Connection," *Irish Times*, October 21, 2011, https://www.irishtimes.com/news/ireland-and-libya-the-connection-1.628509.

18. Heckler family archives.

19. Moffett, "Anglo-Irish Accord."

20. Moffett, "Anglo-Irish Accord."

21. "Northern Ireland Peace Process Testimony at the House International Relations Committee," C-SPAN, March 15, 1995, https://www.c-span.org/video/?63961-1/northern-ireland-peace-process.

22. Heckler family archives.

23. "Northern Ireland Peace."

24. "Northern Ireland Peace."

25. Heckler family archives.

26. Beth Hinchliffe, "A Claim on My Heart," accessed May 20, 2024. https://www.metrowestdailynews.com/story/news/local/2018/08/08/claim-on-my-heart/6527229007.

27. Heckler family archives.

28. Jody McPhillips, "The Ambassador: In Ireland, the Land of Her Forebears, Margaret Heckler Learns to Love the Job She Didn't Want," *Sunday Journal*, November 29, 1987.

29. Carlton Varney, interview by author, Arlington, VA, February 2, 2022.

30. James R. Carroll, "Stars and Stripes in Ireland," *Golden State Report, Washington Connection*, October 1987.

31. Carroll, "Stars and Stripes."

32. Margaret Heckler, Tourism, Ambassador's Speech: American Travel Writers, Date: October 26, 1986, Title: "A Very Special Place."

33. Letter from Pamela Kearney to Ambassador Margaret Heckler, May 12, 1988.

34. Padraic White, interview by author, Arlington, VA, April 21, 2023.

35. "Northern Ireland Peace Process Testimony at the House International Relations Committee," C-SPAN, March 15, 1995, https://www.c-span.org/video/?63961-1/northern-ireland-peace-process.

36. White interview.

37. White interview.

38. White interview.

39. Heckler family archives.

40. Heckler, Remarks.

41. Toast written by Roger Woodworth, July 1, 1989.

42. Lewis, "Hall of Fame."

43. White interview.

44. White interview.

CHAPTER 21

1. Margaret Heckler, interview by author, Arlington, VA, April 10, 2016.

2. Jack Horner, interview by author, Arlington, VA, December 11, 2019.

3. Joe Carroll, "A Bouquet for Mrs. Heckler," *Irish Times*, Weekend Edition, August 12, 1989.

4. Maeve Binchy, "A Bouquet for Mrs. Heckler," *Irish Times*, August 12, 1989.

Index